IT'S NOT ALWAYS RACIST

... BUT SOMETIMES IT IS

IT'S NOT ALWAYS RACIST

... BUT SOMETIMES IT IS

Reshaping How We Think about Racism

DIONNE WRIGHT POULTON, PH.D.

ARCHWAY PUBLISHING

Archway Publishing books may be ordered through booksellers or by contacting:

Archway Publishing
1663 Liberty Drive
Bloomington, IN 47403
www.archwaypublishing.com
1-(888)-242-5904

Because of the dynamic nature of the Internet, any web addresses or
links contained in this book may have changed since publication and may
no longer be valid. The views expressed in this work are solely those
of the author and do not necessarily reflect the views of the publisher,
and the publisher hereby disclaims any responsibility for them.

Any people depicted in stock imagery provided by Thinkstock are
models, and such images are being used for illustrative purposes only.
Certain stock imagery © Thinkstock.

ISBN: 978-1-4808-0588-0 (sc)
ISBN: 978-1-4808-0590-3 (hc)
ISBN: 978-1-4808-0589-7 (e)

Library of Congress Control Number: 2014904138

Printed in the United States of America

Archway Publishing rev. date: 04/25/2014

This book was written in loving memory of my parents, Mr. Wilbur Theophilus Wright and Justice of the Peace Philomen Marilyn Wright with the Ontario Court of Justice (Canada).

Thank you for your teachings, your unwavering support, and your unconditional love. Thanks also for instilling the courage in me to write this book. It never once occurred to me that I could not achieve anything. I am also thankful for your example of openness and respect for *all* people—regardless of any difference.

Mom, before you passed away, you asked me to continue your work. I hope I have made you proud.

Contents

Preface

I want to convince you that not all incidents related to race should be considered instances of racism. And not all people who make comments about race are racists. In this book, I argue not only that we misuse these terms—"racism" and "racist"—but also that this misuse of language damages society. My goal is to convince you that the way to repair the damage and to prevent further harm is to engage in ongoing, open, and honest dialogue. In essence, I am proposing that we do the opposite of what we've traditionally been doing. For example, in virtually all of our public forums, we have a practice of harshly and negatively reacting to every incident related to race without thought for whether or not our reactions are justified. As a consequence of this reactionary response to such incidents, we automatically come down hard on racial offenders and then immediately shut down all reasoned conversation about race—until the next incident. Then the cycle begins again.

Unfortunately, there is a mixed bag of reasons why the United States continues to have problems with race. There is the unquestionably dark history and legacy of slavery that continues to affect our interactions with each other; one scholar calls this "legacy effects."[1] Another part of our problem with race is the fact that indeed there are still ignorant racists with malicious intentions to treat people of color poorly simply because of skin color. Adding to the confusion and pain are erroneous accusations and claims of racism that leave innocent people feeling at a loss, while on the other side, there are legitimate claims of racism that fall on deaf ears, also leaving victims of racism feeling at a loss.[2]

Perhaps our biggest problem—the one that leads to the issues I just mentioned, is that we do not fully understand what makes a particular incident racist. I emphatically state again that not all incidents related to race should be considered instances of racism, and not all people who make mistakes involving race are automatically racists. Ultimately, when we combine all of these reasons, many people are left feeling hurt, angry, confused, guilty, and afraid to say the wrong thing or *anything* about race! As a result, conversations shut down before they even begin, and as a further consequence, we cannot move forward with thoughtful, honest, and sustained dialogue.

The first step toward disentangling the confusion generated by labeling any negative racial incident as an instance of racism is to introduce another word into our everyday lexicon. This term is "bias" or "racial bias."[3] The concept of *racial bias* is distinct from *racism*, and by the end of this book, you will understand why I stress the importance of making this distinction. With this understanding, you will also eventually agree with the necessity of distinguishing these terms and labels as we decipher incidents related to race when they happen. Moreover, you will also learn specific tools and language that will help you critically analyze situations that happen in your everyday life and in society, thereby affording you the opportunity to insightfully break down each situation into its simplest form and to make sense of it.

This book is not filled exclusively with theory and technical terminology. In other words, I don't just talk about race, racism, and bias. I also offer *solutions* and *practical advice* on how to deal with situations related to race. My single most important goal, however, is to create a space for genuine dialogue on race, racism, and racial bias. Therefore, I have to caution you that there will probably be moments in your reading when you feel emotions such as anger, frustration, guilt, mistrust, and confusion. However, I encourage you to keep reading! Rest assured that by the end of this book, you will feel hopeful about the future and at peace in the knowledge that you are not alone.

My Background

Over the last fifteen years of my career, I have studied and researched the dynamics of race; taught in the K–12 and the higher education systems; conducted teacher education workshops; and facilitated talks on race in business and academic environments. It is my experience as an educator, trainer, and researcher that serves as the foundation for my views. This experience also supports the theories I share in this book and how I generally describe our interpersonal and institutional conduct and attitudes related to race. Indeed, during my career, I have had the privilege and joy of meeting and interacting with many people from all walks of life. Through these experiences, I have found that regardless of race, class, gender, sexual orientation, religion, level of education, aptitude, or any other descriptor we use, *all* of us are impacted by race. We all have biases, and we all judge people based on race. However, I also argue in this book that although all of us have racial biases, we are not all racists. Harboring racial bias does not necessarily lead to racist attitudes and actions. And every person who makes a negative comment about race is not necessarily a racist—hence the title of this book: *It's Not Always Racist ... but Sometimes It Is.*

How I Arrived at the Distinction between Racism and Racial Bias

I became interested in the topic of racism and racial bias early in my career. While teaching at a high-needs school in Toronto, Canada, I was surprised at the degree to which many K–12 teachers' racial biases found their way into the classroom—and the lunchroom. It was perplexing to watch my colleagues, who were presumably liberal, thoughtful, educated, and open-minded, be so unaware of the ways in which their racial biases, under certain circumstances, led to racist actions. As time went by, I discovered just how rampant these racial attitudes were—and it eventually hit close to home.

I learned that I, too, harbored racial bias when, twelve years ago, I moved from Toronto, Canada, to Oakland, California. First, let me tell you about the context. While still in Toronto, I taught special education, where the majority of students in my classes were black males who really struggled academically and had problems reading and writing at grade level. So when I moved to Oakland and decided to volunteer at an afterschool program to get to know the city, I automatically, albeit unconsciously, assumed that a young black boy I had just met could not read. I made the personally horrifying mistake of transferring my experience in Toronto—teaching struggling black boys—to a new environment, where I was proven biased. Specifically, while I was helping the young black boy with his homework, I caught myself being surprised that he could read his textbook and answer many homework questions correctly on his own. I unwittingly, yet unfairly, prejudged him.

As someone who has always been open-minded and who prides herself as a fair and aware teacher, I was surprised to learn that I had unconscious biases about black male students when consciously I knew better. It was this experience, coupled with what I witnessed among my teacher-colleagues, that piqued my curiosity about the topic of unconscious and conscious racial biases and assumptions. This curiosity ultimately led me to this area of research.

I moved on to research teacher attitudes about race, earning a master of arts degree in administration and interdisciplinary studies in adult education, specializing in equity and social justice at San Francisco State University. I later wrote my doctoral dissertation on teacher bias. The University of Georgia, where I completed my PhD, granted me permission to utilize a workshop I created in 2004 as the basis for my research. This workshop is titled Think You Are an Unbiased Teacher? Think Again!©

In acquiring empirical evidence to prove my workshop's efficacy to help individuals open up about their feelings about race, and to share them with others, I finished graduate school and have been an independent consultant ever since. In addition to facilitating difficult conversations about race, I also consult on curriculum design, program design and evaluation, and conflict mediation in both academic and business arenas. These experiences, along with my scholarly research, honed my arguments for the distinction between racism and racial bias.

There can be no peace without understanding.

—SENEGALESE PROVERB

Racism versus Racial Bias

If you are lucky, no one has ever accused you of being a racist, and no one ever will. And if you are lucky, you've neither had to, nor will you have reason to, accuse anyone of racism. I use the word *lucky* on purpose, because we live in an age where this label—*racist*—is often arbitrarily assigned. People throw it around with so little thought that when an actual incident of racism happens, it is often trivialized to the point where we don't necessarily believe it. It feels like a version of "The Boy Who Cried Wolf"; we hear false claims over and over, and when there finally is a legitimate claim of racism, it is also dismissed as just another untruth. At best, this error is frustrating. At worst, it is dangerous.

It's easy enough to get caught up in labeling every instance of racial offense as racist. That's because race seems to pop up everywhere as an issue—in the news, in entertainment, and in politics. There are times when I find myself screaming at the television in response to careless, unchallenged comments made on mainstream news shows. On other occasions, I have simply been dumbfounded by substandard analyses of racial incidents in the United States. Moreover, I have also sympathized with people who, in my professional opinion, have been wrongly labeled as racist and, as a result, have been publicly ridiculed, humiliated, and ostracized.

So what is a racist? The dictionary definition of *racist* is a prejudiced person who believes in the superiority of a particular race.[1] The implication of this belief in racial superiority is that

1

one will act in accordance with these beliefs. And what is prejudice? One scholar defines *prejudice* as "negative attitudes, emotion, or behavior towards members of a group on account of their membership of that group."[2] This means that prejudice is a prejudgment about someone, especially when we know nothing about the individual apart from his or her membership in a group. Consequently, the attitudes we have, the emotions we feel, and the behaviors we exhibit all reflect our prejudgments about people. The words *prejudgment* and *prejudice* suggest that rationality is only part of the process of judgment insofar that judgment occurs *prior* to knowledge of all the facts of a situation.

A significant component of the central argument of this book involves the distinction between racial prejudice, which I call "racial bias," and "racism," so I will pay particular attention to it. Especially in today's cultural, social, and political climate, this distinction is really important to make since, over and over, I have seen people being wrongfully accused of being racist when in fact they have only exhibited racial bias. You will learn in this book that racial bias is a normal phenomenon, and although it can be offensive, it is not as severe as racism. Making this distinction is important because, as a consequence of these mislabels of racism, some people have faced unfair criticism and ridicule when they were simply being *human*.

I will also introduce The Poulton Racial Bias Equation as well as The Poulton Racism Equation, which I created by expanding upon a racism equation developed by Pat Bidol in 1970: **Racism = Prejudice + Power**.[3] These equations will help you understand my reasoning behind making this distinction between racism and racial bias. I also use these equations to facilitate my analysis of specific incidents related to race and deciding whether they are indicative of racial bias or racism.

Why This Book Is Timely

After the 2008 US presidential election, some commentators claimed the country had finally reached a "postracial" era. What did they mean by this phrase? Generally, it means that we now live in a society in which race no longer matters. People like Ann Coulter swore up and down that the 2008 election was about racial demagoguery and that America would *never* reelect a black president.[4] Clearly, she and others were proven wrong. However, despite the huge feats of electing and reelecting a black president, research has shown that race is still a significant issue in our society, affecting how we interact and get along with others. Research has also suggested that a fundamental feature of human perception and socialization involves making distinctions among people based on skin color.[5]

Ironically, we want to believe that President Barack Obama, in Dr. Martin Luther King's words, was "judged not because of the color of his skin but because of the content of his character," but I am sure some people did vote for Barack Obama because he was black. However, more in line with Dr. King's dream, I believe the majority of people voted for President Obama because of the content of his character or what I call "relevant factors." These factors include his level of integrity, compassion, intellect, political acumen, education, life experience, and legislative experience. This is not to suggest, however, that President Obama's skin color and life experience as an African American are insignificant, are not a part of his identity, or are not an unimportant part of his presidency. All of us who go to work each day know that we cannot separate who we are from the job we do. In fact, President Obama's comments about the killing of Trayvon Martin and the subsequent acquittal of George Zimmerman are indications of his inability to separate *who he is* from *what he does*. President Obama said he could have been Trayvon Martin thirty-five years ago. He also said that African Americans were upset because of "a history that doesn't go away."[6] Evidently, President Obama identified with Trayvon as a black teenager and shared specific instances when he too faced racial bias while he was just minding his own business as a US citizen. I applaud Obama's comments and his call to action for all of us to begin looking at our individual racial biases. This book is an answer to his call.

Naturally, Obama faced outright criticism from many people who believed he should not have shared his beliefs about the case. Shortly after Obama's remarks, Todd Starnes, host of the radio program *Fox News & Commentary,* called Obama "race-baiter in chief," declaring on Twitter and Facebook that "he truly is trying to tear our country apart."[7] Starnes's interpretation of Obama's words is interesting to me because Obama's message was clear: advocating and promoting peace and understanding. This is a perfect example of my point about "relevant factors." In general, I believe people who are conscientious about their thinking, who strive to be self-aware, and who are not willing to settle for habitual judgments are the ones who search for and take note of relevant factors in any given situation.

Especially with respect to analyzing and evaluating incidents related to race, it is important to search for and identify relevant factors that help us begin to accurately make sense of situations, try to determine whether an incident is indicative of racism, or try to determine if an incident is only racial bias. The heart of making this distinction between racism and racial bias relies on identifying the relevant factors in the concept of racism and identifying the relevant factors in the concept of racial bias. In this book, I heavily reference two Poulton equations that highlight the relevant factors of what I call a racist incident and the relevant factors of what I call a racial bias incident. Ultimately, these equations will help us recognize, evaluate, and make sense of incidents related to race.

Racism = Prejudice (+) Power (+) or (-) Intent
Racial Bias = Prejudice (+) or (-) Intent

In addition to using these equations to help us determine whether an incident is racist or not, I also offer a Five-Step Racism Evaluation Process I developed. We can all follow these steps to help us make sense of incidents related to race the minute they happen, through to how we should "punish" the culprit(s) or racial offender(s) involved.

I must also stress, however, that we, as a society, must stop making our analyses of incidents related to race exclusively after something has happened and in the midst of scandal and controversy. Instead, it would be more beneficial to all of us to have these difficult conversations when cooler heads are prevailing and when emotions are not running high. For example, consider conversations about race in terms of a familial relationship. Most family members know that it is best *not* to have conversations about important issues with siblings, parents, spouses, or partners while tensions are high, when emotions are raw, or in the midst of a chaotic event. But this is what we continue to do on a national scale in relation to race. The reason we do not have meaningful discussions about race and racism is because our timing is off.

Of equal importance is the fact that we are not all on the same page when it comes to understanding key concepts on this issue and with respect to our overall approach to making sense of incidents related to race. If we were all experts on race, and if we were all trained critical thinkers, we would be better equipped to engage in meaningful dialogue about race in the aftermath of racial incidents. But unfortunately, this is not the case. Right now, the general discussion seems to focus simplistically on deciding whether something is racist or not. Surely we can have deeper, more intellectual conversations than this! We need to stop and consider the difference between racism and racial bias and consider the intents and the hearts of those who have displayed behaviors that *might* be racist.

Please keep in mind that emphasis in this book is on the psychosocial behaviors of race—"psychosocial" meaning cognitive (mind) and the behavioral (actions). According to one thinker, focus on this area is invaluable because social psychology has the "potential to contribute significantly to both the dissection and the dissolution of prejudice."[8] I will, however, still touch on the history of race and racism, and institutional racism, including in my professional area of specialization: education. Nonetheless, my aim is not to dwell on the past or on the negative, because we have already seen enough of this. My goal is to move us forward by talking about the things we can do *attitudinally* that will promote understanding, acceptance, and peace across racial and ethnic lines. We can achieve this individually and collectively, and the first step is being open to the idea that our personal beliefs and reactions to others or to different situations could be influenced by race. If we just learn how to engage in meaningful dialogue about race, "much can be gleaned from our unspoken assumptions and how they drive our behavior in racial situations."[9] This book will facilitate this process.

Outline of the Book

In chapter 1, I posit that a clear distinction needs to be made between racism and racial bias. I also argue that a failure to make this conceptual distinction is both morally and socially significant. As part of the foundation for this distinction, I offer concise definitions of race, racism, and racial bias, and then I provide a summary review of scholarly literature on the concept of racism and ultimately argue for the definition I adopt. Moreover, in chapter 1, I introduce critical race theory (CRT) as the overarching theoretical lens I looked through while writing this book. CRT asserts that race is the most important feature of human identity, affecting our perceptions and behaviors toward others whether we realize it or not. CRT will be applied throughout this book, especially in chapter 9 when I stress that children should be taught about race.

I focus my attention in chapter 2 on clearly distinguishing between racism and racial bias by way of my Racism and Racial Bias Equations. In chapter 3, I focus on the fine line between racism and racial bias and how important our critical thinking skills are to making solid judgments about racial incidents. The focus of chapter 4 is how CRT plays out in the way we think about our social environment. This chapter will pull together significant concepts from chapters 1 to 3 so that, combined with chapter 5's brief history of racism in the United States, you'll be ready in chapter 6 to analyze some scenarios and apply your thinking and understanding about the distinction between racism and racial bias.

In chapter 6, I focus specifically on a hit parade of racial gaffes that happened in twenty-first-century US culture. I analyze each racial gaffe and ultimately evaluate and classify them using the two-race equation: racism or racial bias. In this way, we also have the opportunity to see critical thinking about race in action. Remember I argue that we are all racially biased to some extent, so by chapter 7, I hope to have convinced you of this idea. In chapter 7, I discuss the concept of *positionality*, which asserts that race is connected to class and gender. This connection sometimes makes it difficult to isolate race as a sole factor influencing different situations. In addition, I connect this concept with claims that we live in "a postracial society." An analysis of the first black US president in this chapter provides an opportunity to identify some peculiarities of the United States' racial difficulties—difficulties rooted in a sustained history of overt and subtle oppression. I then move on to consider some basic features of critical thinking that are relevant to discussions about race, and your understanding of the distinction I make between racism and racial bias.

By chapter 8, you should have already been thinking about your own attitudes and experiences about race. It's an intimidating prospect for anyone, regardless of racial group, level of confidence, or even desire to honestly think about and potentially question what you think you know. So I encourage you to become comfortable with your discomfort, keep an open mind, and engage in ongoing, honest, and open dialogue about your views, both internally and with a few trusted friends.

Here, I lay out practical steps in reference to what happens after you acknowledge your own racial biases in a process called CHECK. I also discuss further the notion of "positionality"—the intersection of race, class, and gender proposed by scholars.

Now that you have developed confidence in your own thinking about race, racism, and racial bias, you're in a position to think about the next generation and what you owe them. To that end, I use chapter 9 to discuss why it is important to openly discuss race with children, and I propose different methods of teaching children about race. In connection with this topic, I apply adult education pioneer Jack Mezirow's critical thinking strategies.

In chapter 10, I continue the foregoing discussion with a sustained investigation of DIVERSITY.

Decide to be open.
Invite others into your circle of friends.
View others through a lens of love.
Enjoy differences in people.
Respect yourself and others.
Suspend your judgments.
Integrity should be your point of reference.
Treat others the way you would like to be treated.
You are in control of your actions.

This final chapter ends with my concluding remarks, which constitute a sort of summary that should reinforce a number of ideas and skills introduced and developed throughout the book. I hope to leave you with a newfound optimism about the racial harmony we can accomplish together.

In the moment of crisis, the wise build bridges and the foolish build dams.

—NIGERIAN PROVERB

CHAPTER ONE

Race, Racism, and Racial Bias: Why Should We Talk about It?

Racism is an influential force in our society that has motivated individuals to commit horrible acts against people of color, resulting in dire circumstances and even death. In 1955, fourteen-year-old Emmett Till was beaten to death in Mississippi, allegedly for whistling at a white woman. More recently, you might recall the 1991 police beating of Rodney King, which set off days of violence in Los Angeles. It is all but impossible to forget the 1998 horrific and heinous murder of James Byrd Jr., who was killed in Texas because he was black. A group of racists dragged Mr. Byrd along an asphalt road from a pickup truck until he was dead.

These are only a few examples of racist acts among the thousands and thousands that have occurred in the United States, some of which we know about and some that we will never know. Thankfully, not all acts of racism are as extreme as the incidents just mentioned. Acts of racism fall on a continuum from the most horrific on one end, as described above, to subtler forms in our daily interactions with one another. For example, racial discrimination claims were brought against Cracker Barrel restaurants for routinely segregating blacks in smoking sections and refusing to offer them service. The NAACP sued them, and the restaurant chain settled. Specifically, the

> settlement found that black customers at many of the country store-themed restaurants were seated in areas

segregated from white patrons, frequently received inferior service, and often were made to wait longer for tables. Blacks who complained about poor service were also treated less favorably than whites, the settlement said.[1]

This is a perfect example of more subtle (or not-so-subtle) forms of racism and how they can be difficult to discern, which then raises the question of how we can know, for example, that someone is (intentionally or not) treating us in a certain way because of our skin color when interactions are nuanced and perspectives are varied.[2]

Nonetheless, regardless of how racism is manifested, given how profoundly abhorrent it is, if you ask anyone how he or she would feel if someone called him or her a racist, the reaction would be visceral like a sharp slap to the face. As we have learned from the definition of a racist, only someone who believes in racial superiority would not recoil in horror at the thought of being called a racist. However, oddly enough, it appears as if accusations of racism, whether warranted or not, continue to abound in the United States. Here are some examples.

- In 2013, celebrity chef Paula Deen lost a slew of lucrative endorsement contracts and was dropped from the Food Network because she admitted to using the "n-word" on several occasions.[3]
- In 2013, Nicki Minaj accused Steven Tyler of racism when he tweeted a comment questioning her ability to judge on *American Idol*.[4]
- In 2013, Volkswagen released a Super Bowl commercial that involved white people speaking with a Jamaican accent.[5] Another commercial released in 2013, by Mountain Dew, was described as "the most racist commercial ever."[6]
- In 2012, conservative commentator Ann Coulter argued that Barack Obama was elected president of the United States in 2008 only because of liberal white guilt.[7]

- Donald Trump demanded that President Obama produce his birth certificate and college transcripts to verify that he was not lying about his credentials.[8]
- In 2007, radio personality Don Imus called a group of college student athletes "nappy-headed hos."[9]
- A session offered at the 2013 Conservative Political Action Conference (CPAC) sponsored by the Tea Party Patriots was entitled Trump the Race Card: Are You Sick and Tired of Being Called a Racist When You Know You're Not One?[10]

Are all of the aforementioned situations examples of racism? Was it really necessary for there to be a session devoted to "Trumping the Race Card" at the CPAC event?

If we gather a group of people together, some may say all are examples of racism, some may say some are examples of racism, and still others may say none are. In fact, over time, those same people may change their minds about how to think about the examples. Nevertheless, analyses of incidents related to race always seem to fall into two rigid categories: "racist" or "not racist." Most people would be hard-pressed to find a third category to describe incidents related to race. This is why I propose the term "racial bias," which I will explain in coming sections. However, here I will give my answer to the following question: Are all people who exhibit racially offensive behaviors or who make racially insensitive remarks automatically racist? The answer is no! In the next section, I discuss a problem that I have seen over and over.

Not Everything Is Racist!

There are too many events that happen in our society that are automatically and, I will argue, *wrongfully* labeled as racist. Consequently, those individuals involved in the events have automatically been called "racist." How can that be? How is it possible that, in an age of almost uniform social and institutional rejections of racism and racist practices, so many people are accused of racism? Are the examples of racial incidents that I cited above really instances. of racism, or have we lost our understanding of what racism really is? In chapter 6, I offer a complete analysis of many of the incidents mentioned earlier as well as some others. These incidents happened in the industries of advertising, politics, news, sports, and music, all of which represent a problem that exists everywhere. In chapter 6, when I provide my analyses of these incidents, I do declare that some of the incidents are not racist. Make note, however, that in *no way* am I suggesting that at least some of the aforementioned incidents are not offensive in some way. What I am saying is that they are not necessarily instances of racism or racist behavior. They may just be instances of *racial bias*, which is different from racism.

However, before I discuss what I think is the difference between racism and racial bias, it is important to understand what I mean when I reference the following terms and theories that inform this book: race, racism, racial bias, critical race theory (CRT), and race as a social construction.

Race

Setting a foundation with terminology is important to your exploration of this book, and race is the key concept. When I refer to race, I mean simply the skin color of an individual. Race can be self-identified, but it also refers to how our society perceives groups of people. For example, a person might self-identify as biracial—mixed with black and white—but individuals in society will probably simplistically regard this person as black if he or she has a darker skin color. President Obama is a perfect example of how people perceive race. He is the son of a white mother and a black father, and he is considered black.

Additionally, a part of how we judge someone's race is determined by looking at biological characteristics, such as eye shape and hair texture. As a result, categories of persons in this book, such as white, black, Asian, Hispanic, and Middle Eastern, are all superficially related to the physical features and *looks* of a person as well as how he or she is categorized or perceived by society.

Critical Race Theory

Another important conceptual foundation of this book is critical race theory (CRT). I wrote this book while looking through the theoretical lens of CRT, which asserts not only that racism is rife in American society,[11] but also that race is the most salient feature of a person's identity, influencing our perceptions and behavior toward others who don't look like us. Over and above other social factors, such as gender, class, and age, race is believed to have the biggest impact on how we react to situations.

CRT has its origins in the legal system and evolved in the 1970s as a result of civil rights litigation that failed to address racial disparities and, in essence, "racism" that adversely affected African Americans in the United States.[12] However, CRT is widely used in my field of education as a powerful theoretical and analytical framework within educational research. Moreover, CRT is "an important intellectual and social tool for deconstruction, reconstruction, and construction: deconstruction of oppressive structures and discourses, reconstruction of human agency, and construction of equitable and socially just relations of power."[13]

Another key assertion CRT makes is that *all* people are complicit in the system of racism. This means that everyone, including people of color, participate in the system of racism and help to keep it alive. Is this hard to believe? The implication is that people of color also make judgments based on race and, therefore, can also be racist. As you read this book, you will find several examples of incidents related to race that support this assertion made by CRT. Ultimately, CRT "is a framework that can be used to theorize, examine and challenge the ways race and racism implicitly and explicitly impact on social structures, practices and discourses."[14] This is why I use CRT as a powerful lens to help with the analyses and comprehension of many incidents I describe in this book, especially in chapter 6, where I analyze and discuss racial gaffes that have occurred in the United States.

Race as a Social Construction

There are myriad theories about race and racism, and they span a number of different academic research fields. The general consensus of these theories is that race is socially constructed. What does this mean? It means that race is *not* biological or in our DNA, which means it must be sociological. In fact, prior to the eighteenth century, there was arguably no concept of race as we understand it today.[15] Moreover, academic research fields generally agree that social environments best explain our concepts of race. Therefore, race can be considered a fluid concept that might change depending upon the social environment. For example, there was a period in recent US history in which the concept of "passing" was quite prevalent. A black person could "pass" when he or she was light-skinned enough to be perceived as white, thereby enabling him or her to function in the white world. Consequently, these individuals could avoid suffering the same fate experienced by their darker-skinned brothers and sisters. A wonderful film classic that addresses this notion of "passing" and that teaches us great lessons about life and humanity is called *Imitation of Life*. If you haven't seen this movie, I suggest you rent it.[16]

Conceptions of race have shaped our perceptions and have influenced our behaviors toward each other for hundreds of years. Take, for example, an early race taxonomy advanced by Carl Linnaeus in 1735.[17] As you can see in the chart on the next page, the taxonomy reflects a hierarchy in which the European is the most advanced in every respect, while others (Africans, Asians, and Native Americans) are characterized by various deficiencies (according to Western moral values).

Race	Characteristics	Ruled By
Homo sapiens Europaeus	White, serious, strong	Laws
Homo sapiens Asiaticus	Yellow, melancholy, greedy	Opinion
Homo sapiens Africanus	Black, impassive, lazy	Caprice
Homo sapiens Americanus	Red, ill-tempered, subjugated	Custom

EXERCISE 1:
How much do you believe this taxonomy today?

---

1. Grab a piece of paper and a pen and write down the following words exactly as I have written them:

   Native American
   African American/black
   White
   Asian
   Hispanic

2. Now, going with your first thought, rank the races in order of superiority and favorability. The most superior and favorable should be #1.

3. How did you rank the races? Did you have difficulty ranking them? If so, you want to ask yourself why and try to work through

the feelings associated with your responses, which are more than likely to be uncomfortable.

4. Read on.

Did you know "on virtually every socially desirable dimension, the descending order of superiority has been whites, Asians, Native Americans, and Africans"?[18] In some cases, the order of whites and Asians is reversed. However, at one time, "like Native Americans and Blacks before them, Asian Americans were originally stereotyped as 'immoral,' 'oversexed,' 'unclean,' and with 'low standards of living.'"[19] Also, would you be surprised to learn that Native Americans, followed by African Americans, have had the longest and most consistently negative sociopolitical histories of oppression under a white-dominant social structure? As you read on, it should become clear that, in any case, race has a clear relationship to hierarchy, inequality, injustice, and power relations in the United States. It is not difficult to see that race is fundamentally about power and advantage.

Berger and Luckmann

I would be remiss if I discussed the idea of race as a social construction and its influence on us without acknowledging the work of Berger and Luckmann, who wrote the seminal work in the field of sociology titled *The Social Construction of Reality*.[20] The authors' work is critical to the field of sociology and to my argument about racism and racial bias because the authors argue that social processes form knowledge. Berger and Luckmann define knowledge as "the sum total of what everyone knows ... an assemblage of maxims, morals, proverbial nuggets of wisdom, values and beliefs [and] myths."[21]

According to Berger and Luckmann, knowledge is developed through "primary socialization" and "secondary socialization." Primary socialization is the "first socialization an individual undergoes in childhood, through which he or she becomes a member of society."[22] This "first world is constructed"[23] with "every individual ... born into an objective social structure, within which he encounters the significant others who are in charge of his socialization."[24] These "significant others" are imposed upon the person and are usually the mother and father[25] who, in essence, influence how the child views and moves through the world. Therefore, some people are raised in environments where they are exposed to people from different racial and cultural backgrounds, while some do not get this exposure. For example, it is not unusual for Americans to live in communities segregated by economic class and race—and whites are the most racially segregated group in the country.[26] However, as adults, the same people who grew up segregated may seek new opportunities to construct new racial meanings[27] via secondary socialization.

Berger and Luckmann describe secondary socialization as any subsequent process or experience beyond primary socialization that introduces an already socialized individual into new areas of the objective world of his or her society. For example, if someone has the primary socialization experience growing up in a segregated community and later chooses to live in a more racially diverse community as an adult, this choice to live "differently" from first socialized is an example of secondary socialization. Regardless of the type of secondary socialization, one key characteristic of secondary socialization is that it deals with "the acquisition of role-specific knowledge ... [and] the acquisition of role-specific vocabularies"[28] and the internalization of "sub worlds" that are "general partial realities in contrast to the *base world* acquired in primary socialization."[29] Taking a trip to a foreign land and inviting a person of a different race over for dinner are other examples of secondary socialization.

Racism

Before delving into the distinction between racism and racial bias, let's look at the concept of racism, for we need to be clear about what it is in order to better identify what it is not. This is not to say, however, that there is a single definition of the term because the concept is very complex. However, there are specific features that all definitions of racism share, so we can start with those. I begin with the definition of racism offered by Singleton and Linton: "the conscious or unconscious, intentional or unintentional enactment of racial power, grounded in racial prejudice, by an individual or group against another individual or group perceived to have lower racial status."[30] Please note that within this definition is the concept of *prejudice*, which is a prejudgment about another individual. This definition offered by Singleton and Linton best illustrates my thinking about the concept of racism, and I also use it as the central definition to support my overall approach to this book.

Similarly, another scholar asserts that "racism functions not only through overt, conscious prejudice and discrimination but also through the unconscious attitudes and behaviors of a society that presumes an unacknowledged but pervasive white cultural norm."[31] Shirley Chisholm, America's first black congresswoman, eloquently supports this point. She asserted, "Racism is so universal in this country, so widespread and deep-seated, that it is invisible because it is so normal."[32] In other words, if we refer to the discussion of race and the hierarchy of "superiority" that exists with whites at the top, it is not unusual for those racial groups defined as "inferior" to be mistreated by individuals at the top, whether intentionally or unintentionally.[33]

Additionally, racism does not necessarily or exclusively occur at the interpersonal level. Consider, for example, the following three forms of racism posited by one theorist:

- individual racism, which refers to individuals discriminating against others by way of, for example, racial slurs and as a result of feelings of racial superiority
- institutional racism or systemic racism, which refers to social systems and organizations like educational segregation or racial profiling that leads to perpetual unequal treatment among racial groups
- cultural racism, which occurs when white culture or whiteness is considered the norm and superior to other racial groups

Cultural racism promotes, for example, Eurocentric standards of beauty while denigrating other racial groups' physical characteristics, such as skin and eye color, hair texture, and bone structure. Cultural racism can therefore be generically defined as the belief and an enactment of beliefs that one set of characteristics is superior to another.[34] These characteristics include, for example, white skin, blond hair, and blue eyes, which are revered as more beautiful than brown skin, brown eyes, and brown hair. Even within white culture, blond hair seems to be favored—hence the phrase "Blondes have more fun."

So why is all this important to know? Because, as I stated earlier, a fundamental feature of human perception and socialization involves making distinctions among people based on skin color. We are visual creatures, which means we have a natural tendency to prejudge people because of race. And, right or wrong, to help us make sense of our experiences with others, we try to decide to which racial groups people belong by looking at skin color, eye color, hair texture, etc. Consider the following scenario that illustrates this point.

Many years ago, when I first started my career teaching in public schools in Toronto, I was one of a handful of first-year teachers. We went away to a one-day retreat, and one of my colleagues, who looked Asian, happened to have caramel-color skin tone and jet-black hair. I remember a bunch of us were sitting around a table, including my Asian Canadian colleague. We were all talking and having a good time when one of the teachers, an older white male, asked my Asian colleague, "So where did you grow up?" My colleague responded, "Toronto." The teacher, visibly perplexed, asked another question: "So where are you from?" The Asian teacher responded, "I am from Toronto. I am Canadian." The other teacher then became noticeably agitated and, with an elevated voice, screamed, "No! *What* are you?"

The Asian teacher was visibly shocked by the cross-examination in front of a group of people and explained his family background. I cannot remember exactly what country my former colleague's parents were from or his racial makeup, but the point here is that the teacher (cross-examiner) took a while to become satisfied with the Asian teacher's response. He finally got an answer for what he really wanted to know, which was *why* the Asian teacher looked the way he did. In the cross-examiner's mind, how the Asian teacher looked and how he sounded—that is, speaking perfect English—did not make sense, probably because my white colleague expected a Canadian to look a certain way.

What Is a Racist?

In the aforementioned scenario, was the "cross-examiner" racist? To answer the question, let's recall the central definition of racism that I use in this book: "the conscious or unconscious, intentional or unintentional enactment of racial power, grounded in racial prejudice, by an individual or group against another individual or group perceived to have lower racial status."[35] A racist, therefore, is "any person who subscribes to the belief that one race is superior to others and perpetuates this belief intentionally or unconsciously."[36] Given the definitions I just offered, does the cross-examiner fall into the racist category? Is the cross-examiner a racist?

I say no!

I believe the cross-examiner exhibited some obvious bias and racial prejudice about what it is to be a Canadian; otherwise, he would not have asked, "What are you?" which is a dead give-away question people ask when you don't fit neatly into their social or racial categories. I speak from experience! Also, even though the cross-examiner lacked an abundance of tact while questioning the Asian teacher, there was still no evidence that he felt racially *superior* to the Asian teacher. I believe he was just overly curious and felt entitled to know his Asian colleague's background.

I am sure that if you share this scenario with a few people, you will get a range of different interpretations and answers. It's a perfect example of how an incident related to race can automatically be mislabeled as "racist." As aggressive as the cross-examiner was, neither his words nor his actions demonstrated that he felt racially superior to the Asian teacher. Moreover, one key ingredient in the definition of racism I just shared, and that the cross-examiner did not possess, is the *power* to do anything to harm or stifle the Asian teacher. There was no opportunity for the "enactment of racial power."[37] As you will read over and over in this book, one fundamental ingredient of racism is *power*, and the cross-examiner had none. In the coming chapter, you will learn the fundamental difference between racism and racial bias.

Peace is not the absence of conflict but the presence of creative alternatives for responding to conflict—alternatives to passive or aggressive responses, alternatives to violence.

—DOROTHY THOMPSON

CHAPTER TWO

Is It Racism or Racial Bias?
Untangling the Confusion

Now that most of the relevant terminology I use in this book has been introduced and defined, I turn now to further describe the confusion that is created when we call every incident related to race "racist" or "racism." Scholars tend to be quite careful about distinguishing between racism and racial bias, but unfortunately, this distinction has been lost in mainstream discourse. So whenever incidents related to race occur, they are often *not* contemplated or articulated carefully and accurately. Consequently, these incidents usually get labeled as racist because it is the low-hanging fruit. It is easy just to say something is racist when we are racially offended. Further consequences of failing to differentiate between racism and racial bias are increased misunderstandings, conflicts, and breakdowns in meaningful and sustainable discussions about race in the United States.

What I would like to do is bridge the gap between some of the scholarly literature on race, racism, and bias with our ordinary ways of thinking about these concepts. I do not believe these conversations should only be reserved for undergraduate and graduate classrooms in formal educational settings. As an adult educator, I know that much of what we learn occurs *outside* of the traditional classroom. So I am confident that, given our collective experiential knowledge with race, the discussion that follows will not be difficult to understand and will also help us illuminate new ways of thinking about old ideas.

Poulton Race Equations

When we consider early theories about race, like those expressed in Linnaeus's aforementioned 1735 taxonomy, and we couple them with the legacy of European colonization, again it is no surprise that in 1970, Pat Bidol, in the book *Developing New Perspectives on Race*, presented the following racism equation:

Racism = Prejudice + Power

The equation is self-explanatory. Racism is about a person prejudging another on the basis of race and having the integral component of *power* to adversely affect or control the fate of that person. Highlighting these components of the equation is very important because, as you can see, prejudice is an element of racism; the two are not one and the same. I have seen, over and over, people confusing these terms, using them interchangeably and labeling incidents incorrectly. This equation offers a basic way to define racism.

I will reiterate the point again: racism is about power and prejudice, so in order to declare that a racial incident is an instance of racism or that the offender is a racist, these two elements *must* be present. However, although Bidol's racism equation helps us pinpoint whether an incident is racist or not, it falls short in helping us with an important function, which is determining the *intent* of the culprit(s) involved and how the person or people involved in the racist incident should be punished or reprimanded. This is why I developed my racism equations described in the next section.

The Poulton Racism Equation

Not all racist incidents are alike, and there are different levels of racial offenses. Therefore, in order to help us determine how one should be "punished" after an incident related to race, I propose that we must first assess the *intent* of the offender. This is no small task. How, after all, can we get into another person's mind to see what they meant or didn't mean by a comment or action? Let's briefly return to the definition of racism that I stated was the foundation for my approach to this book: "the conscious or unconscious, intentional or unintentional enactment of racial power, grounded in racial prejudice, by an individual or group against another individual or group perceived to have lower racial status."[1] It is important to consider the intent of the racial offender or the culprit before deciding how to punish. Therefore, I have modified Bidol's racism equation by adding the element of intent.

Racism = Prejudice (+) Power (+) or (-) Intent

As you can see, I have added "plus or minus intent" because the question should be asked, "Did the person or people involved in the incident have the *intent* to harm or hurt the victim(s)"? Someone who has negatively prejudged a group of people and has the power to negatively influence the lives of the people in that group, but *not* necessarily with the intent to do so, arguably cannot be as morally culpable as the one who does. I stress again that it is important to discuss the intention of the persons involved because not all racist incidents are alike. We need to stop painting with big, broad strokes, calling all racial offenders "racist" and assigning punishment to everyone in the same manner. For example, I am writing this paragraph shortly after the George Zimmerman acquittal, which completely bumped the Paula Deen scandal out of the news cycle. I believe both the Zimmerman and Deen situations are indicative of racism.[2] However, even though both of them committed racist acts, should they both be "punished" by the public in the same manner? Absolutely not! Paula Deen's situation is mild compared to what Zimmerman did. Zimmerman unnecessarily took a young teenager's life.

In chapter 6, I discuss the Zimmerman and Deen cases in more detail, demonstrating how we can begin the process of deciphering incidents related to race in a more meaningful and less inflammatory manner. The entire chapter is devoted to my analyses of specific incidents related to race that have happened in the United States since President Obama took office. I specifically identify and evaluate whether each incident is indeed racist or a mere expression of racial bias. I make the determination of racism through use of my equation mentioned above, and I determine whether an incident is just racial bias through use of the Poulton Racial Bias Equation.

The Poulton Racial Bias Equation

In order to illustrate my definition of racial bias, I developed the following equation:

Racial Bias = Prejudice (+) or (-) Intent

Like racism, racial bias also has the element of prejudice. However, the element of power is not present because, when it comes to racial bias, people may have prejudices but no power to negatively affect the lives of other people socially, economically, or physically. For example, if you get into an altercation with another person over a parking spot and that person calls you a racial slur and then drives off, that person has *only* exhibited racial bias, not racism. He or she had no ability to affect your life in any way. The person may very well be racist (believing in the superiority of one race over another), but because he or she was not in a position of *power* to not allow you to park in the spot, the *incident* is only an example of racial bias. Also, much like the racism equation, I have also included the element of intent in the racial bias equation. Why? Because, just as I mentioned in the case of racist incidents, I believe it is important to establish the intent of someone's actions before we punish someone who has simply exhibited racial bias. In this case of the angry driver, the use of a racial slur leaves little doubt as to the intent of the person involved. However, much like incidents of racism, not all incidents of racial bias are committed intentionally. In fact, many incidents of racial bias are also done unconsciously.

For example, in my many years as an educator and trainer, I have met some of the most innocuous, reticent people with good intentions that you could ever meet, and yet they have unintentionally hurt others because of racial bias. This is why, at the beginning of my Think You Are Unbiased?© workshops, I lead participants through an exercise using index cards. On one side of the card, participants are asked to write down an example of "victim bias"—a time when they were unfairly judged because of race. And on the other side of the index card, participants are asked to write down an example of "culprit bias"—a time when *they* unfairly judged someone because of race.

> ## QUESTION:
> **Which side do you think people struggle with the most: recalling a "victim bias" example or a "culprit bias" example?**

Social desirability theory[3] teaches us that people are usually unlikely to share their negative feelings about race because it is not socially acceptable. Therefore, if you guessed "culprit bias" as the type of bias people generally have the most trouble sharing, you are correct. People are generally uncomfortable sharing examples of personal racial gaffes, but we have all had them. If we all have racial biases, as I argue, then we have all made racial gaffes, whether intentionally or unintentionally. Therefore, we must look at the intention of "culprits" when incidents related to race happen because not all racial offenders are alike, and not all incidents related to race are alike.

I am simply proposing that we look at the motivations and intentions of racial offenders, just as it is done in the law. For example, in criminal law, when one person takes the life of another, the motivations and intentions of the perpetrator are considered while lawyers try to determine the types of charge(s) to be laid (e.g., manslaughter, murder 1, and murder 2). That individual then becomes eligible to receive a punishment that directly corresponds with the specific charge(s) laid. Why is this done in law? Because not all crimes are alike, and likewise, not all incidents related to race are alike. We must consider the intent of individuals who make mistakes related to race instead of saying everything is racist and, consequently, severely punishing the culprits without completely understanding what happened.

Racial Bias and the Role of Assumptions

We *all* harbor racial biases toward others. In fact, sometimes these racial biases and preferences operate at the unconscious level and without our awareness. This is why I call race an "intangible influence." It can impact our perceptions and actions without our knowing, by operating as either positive or negative assumptions or as a set of assumptions about others.[4]

A perfect example of how assumptions can lead an individual to treat another person unfairly or to harm a person in other ways is the George Zimmerman trial. Prosecutors argued that Zimmerman's assumptions about Trayvon Martin led him to pursue and kill the young teenager. Again, in chapter 6, I offer a robust analysis of the Zimmerman case, but here I agree with the prosecutors who said George Zimmerman's assumptions led him to profile and kill Trayvon Martin.

Although less severe, another example of how assumptions impact us is the scenario I previously discussed involving the Asian teacher. The Asian teacher's appearance confused his colleague— apparently being Asian and Canadian didn't fit his colleague's assumptions about what it is to be Canadian. This type of scenario is not surprising to me because in my field of education, research has shown that educators can have racial biases and assumptions, whether consciously or unconsciously, that can affect how they approach and evaluate students of color.[5] Specifically, it has been shown that race can lead some educators to underestimate the academic achievement of students of color, including having lowered expectations of them,[6] and these lower expectations can also lead to lower evaluations of students of color in comparison to their white peers.[7]

In a later chapter, I focus more on the role of race and racism in the education system, but here it is important to talk about racial assumptions of teachers because they are usually held to an unrealistically high moral standard. Teachers are expected to be infallible and fair. So if teachers are held to this moral standard, yet they still harbor racial assumptions and biases and are sometimes racist, then this is more support for the argument that racial bias is normal and natural. In fact, in response to this revelation that educators need to address how race impacts their pedagogy (teaching) and their perceptions and reactions to race, The Anti-Defamation League, through its World of Difference Institute, offers diversity workshops and other educational opportunities for educators to openly address and discuss racism and anti-Semitism.

Anti-Semitism

It is not a mistake that the Anti-Defamation League addresses both racism and anti-Semitism. Anti-Semitism is defined as "hostility toward or discrimination against Jews as a religious, ethnic, or racial group."[8] Both practices—anti-Semitism and racism—are negative, demeaning, and with devastating consequences for individuals with a history of persecution and injustice. Neither should be tolerated.

When I first moved to the United States after teaching in Toronto, I had the pleasure of working in a private Jewish school in San Francisco, California. While I was already familiar with Jewish culture because of my childhood growing up with parents who had Jewish friends, it was the experience teaching at the school that enabled me to learn more about Jewish culture and the years and years of oppression and devastation they have endured as a people. I identified with the plight of Jewish people because, as a black woman, I am connected to the history of slavery and how inhumanely black people were once treated in the United States. All types of oppression are unacceptable, regardless of the groups being targeted. Therefore, much like when individuals make racist comments, those who also make anti-Semitic remarks should be reprimanded accordingly.

A perfect example of anti-Semitism is the 2006 rant Oscar-winning actor and director Mel Gibson went on during a drunken tirade. "Jews are responsible for all the wars in the world." His comment shocked Hollywood, and he later apologized for what he called "despicable behavior" and sought counseling.[9] But apparently, Mel Gibson is an equal-opportunity bigot with ingrained beliefs about people different from him. It was reported in 2010, for example, that while engaged in a custody battle with his ex-girlfriend for their infant daughter, Gibson said the way his ex dressed made her look like "a pig in heat." He also reportedly said, "If you get raped by a pack of niggers, it will be your fault."[10]

Gibson's statements were—and still are—profoundly offensive and intolerable. It is no surprise that we don't see much of him anymore. Professionally, he has probably hit a wall at every turn that he created himself. Otherwise, it shouldn't be difficult for an Oscar-winning director and actor to find work. Should Mel Gibson be forgiven for his behavior? The public will decide, if they haven't already.

Race in the Workplace

Thus far, I have demonstrated how racism and anti-Semitism can appear in two professional areas: teaching and acting. However, are these instances anomalies? If they have been found in the education system and in Hollywood, then is it possible for racism and anti-Semitism to appear in your workplace? Surely you cannot believe they do not exist in your work environment! The following is a situation revealed by television talk-show host Julie Chen, who shared her experience with racism in the news and media industry.

In September 2013 on the television show, *The Talk*, Julie Chen shared an incident that happened in 1995 when she was a twenty-five-year-old local news reporter in Dayton, Ohio. Chen asked the news director, who was her boss at the time, if she could fill in at the anchor desk on holidays or when people were on vacations because she wanted the experience. The response she got from her boss was unexpected. In a nutshell, he said she would never be at the anchor desk because she is Chinese and the community doesn't relate to her, and that, because of the shape, size, and heaviness of her eyelids, she looked bored and disinterested on camera. Chen said her boss's comments "felt like a dagger in my heart" because all her life her dream was to be a network news anchor. Therefore, if she couldn't make it in Dayton, then there was no way she would make it to New York.

To her credit, even though the incident was hurtful, Ms. Chen decided to think about what she was told objectively and sought the guidance and input from other people, including a high-powered agent who basically told her the same thing. The agent said he would not represent Chen unless she got plastic surgery. The incident clearly and understandably affected her deeply. As a result, she decided to get the plastic surgery because she knew having the procedure was directly tied to her ability to achieve her dream. Evidently, the agent and the news director were *correct*. The agent told Chen that since she was good at what she does, if she had the surgery, she would go right to the top.

In Julie Chen's words, "It [the incident with my boss] felt like a grown-up version of racism in the workplace but I could not challenge him; he was the boss."[11] But was it indeed racism? Let's consider the racism equation:

Racism = Prejudice (+) Power (+) or (-) Intent

Undoubtedly, this scenario has the essential ingredients of racism. The news director judged Julie Chen and decided the audience in Dayton could not relate to her because she was Asian and didn't look like them. And her boss told her she would "never" get to the news anchor desk but *not* because she wasn't good or because she couldn't fulfill the requirements of the position. Instead, she wouldn't get there simply because of her race. Moreover, in terms of intent, it was not clear whether the news director was trying to hurt Chen with his words, nor could we tell his tone of voice in the conversation. But ultimately, his words served as a catalyst for Chen to begin observing herself in video news reports and to ultimately decide to have the surgery that she said was the prerequisite to her career taking off.

I commend Julie Chen for sharing her story because it is an example of the pressures some people of color feel to fit into the dominant culture in order to get a fair shot at professional success. Especially for people who want to be on television, there is an unspoken rule that in order to be relatable and acceptable, you should not look too ethnic but more in synch with European standards of beauty. Right or wrong, this is a classic example of systemic racism that is still ingrained in the United States and, I would say, pretty much everywhere.

This is also an example of the plight that Asian people endure—mostly silently, and probably more often than we would think. This raises the question that Chen stated on the show, namely, did she "give in to the man?" I say no. I agree with Sheryl Underwood's comment that Julie Chen did what she thought was best for her. It is no different from getting our teeth straightened or whitened, putting in hair extensions, wearing makeup, and so forth. We do these sorts of things because, in some way, we want to "fit in" with societal standards. Moreover, remember CRT asserts that we are all complicit in the system of racism, so doing things to conform to society's standard of beauty is just one indication of our complicity.

Conversely, the following scenario is another example of racial bias and racism in the workforce. However, this time it happened to me in the hotel and tourism industry, and unlike the Julie Chen incident, this was much more subtle.

Service, Please!

I once accompanied my husband on a business trip to a conference in Los Angeles, California. We stayed at an upscale hotel chain we normally choose whenever we travel. One morning, I decided to bring my laptop downstairs to the lobby restaurant and work while having brunch. I was busy working and didn't realize that over an hour and a half had gone by and the white female server had not come by to give me a menu, let alone taken my order. In fact, the entire time that I was sitting there, the server did not even greet me. Even after I realized how long I'd been there, she still walked past me a few times and did not even acknowledge my presence. I finally called out to her, but it was clear she pretended not to hear me. I hit my maximum tolerance level a few minutes later when I saw the server, a short distance away, walking with a tray and food to serve other guests whom I know arrived after me.

I immediately got up and walked around to the bar area and asked the bartender for a manager. The bartender was also white, and when I explained the situation to him, he was really apologetic and quite surprised by his coworker's conduct. The manager eventually arrived and I explained the situation to her. I also made it clear that I did not tolerate any type of discrimination and that I believed the server probably overlooked me and ignored me because of my race.

Before the manager arrived, I had thought about every possible excuse for the server's conduct, and I could not think of any. The only plausible explanation was that she assumed, because of my race, I probably could not afford to eat at the pricey hotel. Even if she thought I was uninterested in food or drink, her job was to find out. Why didn't she? Why did she ignore me for almost two hours, even after I tried to get her attention? The manager, who was an Asian American woman, also seemed quite perplexed by the server's conduct and said that she would speak to her and escalate the incident to their human resources department.

One scholar talks about "racial character of stratification," positing that we are all "assigned racial status with the clear purpose of creating or maintaining hierarchies of power and wealth."[12] In the situation I just described, despite the fact that the server was indeed in a position of having to "serve" me (a black woman), the idea clearly made her uncomfortable, and she chose not to do her job. What she didn't know was that *I* knew exactly what was going on, and *I chose* to interrupt her behavior. The server held a position of superiority in her mind, but the reality of her position as a server in the hotel clearly created internal conflict.

This type of inner conflict is a condition in psychology called "cognitive dissonance." Cognitive dissonance is the discomfort experienced when a person simultaneously holds two or more conflicting cognitions—that is, beliefs, ideas, values, or emotional reactions—that sometimes lead to having the overall feeling known as disequilibrium. This state of disequilibrium, or feeling off-balanced, can be manifested as frustration, anger, dread, guilt, anxiety, embarrassment, etc.[13] Cognitive dissonance is one of the most important, influential, and extensively researched theories in social psychology.

The server had a choice to either perform the functions related to her job or unleash her biases (at least temporarily). She made the wrong decision. This idea of cognitive dissonance happens to all of us all the time and is not necessarily always about race. How many times, for example, have you been invited to a family member's house and you don't want to go because you're tired or you just don't want to, but you feel obligated because it's family?

An important takeaway from this discussion is that race *must* influence your workplace, whether you see it or not. Racism, anti-Semitism, and negative racial assumptions are not free-floating forces that function independently of people. There is a reason we are still talking about these issues after hundreds and hundreds of years! There is a reason why, in the United States, there are Title VII laws that prohibit discrimination in the workplace. In fact, one scholar makes a direct correlation to the history of slavery and our current workplace racial dynamics.

Black and White employees may experience conflict due to their shared history of the enslavement of Africans in the United States. Perhaps a White employee doubts the competence of a Black coworker, given that the legacy of slavery does not place Blacks in roles of competence and authority. Black employees may likewise use the legacy of slavery as justification for their distrust or dislike of White colleagues.[14]

It is evident that the history of race "plays a significant part in how we come to construe the world in terms of different social categories."[15]

Race: Its Impact on Our Beliefs and Behaviors

I would love to say that the incident I had with the server at the hotel was an isolated one, but unfortunately, I would not be telling the truth. This type of treatment has occurred often in my life, and likewise for many people of color, this is the norm. People of color often have to deal with passive-aggressive behaviors from individuals who treat them with substandard respect because of race. However, despite the obvious influence of race and the pervasive maltreatment of people of color on a daily basis, race is still not always acknowledged or recognized as a possible factor influencing how we perceive and behave toward "others."[16] Why? Because, as we have already seen, the racial assumptions and biases we have toward others are not always obvious and overt; they are sometimes masked, disguised, and camouflaged by jokes or other word usage, and our negative beliefs and assumptions are not always manifested at the conscious level.[17]

For these reasons, it is difficult for individuals to prove that an incident is related to race, even though race prejudice is "embedded in the social, cultural, and biological collective consciousness of human experience."[18] It is also the reason why, unfortunately, some racial offenders are "protected" even after they have offended. Even when a person of color is convinced that an incident occurred because of race, he or she usually has an uphill battle and the responsibility of convincing others—without a shadow of a doubt—that the situation was related to race.

In my case, the hotel restaurant manager immediately believed what I was saying, but this is the exception. One thing that is consistently true, however, is that regardless of the type of incident related to race, there is the tendency to evoke any of the following emotions within the individuals involved: "fear, distrust, anger, denial, guilt, ignorance, naiveté, and the wish for simple solutions."[19] I definitely had some feelings of anger toward the server at the hotel lobby restaurant, while the server apparently denied ignoring me and supposedly felt guilty. This denial of the influence of race among some white individuals is the key element in the concept of colorblind ideology that serves to "dodge, suppress, and ignore matters related to race altogether."[20]

Colorblindness

Colorblindness is not physical blindness or an inability to see color[21] but "white resistance to seeing."[22] Research has shown that when white people are pressed, they reveal their awareness of the advantages and privileges afforded to them simply because of their skin color.[23] The self-inflicted blindness to race and resistance to seeing it unless pressed suggests that there is an ongoing series of decision points for some white people when it comes to race.[24]

One such decision point or option that is afforded to white people is the ability to remain silent when incidents related to race occur. This silence is indicative of colorblind ideology because it reflects the position of privilege that white people have to ignore race when they so choose.[25] That said, however, I don't necessarily believe that white people always choose to ignore race because they don't want to acknowledge their positions of privilege. In fact, in my work as a trainer, I have encountered many white workshop participants who use colorblindness as a defense mechanism. If they don't acknowledge race, then they don't have to talk about it—and ultimately, this decision shields them from saying the wrong thing.

In fact, in my many years of facilitating workshops, I have encountered many white participants who have difficulty thinking in terms of race, especially when analyzing case studies while looking through a racial lens. As a result of this difficulty, many participants say, they "don't see race" while analyzing the case studies but at times will admit they "only see gender." The participants say they only see gender because it is easier to talk about gender than it is to talk about race. This should not be a surprising disclosure, since there are much steeper penalties from the public when a person says the "wrong" thing in relation to race versus in relation to gender. Given this reality, of course some white people are afraid to acknowledge and talk about race. I would be afraid too! However, perhaps the best way to move forward is to become *more* conscious of race and its impact on equal opportunity.[26]

Moreover, as a result of my understanding of colorblindness and the fact that some white people use it as a defense mechanism, I don't attach any judgments to workshop participants who are colorblind or who struggle to discuss race. Instead, when I recognize this in participants, I reiterate that it is understandable for individuals to be afraid to admit they have racial biases, and equally terrifying is sharing them publicly in discourse with others. Invariably, participants eventually feel safe enough to share their beliefs because I always establish a psychologically safe environment before I facilitate any discussions. I do this by setting ground rules for discussion and explaining what it means to engage in dialogue, especially in relation to such a potentially volatile topic. The American sociologist and emeritus professor of adult and continuing education at Teachers College, Columbia University, Jack Mezirow asserts,

> Discourse is that type of dialogue in which we participate with others whom we believe to be informed, objective, and rational to assess reasons that justify problematic beliefs. Discourse leads to a best tentative judgment that

is always subject to new insights, perspectives, evidence, or arguments. The quality of this assessment is, itself, enhanced through free, full participation in a continuing discourse involving critical reflection on assumptions with an increasingly broad and more diverse group of informed and open-minded participants having the widest range of views possible.[27]

In general, it is difficult to consider alternative ways of thinking about issues when you are used to thinking one way. And this is especially the case when asked to discuss such an inherently challenging topic that evokes intense negative emotions *and* with stiff penalties attached. It's true that some white people refuse to see race because they don't want to acknowledge the privileges they have over people of color. I also know from my professional experience that there are whites who also choose to be colorblind because they struggle with how to address and talk about racial disparities and fear potentially saying the wrong thing. This does not mean that colorblind racism is right. I am saying that it is important for white people to talk about race—especially because it is difficult. However, the proper environment must be established and with clear parameters and guidelines in order to facilitate these difficult discussions. Moreover, one other thing I do during the "ground rules speech" that helps establish a safe environment is share my embarrassing experience of unconsciously prejudging the ability of a black boy when consciously I should have known better. This sharing of my personal experience of "culprit bias"[28] inevitably breaks the ice and allows participants to also feel comfortable sharing their vulnerabilities.

Can People of Color Be Racial Offenders?

I have stated over and over that we are too quick to label every racial incident as racist. I also believe we move even more quickly to come down hard on individuals who make any mistakes involving race.

However, what if a racial incident involves a person of color as the culprit? Can people of color be racist? The answer is yes. But before I delve into a detailed explanation of my stance, I must first state that even though there are people of color who, by Bidol's definition (**Racism = Prejudice + Power**), can be racist, in comparison to whites, the number of people of color in positions of power with the ability to oppress, stifle, and prevent the progress of other people of color is miniscule.

Overwhelmingly, white people continue to be in control of the majority of society's institutions, from education to Fortune 500 companies—simply because of systemic racism. In fact, the 2010 Alliance for Board Diversity's (ABD) Census supports this claim when it reported, "White men continue to dominate corporate boards and have, in fact, increased their presence since 2004. Women and minorities are still vastly underrepresented."[29] Further, the following 2010 statistics offered by the ABD illustrate the disparity between the number of whites and the number of minorities holding director positions at Fortune 100 and Fortune 500 companies.

Director Positions at Fortune 100 Companies

White Men	White Women	Minority Men	Minority Women
72.9%	14.5%	9.1%	3.6%

Director Positions at Fortune 500 Companies

White Men	White Women	Minority Men	Minority Women
77.6%	12.7%	6.8%	3.0%

These statistics are important, because they show the gap between whites and minorities holding positions of power, thereby highlighting the potential opportunities for both groups to abuse their power—as is required for racism to occur. In the past, Bidol's racism equation was criticized because it was said to only be applicable to white people. However, at that time, the people in power were all white, so the criticisms are questionable. However, as time has gone by, more and more minorities in the United States have acquired economic wealth and have ascended to positions of power where they can potentially adversely affect others on the basis of race. For example, it was reported that more cases of discrimination against whites are emerging. In Fulton County, Georgia, a black female commissioner was reported to have said that there were "too many white boys on staff" when she denied a white applicant a director's position after he served as the interim director in the same position. The white applicant sued and was awarded over a million dollars.[30]

Likewise, Trayvon Martin's death was a case of one person of color committing a racial offense—in this case, racial violence against another person of color. Even though Zimmerman describes himself as white, he looks Hispanic and his mother, who testified at his trial, is Hispanic. Zimmerman abused his position as a neighborhood watch coordinator by racially profiling, pursuing, and then killing Trayvon Martin. And fortunately for him, despite being a person of color himself, Zimmerman clearly had access to some degree of institutional power, probably because of his father's position as a white man and as a magistrate. From day one after the killing, Zimmerman was treated with kid gloves; he was not arrested for forty-six days. If Trayvon's name were Travis, this case would have been handled very differently. And especially if Zimmerman were a black man, the case would have been handled differently. And the verdict would have been different.

Let's look at another incident that happened in 2012 involving ESPN commentator Rob Parker, who questioned the "blackness" of

Washington Redskins quarterback Robert Griffin III, also known as RGIII.[31] On the show *First Take*, Parker made ignorant, stereotypical remarks about RGIII, declaring that he "wasn't black" and called him a "cornball brother" because he had a white fiancée and was rumored to be a Republican. Parker was eventually fired for his remarks.

What is interesting is how this incident was described as "racial" and "racially charged." But why not "racist" or even "racially biased"? If the culprit involved in an incident related to race is also of color, is the racist label not suitable? What if Parker were white? Do you think he would have been called a racist? Most definitely! The problem is that people don't seem to know how to make sense of situations when people of color make racial comments about *other* people of color. Why? Because there is an inherent belief that people of color should "know better" since they have faced discrimination themselves. But again, these types of scenarios should not be confusing if you remember the basic thesis of critical race theory (CRT). CRT posits that we are *all* complicit in the system of racism and that all people participate in keeping racism alive. Moreover, when it comes to people of color, it is important to recognize the following:

> Oppression does not make us immune from hurting others. All too often, it serves as a lesson in how to behave once we get whatever power we can. The hierarchal and competitive nature of our society gives everyone plenty of opportunities to experience both sides.[32]

There have been times when people of color have walked into the room before I was about to present my workshop Think You Are an Unbiased Teacher? Think Again! and have asked, "Is this workshop for me too?" My response is always the same: "Absolutely!" Unfortunately, there is a pervasive misconception, mostly among people of color themselves, that people of color cannot be biased, exhibit oppressive behaviors, or even be racist. I have seen otherwise in my work as an educator, trainer, and researcher, and there is plenty of documented evidence from a variety of sources. I wrote this book for *all* of us because we *all* struggle, regardless of race, with these issues.

Let's return again to the Parker incident. Were Parker's words racist? Was his firing justified? To answer these questions, let's reference my Racism Equation: **Racism = Prejudice (+) Power (+) or (-) Intent**. Were his words prejudicial? Yes, they were, and in fact, they were stereotypical. Parker had a specific stereotype about "brothers" and what they should do in order to show they are "down for the cause," whatever that may mean. Parker also used his power inappropriately, by way of his public platform, to make disparaging statements about RGIII. Therefore, when we analyze the incident while considering the equation, Parker made prejudicial and stereotypical remarks. When this is coupled with his abuse of power, publicly making such insulting remarks and suggesting that there is a set way that a black man can "prove" that he is "a brother," we can conclude that his comments were racist. Moreover, Parker's comments are indicative of "internalized racism," also known as self-hatred or "internalized racial oppression," which is a phenomenon sociologists define as follows:

> The individual inculcation of the racist stereotypes, values, images, and ideologies perpetuated by the White dominant society about one's racial group, leading to feelings of self-doubt, disgust, and disrespect for one's race and/or oneself.[33]

This area of research, self-hatred, is not widely known and is not particularly welcomed or embraced because, on some level, there is a belief that victims of racism are being punished or blamed for their thinking. This is not my intent. I am merely pointing out that none of us is immune to the effects of racism because we all live in a racist society. Internalized racism is an expected consequence of racism.

> Like *all* forms of internalized domination, internalized racism is *not* the result of some cultural or biological

characteristic of the subjugated. Nor is it the consequence of any weakness, ignorance, inferiority, psychological defect, gullibility, or other shortcoming of the oppressed.[34]

This said, however, I still believe we all have a responsibility to learn how to think critically about what we think and what we say. This brings us back to the element of *intent* in the racism equation and in reference to the Rob Parker incident. Apparently, Rob Parker's comments were not said off-the-cuff during the show but were prepared beforehand. This means that he intentionally wanted to say *exactly* what he said. However, I do not necessarily believe he understood the gravity or the implications of what he was saying and how racially insulting his words were. Bottom line: his words were mean-spirited and were racially offensive, so it is not a surprise that he lost his job. And does Parker deserve another chance? I believe he does. He publicly apologized for his remarks, and hopefully he has learned a lesson from this mistake, which was in essence racially stereotyping RGIII.

How Stereotypes Influence Our Thinking

Historically, the word *stereotype* is derived from an aspect of the printing process in which a mold is made in order to duplicate patterns of pictures on the page. Pulitzer Prize–winning political journalist Walter Lippman "saw the suitability for the term to be used in reference to people. He believed people used cognitive molds to reproduce images of people or events in their minds that he called 'pictures in our heads.'"[35] In other words, Lippman believed that we respond to the perceptions we have about the world rather than the world itself. Similarly, there are various ways that stereotypes influence our judgments or recollections of social situations, and in any context in which social categories are psychologically available, stereotypes will come into play more or less automatically.[36]

Preeminent social psychologist Gordon Allport defines and

explains stereotype development in his 1954 classic treatise, *The Nature of Prejudice*:

1. Stereotypes are the perception that most members of a category share some attribute and that stereotyping arises directly out of the categorization process.

2. Stereotypes can originate from the culture in which people are socialized, from real cultural or socioeconomic difference between groups and also cognitive bias, which seems to result in an *illusory correlation* between minority groups and infrequently occurring attributes. Put simply, illusory correlations describe the natural inclination for people to assign positive attributes to people who appear to be within their "in-group" status while those who appear to be in the out-group are more likely to be ascribed negative attributes/ stereotypes.

3. Stereotypes can influence people's judgments of individuals. A useful way of viewing stereotypes is as hypotheses in search of confirmatory information. Much evidence exists for this confirmation-seeking nature of stereotypic expectancies.

4. Stereotypes also influence attributional judgments about the causes of in-group and out-group actions. A typical finding is that positive and negative behaviors by the in-group are attributed internally and externally respectively; for out-group behaviors the reverse applies.

5. Stereotypes may be used more if people are cognitively or emotionally preoccupied with other concerns. The reason is that distractions are thought to consume cognitive attention, thus paving the way for the laborsaving afforded by stereotyping.

6. Stereotypes can have self-fulfilling properties (as previously described), creating in the targets of their focus the very attributes hypothesized to exist. These self-fulfilling prophecies have been observed in educational contexts.

7. Stereotypes change in response to disconfirming information, but the patterning of that information (concentrated in a few exemplars or dispersed across many) and the valence of the stereotype undergoing revision are important factors determining the extent of change.[37]

If we relate these definitions of stereotypes back to the subject of race and racism, it is clear that racism, at the overarching and systemic level, can involve either conscious or unconscious stereotypical thinking that ultimately biases us to others at the social level. Conversely, it is important to also know that our prejudices can lead us to rely on our stereotypes when judging people. Either way, a stereotype, whether prejudiced or not, is a cognitive association of a social category with certain characteristics. Stereotyping is nothing more than a mode of generalizing. The problem, of course, is that it tends to be offensive at worst and merely inaccurate at best. The Rob Parker incident is a perfect example of how one can get into trouble when one stereotypes.

One caveat to this discussion is that prejudice and stereotyping could be either positive or negative. However, because this book focuses on disentangling racism from other ways in which race is involved in negative assertions and actions, it is reasonable to restrict the focus to negative prejudice. Nevertheless, we should not forget that people also exhibit *positive* prejudice and this may be just as harmful as negative prejudice. For example, I have taught Asian students over the years at all levels of education who have articulated that they feel overwhelming pressure to succeed academically because of the pervasive stereotype that all Asians are smart.

As human beings, we have a wonderful capacity to abstract from the particular, and this capacity is arguably what makes human beings the most dominant creatures on earth. However, generalizing doesn't always go well, especially when we first meet someone.

Hello. Nice to meet you!

It is true that one of the ways we make sense of our world is by classifying or categorizing things and people. Simple examples include noticing the difference between a dog and a cat based on the way they look. Or if we see someone wearing a skirt, we classify that person as female. However, we should ask, "Are all cats alike? Are all dogs alike? Are all people who wear skirts female?" The answer to each question is no. For example, an Irish male friend wore a kilt to my wedding.

I ask these questions because we have to understand that "stereotyping arises directly out of the categorization process."[38] Regardless of what we are judging or categorizing, we should not believe that *all* of what we see in a particular category is the same. For example, Rottweilers have a reputation for being dangerous dogs, but do we classify all dogs as dangerous? Do we even believe that all Rottweilers are dangerous? We make distinctions between breeds of animals and even between animals within a breed. I argue that we need to also make distinctions among types of people as well— including those within racial groups, because no group is monolithic. Moreover, we have to remember that, when we meet a person for the first time, we have at our disposal not just our preconceptions about his or her group membership but also information about the way he or she actually appears, dresses, and behaves, which may not be consistent with the group stereotype.[39] This is when we have to consciously work through our preconceived notions and stereotypes and try to look at the person as an individual and not as part of a group. I realize what I am asking people to do is very challenging, but I stress this necessity even more when we encounter a person for the first time and that person reminds us of a negative event or situation involving someone who looks like that person.

It is important to understand that just because something negative happened with one particular person from a specific racial group, this does not necessarily mean that associations with *all* people from that particular racial group will inevitably yield negative experiences. For example, suppose you went to the grocery store and purchased a container of raspberries. In the store, on the surface, they all looked ripe and fresh, but when you opened the package after you got home, you discovered that many of the raspberries were actually rotten. Disappointed, you would not eat that particular batch of raspberries and would probably throw them out. But would that experience keep you from ever buying raspberries again? Of course not. You would try again and buy another batch at some point. This is what I propose we do with people.

We cannot let a few rotten raspberries keep us from trying raspberries again. There are too many people in the world for any of us to definitively say that *all* people from any particular race are the same. We need to keep looking for exceptions to our beliefs, especially when they involve negative perceptions or attitudes toward others. Let's return to the analogy.

Now suppose you have another bowl of raspberries. Let's say there are almost one hundred raspberries in the bowl. You pick one up, inspect it, and declare it ripe. Then you pick up another, inspect it, and declare it ripe. After picking up five raspberries, each of which is ripe, you declare, "All the raspberries in this bowl are ripe." This is a perfectly ordinary thing to do. It's not scientific, but it tends to work quite well for us when we are selecting food. Why not do this in our daily lives? If we're going to make assumptions, let's try to make them as positive as possible. We need to assume that all people, like the raspberries, are good. And if we happen to have a bowl of raspberries and many of them are ripe but we suddenly encounter a few not-so-good ones, then we need to keep looking for more good ones.

In essence, what I am suggesting we do is consider the consequences of uncritically holding on to our "mental models."[40]

These are deeply ingrained assumptions, stereotypes, or pictures we have in our heads that, although they are often unconscious, influence how we understand the world and how we act toward others. We should strive to be open to the idea of new experiences and people, and this will hopefully lead us to become habitually flexible and open to new people and new experiences.

Jack Mezirow says it is important to

> search for more dependable beliefs and understandings— those producing interpretations and opinions that are more true and justified—by assessing the intentions, experience and character of others communicating with us and by becoming critically reflective about the assumptions supporting the beliefs, values, feelings and judgments of those others, as well as about our own.[41]

When we put these words in terms of race and cognition, even though, when we meet someone for the first time, we (a) look at that individual's race, (b) make assumptions and draw inferences about that person because of race, and (c) behave either positively or negatively toward that person, this does not have to be an inevitable, uncontrollable process. While I agree that indeed sometimes we do and say things unconsciously, I still believe we can learn to control our assumptions about others. In fact, for almost a decade, my workshops have focused on helping individuals recognize and challenge their racial assumptions about different people. Among the many topics, I also discuss how these assumptions can have dire consequences for everyone, especially people of color, who also have to contend with systemic barriers in society's institutions.

The Burden to Prove

The experience of racial assumptions is perhaps most difficult for people of color, because even though they experience the consequences of those assumptions on a daily basis, they still have the burden of "proving" it. What is unseen is hard to prove. Recall, for example, the scenario I shared earlier when I made the mistake of unfairly assuming that the young black boy I was tutoring could not read. He would have had a lot of difficulty *proving* it, especially if I were to deny the truth. Similarly, had the Los Angeles hotel restaurant manager not believed me when I told her that the waitress ignored me for almost two hours, I would have had a hard time proving the server was racially motivated. Also, another example of the burden to prove is the Trayvon Martin case. We all know how hard it was to prove that George Zimmerman's assumptions led him to racially profile Trayvon Martin and eventually kill him. As I have said, race is an intangible aspect of our interactions and typically is an influence that one cannot necessarily see unless it is blatantly articulated through word or action. In the Zimmerman criminal case, ironically, I believe both were clearly present, yet Zimmerman still got off.

Additionally, compounding the problem of proving that an incident happened because of race is the fact that the assumptions we have about race are typically disguised by language type and use. For example, using the pronoun *them* or *they* in reference to some generalization about a group can be considered racially charged under certain circumstances and is typically identified by way of tone of voice. George Zimmerman's comment to 911 dispatchers—"These assholes, they always get away"[42]—is a perfect example of this. We all know that no racial group is monolithic, so using the word *they* or *them* automatically puts everyone in the same box and does not acknowledge or respect individuality. Using the word *some* is much safer.

In chapter 6, I further discuss this topic of language and how it can be used to mask or veil our assumptions and true feelings—especially when it comes to race. Also, later in this book, I will teach you how to recognize your assumptions and I will teach you how to interrupt your assumptions *before* they translate to behavior. Yes, making assumptions is a normal phenomenon, as I have argued, but I believe we can learn to manage our automatic assumptions by becoming more introspective. It is also important for us to understand *how* we learn and how to open ourselves up to new ideas and teachings. In essence, I am talking about what is going on in our heads.

Tell me and I forget. Teach me and I remember. Involve me and I learn.

—BENJAMIN FRANKLIN

CHAPTER THREE

How Do Adults Learn?

Some scholars suggest that "situated cognition is based on the idea that what we know and the meanings we attach to what we know are socially constructed."[1] In other words, "The self cannot be adequately understood apart from the particular social context in which they are shaped."[2] Situated cognition means that learning is inextricable from the situation in which the learning process occurs.[3] Put simply, if we relate these points back to the theme of this book, we see that, because society is so obsessed with race and because we live and learn *within* this society, then we must also be preoccupied with race.

Situated cognition is based on three key ideas:

1. Learning and thinking are generally social activities.
2. Thinking and the ability to learn "are profoundly structured by the availability of situationally provided 'tools.'"
3. Our thinking is influenced by our interaction with the setting where learning takes place.[4] In other words, "Learning and knowing are intimately linked to real-life situations"[5] or the "context" in which something takes place.

Context

There are two important dimensions to the contextual approach to learning: the "interactive" and the "structural."[6] First, the interactive dimension acknowledges that learning is a product of the individual interacting with the context. That context, in turn, is most effective when it involves real-life situations like role-playing and simulations. The structural dimension of context takes into consideration the social and cultural factors that affect learning, such as race, class, gender, ethnicity, and power and oppression.[7] Clearly, the structural dimension of context—namely race—is informed by Critical Race Theory's (CRT) assertion that racism and prejudice are everywhere.

To see these concepts in action, let's refer back to the incident in which I unfairly prejudged the young black boy I was working with in California. Prior to meeting him, I *learned* through my experience teaching in Toronto that some black boys cannot read at grade level. Then when I changed environments and met the black boy in California, I transferred my experience and assumed that he also could not read at grade level. I made a terrible mistake by transferring what I *learned* in one context (Toronto) and added it to a new context (California) without realizing. The lesson here is we cannot assume that what we've learned in one situation or environment will automatically be true in another situation or environment.

On one hand, transferring previous experience to a new, seemingly similar one is a part of how we make sense of our world and how to get used to a new environment. If we couldn't make connections between events, we would have no experience to speak of—everything would be fragmented. This doesn't mean, however, that we're always good at using our cognitive apparatus. Just as it's an error to generalize from one or two experiences with similar people to the entire group, it's also an error to believe that similarities transfer from one experience to another. This is why, as much as possible, it is important to look at each situation or context as new and not assume anything. We need to develop "contextual awareness," as one scholar calls it, which is when the assumptions undergirding our ideas and behaviors are seen to be culturally and historically specific.[8]

Disorienting Dilemmas and Perspective Transformation

The incident I just described involving my prejudgment of the black boy would be classified by pioneer adult educator Jack Mezirow as a "disorienting dilemma."[9] A disorienting dilemma is described as some type of life crisis or incident that has left a person profoundly changed. As a result of the incident, the person realizes that his or her thinking or approach to something or someone is flawed, and as a further consequence, that person has gone through a perspective transformation and is no longer the same as a result of the incident. In my case, I realized how important it was to enter every new environment with fresh eyes (as much as possible) and not to assume or anticipate anything.

Another event I would classify as a "disorienting dilemma" involved Republican senator Rob Portman, who reversed his opposition to same-sex marriage after his son came out as a homosexual. The revelation of his son's sexual orientation directly led to the senator's perspective transformation or change in thinking on the matter of gay rights. Moreover, another important point to know about the notion of a "disorienting dilemma" and a "perspective transformation" is that the terms come from a body of literature in adult education called transformative learning.

Transformative Learning

Transformative learning is concerned with how people *make meaning* from the experiences they have and how they change as a result of those experiences. It is the process of becoming critically aware of how and why our assumptions have come to constrain the ways we perceive, understand, and feel about our world, changing these structures of habitual expectation to make possible a more inclusive, discriminating, and integrative perspective, and finally making choices or otherwise acting on these new understandings.[10] Thus, the process involves a critical assessment of the assumptions we have taken for granted—assumptions that have supported our beliefs, feelings, and prior judgments.[11]

Needless to say, this is an incredibly difficult process that requires an individual to distance himself or herself in such a way as to look dispassionately at who one is. It's as if one becomes a frog on the dissection plate. Through the process of removing and cataloging our innards—those attitudes, beliefs, etc.—we create new meaning for ourselves.

Mezirow's Perspective Transformation Model helps explain some of the phases of the transformative process that yields clarification of new meaning.

1. a disorienting dilemma
2. self-examination with feelings of fear, anger, guilt, or shame
3. a critical assessment of assumptions
4. recognition that one's discontent and the process of transformation are shared
5. exploration of options for new roles, relationships, and actions
6. planning a course of action
7. acquiring knowledge and skills for implementing one's plans
8. provisional trying of new roles
9. building competence and self-confidence in new roles and relationships
10. a reintegration into one's life on the basis of conditions dictated by one's new perspective[12]

Perspective transformation does not always happen in that exact order, but this is not essential for the theory's instructive value. To some degree, I would like readers of this book to reassess their thinking and begin their own process of perspective transformation by beginning to look at incidents related to race beyond simple "racist" or "not racist" categories. However, I know full well that in some cases there will be outright opposition, in some cases there will be a little resistance, and in some cases, full acceptance. Nonetheless, I am not measuring the "success" of this book by counting how many people agree with my opinions because I know there are always levels of readiness to learning new things. Much like in my diversity training workshops, my goal is to only present information with the understanding that some may "get" the message immediately, some down the road, and some never.

This conversation is likened to a question asked in transformative learning theory: do mere experiences or "critical incidents" automatically lead to perspective transformation? I would say no. We all know some people who do the same thing over and over and never get the lesson. The point is that people learn things and get things when they are ready to get them. Bottom line: I think an experience or a critical incident has to be so profound that it forces an individual to change his or her perspective and behavior.

Critical Incidents

The term *critical incident* is self-explanatory. It is an incident in your life that is of great importance; it is critical. However, it differs from a disorienting dilemma because critical incidents do not necessarily lead to a perspective transformation or a change in behavior. We all have at least one friend in our life who seems to continuously encounter or create the same type of critical incident in his or her life, such as repeatedly choosing abusive boyfriends. And yet this person does not learn from the experiences or come to any realization that even though the boyfriends are rotten, there's something problematic about repeatedly choosing the same type of person. This individual needs to *learn* from the experiences by looking inside, figuring out what contributes to these choices, and beginning to make positive shifts in perspective and in behavior. Nonetheless, critical incidents are widely used in educational research, including in my own, in order to "assist learners to understand why they think, feel, and believe" what they do.[13]

Another example of a person I believe experienced a disorienting dilemma is TV veteran and icon Larry King. King was being interviewed on CNN by television host George Stroumboulopoulos when King shared a scary situation that prompted him, after several attempts, to quit smoking cold turkey.[14] King described a time when he was feeling so unwell he decided to go to the hospital. However, he apparently was not too sick to smoke on the way to the hospital! Upon arriving at the hospital, King learned that he was having a heart attack and subsequently had bypass surgery. King further described the ride home after his ordeal and stated that he threw away the pack of cigarettes he had in his shirt and never smoked again. Evidently, King had enough of a scare, or a "disorienting dilemma," that made him quit smoking for good.

I share this scenario because all along King said he knew he needed to quit smoking and had tried in the past. However, it took facing death to make him stop. Evidently, there was a shift in King's perspective on smoking, fueled by the heart attack that led him to change his behavior and stop smoking. But of course, not all people who have heart attacks decide to change their behaviors as a result. Case in point, I have a girlfriend whose father had several heart attacks but continued smoking thereafter. A person has to want to change his or her behavior and *decide* that it is worth the effort. What is a disorienting dilemma for one person is not necessarily for another. It is very individual and no one can force another to change his or her perspective on anything.

We all know some people who, regardless of your effort, will never try to even consider your opinion or perspective on something because they are right. I say do as I do; don't waste your time or energy. One scholar brilliantly sums up this type of behavior by calling it "tribal thinking," which is the assumption that others have myths but we have the *truth*. It is arguably the case that "even facts are artifacts of a particular historical period or a historian's bias ... [therefore] the key recognition here is that there is no such thing as pure objectivity"[15] and "there are any number of tribes, each believing its own truth to be paramount."[16]

Given this point, it is no surprise that there was such a chasm between the reactions of some blacks versus those of some whites in relation to the George Zimmerman acquittal. President Obama also used the word "context" in his remarks after the verdict, saying in a nutshell to the public that there was such reaction from the black community because of the history of black people and the context in which they are treated in society because of color. But as President Obama stated in his remarks, despite the massive gap in reactions between blacks and whites, all is not lost, and peace and understanding can still be achieved by addressing this issue, for example, in churches and in educational institutions. Also, one other point President Obama made that was poignant was that it was pointless to gather politicians and talking heads together who have their positions and are not willing to budge.

This is, in essence, what I am saying. It is best to focus your energy on those who are open to new perspectives and new learning opportunities—put simply, those individuals who strive to achieve emotional self-actualization. Some people are just unwilling to learn new lessons, and this is okay. And it especially has to be okay if those persons are your spouses or family members whom you wish to remain in your life. Then you will have to learn how to deal with it and meet them where they are. Nonetheless, those who do choose to consider alternate perspectives and learning opportunities do so through a process called critical reflection.

Critical Reflection

According to Mezirow, "By far the most significant learning experiences in adulthood involve critical reflection, reassessing the way we have posed problems, and reassessing our own orientation to perceiving, knowing, believing, feeling, and acting."[17] It is like the discipline of working with mental models, which "starts with turning the mirror inward; learning to unearth our internal pictures of the world, to bring them to the surface and hold them rigorously to scrutiny."[18] Moreover, critical thinking is not a "tribal value" because "it threatens existing authority and elevates the individual above the group."[19] This means that individuals are willing to go against the grain and attempt to consider alternative ways of looking at things. This is a challenging task, especially when individuals believe that they *know* everything.

We have probably all heard the saying "Common sense is not common." I have encountered too many people who believe, because they have achieved an advanced degree or because they have gone to a great university, they don't need to *learn* anymore. They are too rigid and, in this sense, too elitist to consider the perspective of others—especially those with less education or who didn't go to the *right* school. Adult education teaches us that we should all be lifelong learners and that education and learning can happen anywhere and from anyone. As an adult educator, I believe in this philosophy, and it coincides with how I was raised. My parents taught me to treat all people equally regardless of profession, position, aptitude, or ability. Whether it's the president of a company or the janitor who is cleaning floors, I treat everyone equally. At the end of the day, we are all mortal, and we all pass away. As my wise mother-in-law says, it doesn't matter how high our tombstones will be in the cemetery; we will all be in the ground. Death is the great equalizer, so why not treat people equally when we are alive?

The sense of morality that was taught to me by my parents directly coincides with the outstanding and influential work of Chris Argyris, an American business theorist and professor emeritus at Harvard Business School. Argyris brilliantly makes the distinction between "single-loop learning" and "double-loop learning" among professionals during the leaning process.[20] He argues that in order for learning to take place that is meaningful, individuals must look inward and not only rely on "single-loop learning." A person engaging in single-loop learning repeatedly tries to address a problem but is too rigid to make any adjustments or modifications to the methods used, and the person never questions the goal itself.

Argyris analogizes this concept to a thermostat that is set to automatically turn on whenever the temperature in the room falls below sixty-eight degrees. Instead, he asserts that professionals should look beyond the automatic and become "double-loop learners," asking, "'Why am I set at 68 degrees?' And then explore whether or not some other temperature might more economically achieve the goal of heating the room."[21] It ties in to the old adage, "If it ain't broke, then don't fix it." And it is also represented by Paula Deen's words, "I is what I is," stated in an interview with Matt Lauer on the *Today Show* after the scandal broke regarding accusations of her use of the "n-word" and creating an unpleasant work environment. If Paula Deen wants to *recover* from the scandal and repair her reputation, she will have to make personal adjustments and be open to new ways of seeing things, or she will not survive. The implication of "I is what I is" is "Take me or leave me." Well, the public and the law will not accept her behavior as is. Learning involves both the detection and correction of error.[22]

The following are two other examples of words from a rigid person demonstrating the type of reasoning (or lack thereof) that does not consider alternative ways to view a situation:

EXAMPLE #1

Flawed Reasoning
"If I have four quarters, then I have a dollar. So if I have a dollar, then I must have four quarters."

Explanation
No. There are ways to make a dollar with coins other than quarters. Therefore, having a dollar doesn't mean you have four quarters.

EXAMPLE #2

Flawed Reasoning

"If I have four quarters, then I have a dollar. I don't have four quarters, so I don't have a dollar."

Explanation

No. Just because you don't have four quarters does not mean you don't have a dollar. There are ways to make a dollar using coins other than quarters.

It is tempting to come down hard on people with this type of reasoning, but much like the caveat I shared when discussing white people who are "colorblind," we need to show compassion and patience here. Again, it can be a scary process rethinking what you think you know and being open to change and potential criticism. This is why, even when some people realize that their thinking is "flawed," they pretend to be perfect and refuse to address their limitations. It is important to be patient with people and hear them out. However, the onus is also on the individuals to take a risk and admit what they think. Influential scholar Dr. Peter Senge, senior lecturer at the Massachusetts Institute of Technology (MIT), explains that working with mental models involves the inclusion of "the ability to carry on 'learningful' conversations that balance inquiry and advocacy, where people expose their own thinking effectively and make that thinking open to the influence of others."[23]

However, the operative word here is "expose." People have "mental maps" that help them act in different situations, and these maps govern the actions of people rather than the theories people say or explicitly "espouse" in order to get others to think what they would like.[24] Put simply, there are theories for what people *say*, and there are theories for what people *do*. Unfortunately, few people are aware that the maps they use to take action are not the ones they explicitly espouse. And even smaller numbers of people are aware of the maps or theories they do use.[25] Therefore, the ultimate goal is for people to learn how to make what they do and what they say more congruent. This is accomplished by engaging in the aforementioned "learningful" conversations that are particularly useful if coupled with an individual's willingness to critically reflect on his or her beliefs and behaviors and with the ability to let go of rigidity, ego, and elitism.

Critical reflection can also be described as *consciousness raising*, "the simultaneity of remembering and understanding that occurs in consciousness raising always constitutes *critical (self) reflection.*"[26] For example, one theorist surmises,

> If in the course of consciousness-raising ... a woman responds strongly, it is not because she has found something new to bitch about, but rather she has found something old to bitch about, because she perceives something old in a new way.[27]

This thought is consistent with another researcher's insistence that "critical reflection and feelings should not be viewed as separate but instead as operating in an interdependent relationship, with each relying upon the other in the search for clarity and understanding."[28] In my work, this connection between reflection and feelings is inevitable because I address such a historically significant and painful topic. However, because race and racism can evoke such negative emotions, I caution my participants to not get *stuck* in their emotions but to speak up when they feel rumblings inside. Otherwise, these negative emotions can fester and will hinder progress.

Bottom line: one intended outcome for this book is that people learn how to make what they do and say more congruent. Those people who are willing to be vulnerable enough to reconsider what they think they know, and who are open to learning new things through sharing their views with trusted others, are more likely to achieve this state of congruency and authenticity. If you feel like you are "pretending" when you are at work or in public, and you struggle with your biases, then this is how your *work* should begin. Moreover, this questioning of what we think we know is also important as you read this book. I know some of you probably do not believe you need to learn more about this topic, and some of you probably believe you do not harbor any racial biases. But a key component in most of prejudice, discrimination, and racism is that it does not require intention but happens automatically.[29]

In the next chapter, I show just how easy it is to have a misstep with race, even when you think you are being careful.

To get lost is to learn the way.

—AFRICAN PROVERB

CHAPTER FOUR

The Fine Line between Racism and Racial Bias

Now that we have made a clear distinction between what constitutes racism and what constitutes racial bias and what is happening to us cognitively, in this chapter I discuss how easy it is to have a racial misstep, even when you have the purest intentions. Take, for example, MSNBC's liberal commentator Chris Matthews, whom I believe is a smart, fair-minded orator. Matthews made a racially charged comment a few years ago[1] after President Barack Obama made his State of the Union speech. Matthews said, "I was trying to think about who he was tonight. It is interesting, he is 'postracial' by all appearances; you know, I forgot he was black tonight for an hour." Matthews later "clarified" his comments on *The Rachel Maddow Show*, saying, among other things, that he believed what the president has been able to do, moving beyond the black and white, was wonderful, and he was "loving it."

Was Matthews's initial comment racist? Let's consider the racism equation to help us decide: **Racism = Prejudice (+) Power (+) or (-) Intent**. Yes, Matthews's comment had the ingredient of prejudice because if he forgot Obama was "black" and said that Obama was "postracial," then the implication is that, for an hour, Obama spoke well like white people do. Also, given his position to influence people—serving as a commentator and analyst on a well-known television channel, there is no doubt that the crucial element of power is satisfied. Matthews unfortunately, and I believe unconsciously, made a sweeping generalization about black and white people and their general abilities to articulate. We all know that not all black people speak Ebonics, and we all know that not all white people speak well. I am also certain that Matthews knows this too.

Without realizing, by his comment, Matthews intimated that it was unusual for a black man or a black person to bring the country together or to speak well. His comment was also tinged with a little white hegemony, suggesting that Obama was not black but was "one of us" for an hour because he appeared to bring the country together beyond black and white. This is not something we would say of a white president (e.g., "I forgot for an hour that President George W. Bush was white.") This said, I understand that the uniqueness of a first black president does push us to make black versus nonblack comparisons, and Matthews likely meant that there was a period of time when President Obama's blackness was not seen. Even then, however, one wonders what is implied about all the other times Matthews doesn't forget the president is black!

Matthews's comment is a perfect example of how unconscious racial bias can spill into the territory of racism without someone knowing. This is why I include "intent" in my equations. Sometimes, we say and do things that are deemed offensive or racist without intending to do so. Therefore, even though I evaluated Chris Matthews's comment as racist, I do not believe Matthews *intended* to be racist or to use his platform to hurt Obama. I think he was caught up in the moment and said exactly what he thought, which happened to be offensive.

I respect the fact that Matthews said what he thought, even if I take issue with the bias expressed. He also immediately clarified his point, so should he have been ostracized or punished for his comment? I do not believe so. Chris Matthews was just being human. It's difficult to talk about a mistake, such as the one Matthews made, and the fact that he was willing to confront it and admit it is a great first step in the process of recovering from it. This incident is a perfect example of how anyone—even a liberal commentator—can unintentionally make a mistake because of unconscious racial bias. The even larger point I would like to make is that we need to analyze each racial gaffe individually as it occurs because no two situations are identical. Therefore, we cannot "punish" all racial offenders in the same manner. This is why I believe my Racism and Racial Bias equations are among the legitimate tools I offer to help us assess and evaluate what has happened.

Chris Matthews had three things going for him that night that I think minimized the firestorm that would have come his way had he not clarified his comment: the ability to self-reflect, courage, and a national platform. Evidently, after he made the racist comment, Matthews was told what he said was offensive. To his credit, he must have immediately engaged in self-reflection and found the courage to correct what he said. He was also fortunate to be able to do it on Rachel Maddow's show. I like the way Chris Matthews handled the situation, and we can all learn from his example. When we make inevitable mistakes, we should conduct a self-analysis, find courage to say we were wrong, and clarify and correct whatever it is as soon as possible. This formula for peace helps us get back on track after we have made a racial gaffe. Quite frankly, these steps don't work just with racial incidents. As adults, this is how we should behave after we make *any* kind of mistake.

Are We in a "Postracial" Society?

This incident involving Chris Matthews raises a key question: are we in a postracial society? A definite indication of us moving in the right direction when it comes to race is the election and reelection of our first black president, Barack Obama. When we consider the historical journey of the United States from slavery until today, it is really remarkable how far we've come. It was *thinking* and *objective* individuals who voted for the right person to achieve the presidency in 2008 and again in 2012. Barack Obama was the best person for the job, and he just happened to be black. He was elected because voters did not let the superficial (skin color) negatively influence their judgment and keep them from making the right decision.

However, as wonderful as it is that US voters elected a black man as the president of the United States, I still do not believe we now live in a postracial society. What is a postracial society anyway? I have repeatedly made the argument that race issues are entrenched in our society, and this is evidenced by the incessant number of incidents related to race and racial accusations that happen on a regular basis. Every other day, there seems to be some race incident in the news. Also, the fact that I was motivated to write this book because of the lack of understanding about race I have seen in the media and in my work is clear indication that we are not *beyond* race.

I believe the idea of a postracial society came out of our desperate desire to move beyond race. To the world, electing Barack Obama was an assurance, a declaration that the United States has moved in the right direction. And I will say, as a black woman from a country that prides itself as being truly multicultural and inclusive, that the US election of a black man showed Canada up! In fact, if we compare the amount of racial diversity in the federal governments of both countries, the United States puts Canada to shame.

However, despite how far the United States has come electing a black president, it still has a long way to go. One thing I will say that Canada does better than the United States is regulating hate speech. Like the United States, Canada operates under free speech principles, but Canada wisely puts limits on what its citizens can say publicly. You can say what you want in Canada, but when it spills over to the area of hate speech, you have broken the law. I proudly share that my dearly departed mother, former justice of the peace, Her Worship Philomen M. Wright, played a significant role in conceptualizing and writing multicultural and employment equity laws in the province of Ontario. In Canadian law, it is universally believed that hate speech is a prerequisite to hateful actions. Therefore, Canada enacted laws against hate speech of any kind.

This is why moving from Toronto to Texas then to California, and now living in Georgia for the last ten years has been an interesting journey. Imagine my alarm and distress in 2012 when a local television news station in Atlanta reported a story involving a business owner in Paulding County who declared on the marquee outside his business, "I do not support the 'n-word' in the White House." This type of public display of hate is *never* acceptable in Canada about anyone, let alone about the leader of the country. Evidently, both Canada and the United States have strong points in reference to their handlings of race relations, but both could learn a little more, especially from each other. If the United States were really a postracial society, the individual in Paulding County would not have mentioned the race of the president of the United States of America in such negative and incendiary terms.

More evidence for why I do not believe we are in a postracial society is the fact that we are calling Barack Obama the first *black* president. As you probably already know, Obama was born to a white American mother and a black Kenyan father. Even though genetically he is as much white as he is black, we still call him black. Why is this so? Because as I said at the beginning of this book, our society is fixated on the outside—*race* and color. I have also answered this question pretty often in my work as a trainer. Many people don't understand why President Obama is called black when his mother is white. My answer to this question is usually pretty simple: because we judge people based on what we see.

However, I still caution the adults I train, advising and teaching them not to rely solely on what people look like to decide what kind of people they are, to which race they belong, or to decide how they should be treated. You would be surprised to know how many people we observe and believe are of a particular race, but they are not. This speaks to the complexities of categorizing people using what some scholars call an "additive model"[2] that places people in either/or categories. These thinkers do not believe people can be dichotomized so easily as "black or white." I agree. Bottom line: we cannot *assume* that we know anyone simply by looking at him or her.

We almost need to approach people as if they are imposters, looking beyond what we see, and try to get to know the person before we make judgments.

It is clear from this chapter that there are times when we say and do things related to race and we don't realize how offensive we are being. But when we are told we are being offensive, we need to be mature adults and apologize. According to critical race theory (CRT), we live in a racist society that affects *all* of us, so we are *all* bound to make mistakes. Therefore, the goal is for us to keep moving forward, especially after we've made missteps, and not be hindered by history.

When I despair, I remember that all through history the way of truth and love have always won. There have been tyrants and murderers, and for a time, they can seem invincible, but in the end, they always fall. Think of it—always.

—MAHATMA GANDHI

CHAPTER FIVE

Why History Matters

At times, it seems as if every interaction involving people of different races becomes a racial interaction and not anything else. This is partly understandable, given the United States' troubled history with racism and the fact that racism still exists today. Legal racism in the United States has been practiced against Native Americans, blacks, and others since colonial times in the form of the little-known practice of peonage[1] and Jim Crow laws. Additionally, discrimination against other groups—for example, Jews, Latin Americans, and Asians—complicates the picture of racism and racial prejudice. That's because some of the underlying reasons they faced discrimination were based on cultural rather than racial prejudices. This idea is usually associated with ethnocentrism.[2]

Despite the fact that US history also includes the mistreatment of other racial groups outside of slavery, US history seems to be synonymous with the institution of slavery. If you ask a group of people about US history, more than likely they will mention slavery, probably because of how barbaric and inhumane it was. Even while facilitating my workshops addressing racial biases, the conversation usually becomes an exclusive discussion of black and white, even when participants of other racial and ethnic groups are present. When I point out my observation of this dynamic to participants, they are always surprised, and this revelation inevitably opens up a clear opportunity for discussions to go beyond white and black. As a result, nonblack and nonwhite participants feel validated because their experiences are recognized and acknowledged as an integral part of race discussions.

Let me be clear: in no way am I trying to minimize slavery. People should know that as recently as 1968, black people were lynched by white mobs made up of average men, women, and children who considered themselves civilized, religious, and upstanding people. At one time, whites even traded lynching event *postcards*, often sending them through the US mail. In 1908, the postmaster general banned the postal service from handling the cards,[3] but the practice continued through other means. Unquestionably, slavery was despicable and inhumane. However, I also think it is important to remember how other groups of people (e.g., Jews, Native Americans, and Chinese) have been treated inhumanely either in the United States or around the world.

This said, given the heinous nature of slavery and the fact that there are still people alive today who remember the lynching, who experienced segregation, who had great-grandparents who owned slaves (Paula Deen), and who felt or still feel deep-seated hatred toward blacks, it is no surprise that race discussions in the United States always seem to take place in a dichotomous manner—either "black and white" and "racist or not racist." Also, we have to keep in mind that the Civil Rights Act was only passed, as of 2013, fifty years ago. Changing laws doesn't mean there will be changes in attitudes. Especially when we consider the words of one of the country's Founding Fathers, Thomas Jefferson, it is no surprise how much race still influences and divides us today. By Jefferson's own words, it is evident that even as he was debating the moral rightness of the practice of slavery, there was less doubt about the idea that whites were racially superior to blacks.

> Deep rooted prejudices entertained by the whites; ten thousand recollections, by the blacks, of the injuries they have sustained; new provocations; the real distinctions which nature has made; and many other circumstances, will divide us into parties, and produce convulsions,

which will probably never end but in the extermination of the one or the other race ... The first difference which strikes us is that of colour. - Whether the black of the negro resides in the reticular membrane between the skin and scarf-skin, or in the scarf-skin itself; whether it proceeds from the colour of the blood, the colour of the bile, or from that of some other secretion, the difference is fixed in nature, and is as real as if its seat and cause were better known to us. And is this difference of no importance? Is it not the foundation of a greater or less share of beauty in the two races?[4]

These words show us just how extensively the issue of race has been entrenched in our society. Even though we no longer believe in the sort of fallacious belief expressed in the idea that nature justifies, or at least leads to racism, one point Jefferson made that is still *valid* and that is consistent with what I've been saying in this book is "the first difference which strikes us is that of colour." Unfortunately, the first thing we see when we meet another person is skin color. We should not deny the fact that there are psychosocial dynamics of race that affect all of us all the time, and sometimes to the point that it can create conflict with others. This conflict is due to what one scholar calls "legacy effects."

> Black and White employees may experience conflict due to their shared history of the enslavement of Africans in the United States. Perhaps a White employee doubts the competence of a Black coworker, given that the legacy of slavery does not place Blacks in roles of competence and authority. Black employees may likewise use the legacy of slavery as justification for their distrust or dislike of White colleagues.[5]

Moreover, racial conflicts also occur outside of the traditional workplace. For example, you might recall that actor Michael Richards, who screamed the "n-word" out of frustration when he was heckled by some black patrons during a standup routine. Or even the recent incident with NFL player Riley Cooper, who had a conflict with a black security guard at a concert and said he "will jump that fence and fight every nigger here." Sometimes, when whites are put in a vulnerable position outside of their normal status "at the top" of the hierarchy and have to answer to blacks in authority (e.g., a security guard, black spectators who have paid money for a comedy show, or in my case, a black customer in an upscale restaurant), this can yield very nasty results. Conversely, a white friend of mine shared the following scenario with me, which elucidates the distrust of whites felt by blacks.

ID Please?

A white female employee in a clothing store was checking out customers at the register. All around the store, including three posted around the registers, signs read, "ID is required with all credit card purchases." The white employee called the next customer in line, who was a white woman. She walked up with her credit card and ID in hand to make her purchase. The white employee finished the transaction and then called the next person in line, who was an older black man. The white employee rang up the black customer's total, and the black man handed the white employee his credit card. The white employee politely asked, "May I see your ID please?" The black man began to spew racist and sexist comments, calling the white employee a "white racist" and a "fucking bitch" because she asked *him* for ID and not the white woman. Evidently, the black man was not aware that the white customer before him walked up to the register prepared with her ID handy, so the white employee didn't have to verbally ask for it.

I asked my friend how she dealt with the situation. She said it happened so fast and she was so shocked that she couldn't say anything. However, the incident left her feeling really sad and hurt because she had done nothing wrong and she was wrongly accused of racism. This scenario is a perfect example of the level of distrust that some blacks have toward whites because of racial history. It is also a perfect example of false claims of racism when it was only a misunderstanding. Nonetheless, all of these incidents exemplify how much race is just beneath the surface and how conflict (both internally and externally) can bring out people's real feelings. They also exemplify what we've learned about stereotypes being used more when people are cognitively or emotionally preoccupied with other concerns.[6]

Blurred Racial Lines

Even though we have a history that distinguishes us along racial lines and makes us mistrust one another, these lines are not necessarily clear-cut all the time. For example, one thing Riley Cooper didn't realize is that perhaps there was an "n-word" in his company that he didn't know about. "Black" people come in all shades—from blue-black on one end of the continuum to whiter than white—the albino—at the other end. You can't necessarily tell who's who just by looking at skin color. Or maybe Riley Cooper just had an ethical white person in his company who did not condone what he said and decided to share the video. The bottom line is that we cannot look at people and decide, based on their race, whether they are "one of us" or "one of them."

I am speaking of the "the confusion that exists with respect to the definition of race."[7] Consider the ancestry of blacks who were African descendants in the United States during the era of slavery. Of these, "the majority (72 to 83 percent) have at least one known white ancestor."[8] Moreover, "the average American black is about as far removed from the pure Negroid type as he is form the pure Caucasian type."[9] Additionally, another example illustrating the difficulty of categorizing people is with respect to racial ambiguity of racial classifications. In the past or even today, some blacks escaped racial oppression because their physical appearance permitted them to "pass" into white groups. In addition, although not appearing in relevant literature, "passing" may also occur among Asians and

Native Americans. In fact, increasing numbers of young people refuse to classify themselves as white, black, etc., opting instead for a multirace self-identification. This is probably a reason there are now census questions that allow individuals to identify with multiple classifications.[10]

Interestingly, I recently met an older white woman in a café while I was writing this book in a suburb of Atlanta, Georgia, and said she refuses to say she is "white." She said she and her husband, who is also white, always write "none of your business" whenever asked to disclose their race in a survey or questionnaire. Righteously indignant, the lady declared that she and her husband do this because they are sick of the divisiveness that exists because of race. In their minds, they believed if they didn't reveal their racial identities, then they were not contributing to the madness around race that she said has gotten worse in recent years. This is an example of a "wish for simple solutions" when it comes to race.[11]

Lastly, just to underscore my point about our not knowing who's who and the fact that we need to question who is "one of us" versus "one of them," I am happy to share that I am the proud aunt of two nephews and one niece who have interracial parents. Why is this relevant? Because, interestingly, when my daughters, who were born to two black parents, take pictures with their interracial cousins, you cannot tell whose parents are interracial and whose parents are not. All of the kids have the same complexion. I am sure this is why I am often asked whether my husband is white or not. On the face of it, I am usually not bothered by the question since my children happen to have lighter skin than mine. But when I sense that I am being judged harshly or looked down upon because of the prospect of having a white husband, I usually throw the question back in the person's lap and ask, "Why do you ask?" This forces the person to share his or her beliefs and assumptions, and I reciprocate with tact and education. In my world, there is no "us" and "them" because we are all family, including my friends of different races.

As you can tell, my aim here was not to harp on the past, even though the past is important to remember so we do not repeat the same mistakes. I merely wanted to briefly share how our history with race still affects us today. Again, I wrote this book because it is unacceptable to me how we have been dealing with this issue of race, and it's time to start changing how we speak to one another within and across racial lines. This cannot happen unless we individually and collectively address what's going on in our minds as we interact with different people. We also have to remember that we cannot decide "who" people are or what is in their hearts simply because of their racial identity. Furthermore, we cannot move forward unless we learn to be proactive and have honest discussions about race and racism on a regular basis rather than in reaction to every incident. Lastly, we also have to stop calling everything and everyone racist, which begs the question: are we all a little bit racist?

Is Everybody "a Little Bit Racist"?

As I have repeatedly claimed in this book, harboring racial bias is normal and natural. However, is being a "racist" normal and natural? To answer this question, let's consider an excerpt from the song "Everybody's a Little Bit Racist" from the hit Broadway musical *Avenue Q*.[12] The introduction is a terrific example of what I am talking about—the need for us to learn to make conceptual distinctions between racism and racial bias. Consider these words from the first chorus:

> Everyone's a little bit racist ...
> Look around and you will find
> No one's really color blind.
> Everyone makes judgments based on race.

Take a moment to reflect on these lyrics. Based upon what you have learned thus far, would you say these lyrics better describe racism or racial bias? If you picked racial bias, you are correct. These lyrics better describe the category of racial bias because it says we all make judgments based on race. This is a perfect example of how the terms *racial bias* and *racism* are used interchangeably and incorrectly. This adds to our confusion.

Nonetheless, it is time for all of us to admit it. We all have biases about people from different racial groups, and if you are reading this paragraph while screaming, "No, I do not!" then you are not being truthful to yourself. Even researchers have argued the normalcy of harboring racial biases by stating, "The persistence of prejudice, even among those who renounce prejudice, may simply be that responding without prejudice is sometimes difficult."[13] However, despite the "normalcy" of prejudice, we are afraid to admit it, which is no surprise. Social desirability theory teaches us that people are usually unwilling to report their negative attitudes toward others, even when they are aware they make assumptions based on race, because it is not socially acceptable.[14]

Are you now convinced that you might harbor racial biases? If not, here's a question for you: do you make comments about others in the privacy of your own home that you would never say in public? If yes, this is a telltale sign that you probably have biases. But don't feel bad. Again, research tells us that we all have biases.

So the song "Everybody's a Little Bit Racist," despite its catchy title, is an example of how we mix up key concepts about race. This is why I insist we need to introduce the concept of racial bias into our discussions and our analyses of incidents that happen. However, in light of the history of slavery and racism that exists today, would you agree that "every white person's a little bit racist"?

"White" Does Not Mean "Oppressor"

Not all white people are racist, bad, or oppressors of people of color. In my work as an educator and workshop facilitator, I have met countless white men, in particular, who have shared that they feel demonized because of who they are. I believe this, and I am sympathetic to it. As I mentioned earlier, it is important for us to look for exceptions to the so-called "truths" that we believe. Men like Brad Pitt, Bill Gates, Matt Damon, George Clooney, Bono, and former United States President Bill Clinton are all white men and are known to do a lot of good for people of color in fighting for human rights. And I'm sure you can look beyond celebrity into your own communities and circles and find more examples.

Much like I stress that all minority groups should not be viewed or treated as monolithic, neither should white men. In fact, in my life, I have met many white men and white women who are responsible for helping me when, quite frankly, some of my own people wouldn't even help when they were in a position to do so. Fortunately, my parents were forward-thinking, positive people who raised me to take individuals as they come. While I was growing up, it was not uncommon to have people of all races in my home, and it was not uncommon for my parents to have friends of different races. This is why I live by the motto, "No person is my friend because he is black, and no person is my enemy because she is white." Both black and white people alike have burned and benefitted me. Color does not unequivocally mean consciousness, and whiteness does not unequivocally mean wickedness.

The lesson here is that race cannot be the only criterion we use to judge people and to anticipate what they will and will not do. To reiterate a point previously made, we cannot assume that someone black automatically falls into the *oppressed* or *victim* category, and we cannot automatically assume that someone white is automatically an *oppressor* or a *culprit*. In fact, in the next chapter, I offer my analysis of several incidents related to race that I classify as either examples of racism or racial bias. Some of the culprits in these incidents are people of color, proving my point that it is foolhardy to assume someone's mind-set or to try to determine how someone will react to or behave in any given situation simply because of skin color.

Success does not consist in never making mistakes but in never making the same one a second time.

—George Bernard Shaw

CHAPTER SIX

A Hit Parade of Racial Gaffes

Now that we have a good idea of what racism and racial bias are, and what distinguishes one from the other, we are in a better position to correctly identify one versus the other when incidents related to race occur. And helping us do so is the conceptual and analytical framework of critical race theory (CRT), which teaches us why it is important to look at incidents through a racial lens as we think about and evaluate what we and what others say and do.

This chapter is particularly important because it is the beginning of the "practical" part of this book in which we start applying what we have learned. Specifically, in this chapter, we take a close look at specific examples of racial gaffes—comments or actions—that have occurred here in the United States. For each gaffe, you will have an opportunity to apply your knowledge and evaluate the incident as either racial bias or racism. I then offer my analysis of each incident and evaluate them as either clear examples of racism or clear examples of racial bias.

Without question, all of the racial gaffes in this chapter committed by individuals fall into at least one of the categories of lacking sensitivity, lacking critical thinking skills, or harboring unconscious and conscious assumptions. However, as awful as some of these incidents may seem, they don't all necessarily equate to racism as I have defined it. Remember, using my racism equation **(Racism = Prejudice (+) Power (+) or (-) Intent)**, we know that when an individual has racial bias *and* uses his or her power in unacceptable ways to negatively impact another's life, whether institutionally or personally, that person has exercised racism. However, lacking that power, there is only racial *bias*—hence, the racial bias equation **Racial Bias = Prejudice (+) or (-) Intent.** Remember racism can exist at the institutional level (e.g., Jim Crow laws and college and university admissions policies historically) and social club membership requirements. However, my focus here is on the psychosocial, interpersonal behaviors of individuals who prejudge others on the basis of race and on those who sometimes wield their power, adversely affecting the lives of people of color physically, socially, or psychologically.

What Can We Do When an Incident Related to Race Occurs?

In general, when an incident related to race happens, we can take the following steps to help narrow down what it is (racism or racial bias), evaluate the severity of the situation by determining the racial offender's intent, and then assign an appropriate "punishment."

Remember the distinguishing factor that separates racism from racial bias is *power*. However, I still believe that someone could be in a position of power and not realize that he/she has said or done something that is illustrative of racism (e.g., the Chris Matthews incident discussed earlier). We have to consider each incident individually as it happens because no two incidents are identical.

The Racial Gaffes

Below, I have catalogued a list of incidents related to race that we have seen play out in the media, whether on the radio, on television, or on the Internet. All have occurred since the United States elected its first black president, Barack Obama, and these incidents took place in diverse settings, including in the workplace and in politics. Together, we will go through each incident, and you can apply the knowledge you have accumulated thus far by determining whether each incident is an example of either racism or racial bias.

Steps to follow when classifying and analyzing an incident related to race

1. Decide if the incident is racism by comparing the incident to the racism equation.

2. Ask yourself, "Is the element of racial prejudice present? Was power exerted?"

3. If both elements are present, *then* you can call it racism. If both elements are not present, then it must be racial bias.

4. Regardless of whether the incident is racism or racial bias, establish whether the individual(s) involved intentionally or unintentionally* hurt the victim(s). Sometimes, people have unconscious biases that influence how they think and behave toward people without realizing it.

5. Decide the "punishment" by taking into consideration the following:
   a. Is the person apologetic? Did the person apologize and show remorse?
   b. Does the person say offensive things over and over, or was this done out of character?
   c. Was the comment premeditated, or was it done off-the-cuff or unconsciously?

   *Establishing intention can be considered a very subjective endeavor, but asking the preceding questions would help you figure it out.

- Ann Coulter's comment about black conservatives
- Former Mexican president, Vicente Fox's comment on black workers
- Juan Williams's comment about Muslims on planes
- John Sununu's and Rush Limbaugh's comments about Colin Powell

- Trayvon Martin
- Don Imus's comment about "nappy-headed hoe"
- Rick Perry's reference to Herman Cain as "brother"
- Rush Limbaugh's "uppity" comment about Michelle Obama
- Brad Paisley and LL Cool J's "Accidental Racist"
- Nicki Minaj's response to Steven Tyler's "cornfield" comment
- Paula Deen's discrimination and harassment lawsuit

It is important to note that this list is not exhaustive. I also deliberately chose these incidents since Obama took office in order to refute the idea that we have entered into a postracial society. I agree that Obama winning two elections is clear evidence that racism did not keep him out of the White House. However, this does not mean that racism is dead, and it does not mean that our society no longer has racists. In fact, I think we have become hypersensitive to race since Obama took office. This is disappointing because I, like many, had great hope that we would seize the opportunity to engage in intelligent dialogue about race. However, evidently we don't know how to have civil discourse on race because we don't understand key concepts related to race and racism, and quite frankly, we rely too much on the opinions and interpretations of disgruntled and misinformed talking heads and politicians who spin stories and spew venomous rhetoric in order to reinforce their personal agendas. President Obama is a Harvard-educated lawyer, brilliant, deliberate, and thoughtful, with a background of extensive public service, stability as a father and husband, and someone whose character is generally agreed to be solid. Yet he has faced unprecedented and unyielding opposition and cantankerousness from some members of Congress and beyond.

We need help, and this is why I wrote this book. This book is an invaluable tool we can *all* use to individually learn more about the psychosocial dynamics of race and how to evaluate situations when they occur *for ourselves*. It is time we use our individual sensibilities and think for ourselves rather than accept, absorb, and regurgitate the words of others without any scrutiny. This is what critical thinking is all about.

Ann Coulter

On a 2011 episode of Fox's *Hannity*, Coulter claimed that political liberals don't like black conservatives. She said,

> Our blacks are so much better than their blacks. To become a black Republican, you don't just roll into it ... and that's why we have very impressive blacks in the Republican Party.[1]

APPLY YOUR KNOWLEDGE

What do you think about the comments made by Coulter? Racist or racially biased?

Consider the two race equations to help you decide:

Racism = Prejudice (+) Power (+) or (-) Intent
Racial Bias = Prejudice (+) or (-) Intent

My Analysis

Coulter's argument suggests that being a black conservative is more difficult than being a black liberal because, apparently, there are implicit tests or standards that black Republicans must pass or meet in order to get into the party. This, supposedly, is in contrast to nonthinking black liberals who wake up and just arbitrarily decide they support a particular philosophy and political party. Interestingly, Coulter elucidates an invisible social hierarchy (at least in her mind) in which black conservatives have superior standing to black liberals.

Then there is her claim that black Republicans are "impressive" in a way that black Democrats are not. What could that mean? Her "accolade" is backhanded, patronizing, and demeaning. A child who learns how to perform a cartwheel for the first time is impressive. A prospective college student who scores perfectly on the SAT is impressive. If something is "impressive," it is considered extraordinary or remarkable. Is that how you describe a subgroup of a race, as Coulter did? Leaders of the civil rights movement like Dr. Martin Luther King, Reverend Al Sharpton, Reverend Jesse Jackson, and Congressman John Lewis (to name a few) are "impressive" because they stood up for equal rights and literally paved the way for us to get to a place where we could elect a black president. Mere participation in a political party is not, in itself, impressive. Hence, her comment is patronizing.

Coulter's comment is also demeaning in that it reveals a subtle subtext that suggests blacks are generally mediocre or inherently worse than everyone else—and only a few can rise to the level of being "impressive." Indeed, it is probably true that it is less common to meet a black conservative than a black liberal. However, just because something is rare does not automatically mean it is more valuable or more impressive than something that is not. Maybe in the world of mining this is true, because there is a search for unique diamonds and precious gems, but we are talking about people, not baubles.

I also believe Coulter's comment is offensive to all black people, including those within her party. Evidently, despite the collective title "Republican," Coulter still views her black conservative colleagues as outsiders. Perhaps she was trying to compliment black Republicans, but what does she mean by "our blacks are so much better than the Democratic blacks"? Has she ever publicly said, "Our whites are so much better than the Democratic whites"? Not to my knowledge. Why does Coulter single out one racial group anyway? Why make this distinction? It is one thing to distinguish between people in political parties, but making distinctions between individuals within a specific racial group is reckless.

Neither group—Democratic or Republican—is monolithic. Neither group, black Democrats or black Republicans—is monolithic. Her standpoint is largely problematic because it is influenced by her racial biases, whether she is aware of them or not. In my workshops and talks, I always stress to audiences that they will get into trouble when, and if, they make sweeping statements and judgments about groups of people. The one sweeping statement I say you should always remember is that whatever theories you have about certain people, you have to understand that there are always exceptions to what you think you know.

I also liken Coulter's comment to a comment made by one of my teachers when I was in high school. After a test, this teacher pulled aside one of my peers, who was also black, and praised him for getting the highest grade out of all the black students in the class. Why was it necessary for this teacher to make this distinction between the academic achievements of black students and white students in a class? Rather than promoting and facilitating the academic achievement of all his students, race was clearly in the fore of the teacher's mind. Regardless of whether or not the teacher was trying to find a way to congratulate and encourage good work in black students, the approach was inappropriate.

Regardless of the intent of my former teacher and that of Ann Coulter, I believe their comments are examples of racial bias, not racism. Yes, undoubtedly their comments are both offensive and have an element of racial prejudice, but neither one used their power to control or keep anyone down, which is the definition of racism. It is also important to point out that in both of these instances, the teacher and Ann Coulter showed favorable bias toward some blacks. The teacher might have believed he was giving a compliment to the black student, just as Coulter probably believes she was complimenting her fellow black Republicans. Just as I stated earlier, racial bias can be favorable or unfavorable, positive or negative, which is why it is important to look at the intent of behavior. In both cases, when I consider the element of intent, I don't necessarily believe the teacher or Coulter meant to offend or hurt anyone.

Another Coulter Comment

Let's consider another racial gaffe made by Ann Coulter during an early 2013 interview on Fox's *Hannity*[2] during a debate over gun control. Coulter said, "If you compare white populations, we have the same murder rate as Belgium. So perhaps it is not a gun problem; it is a demographic problem."

APPLY YOUR KNOWLEDGE

What do you think about Coulter's comment? Is it racist or racially biased? In addition to looking at the race equations to help you decide your answer, also keep in mind that racism and racial bias are not always straightforward and obvious; they can also be subtle and covert.

Racism = Prejudice (+) Power (+) or (-) Intent
Racial Bias = Prejudice (+) or (-) Intent

My Analysis

The implication of Coulter's argument is that the problem in the United States is not guns but the nonwhite demographics that use them. There are several problems with her reasoning. First, Coulter did not provide the source of her statistics. Second, she overlooked competing statistics that would undermine her claim, because if you widen the search to include additional European countries, the murder rate comparisons don't match up.[3]

In a nutshell, Coulter was supposedly talking about murder, but in actuality, her words reflected a racist attitude because she sent the veiled message that it is people of color who are most responsible for high murder rates in the United States. Since when do we separate and analyze the behaviors of specific populations of people when trying to compare countries? We need to be critical thinkers and listeners at all times, even when it is uncomfortable. We must read between the lines and not be quick to accept—uncritically—anyone's word. Did Coulter actually sit down and statistically figure out which populations commit more murders in the United States? And if so, how far back in history did she go? Also, did she consider the circumstances of each killing, which may include self-defense, domestic disputes, and random killings? As critical thinkers, it is imperative that we ask these sorts of questions and search for other possible explanations. Her analysis is nonsense. It's like me saying, "Gee, I would really weigh less if I didn't have to factor in the weight of my arms." When measuring the "whole" of something, you cannot arbitrarily leave out certain parts in order to manipulate the outcome.

Coulter's gaffe is also an interesting one to analyze because it is a perfect example of why it is important to not only pay attention and listen to what people say but to also pay close attention to what they *don't* say. Be cognizant of hidden messages when people speak. We should ask ourselves, "What is obscured? Veiled? Subverted? Hidden? Or surreptitious?" This is necessary because language is very powerful, and people do not always use it innocently or for positive purposes. This use of language, or what some scholars in academia call "text," is always important to keep in mind because not all texts are arbitrary or random. Humans generally use texts in key social institutions like families, schools, workplaces, and in this case, the mass media in order "to make sense of their world and to construct social actions and relations required in the labor of everyday life. At the same time, texts position and construct individuals, making available various meanings, ideas, and versions of the world."[4]

To tie this idea back to Coulter's reasoning, using text in this way revealed a clear desire to imagine a different version of her world, one that is better, or all white, since apparently it is people of color who are responsible for high murder rates in the United States. Also, if we refer back to the racism equation **Racism = Prejudice (+) Power (+) or (-) Intent,** it is clear that Coulter's reasoning includes the ingredients of racism. Coulter used her power as a public figure to propagandize these thoughts—and illogically, to boot—on national television. Her statements were damaging because they conveyed the underlying and specious reasoning that people of color should be feared since they are most responsible for the high murder rates in the United States. With comments like these, the incredible spike in gun sales in the last few years since Obama took office does not surprise me.

To reiterate a related point I made earlier, it is important to recognize how we, as humans, use language or text to communicate. It is suggested that "every waking moment is caught up in engagement with text of some kind: from children's stories to political speech, from television sitcom to casual conversation, from classroom lesson to memorandum."[5] Again, "text" is "any instance of written and spoken language that has coherence and coded meanings."[6] It can also be on a continuum from simple and straightforward on one end to complex and convoluted at the other, as is the case with Coulter's dubious assertions.

Vicente Fox

I liken Coulter's brusque style of communication to that of former Mexican president Vicente Fox, who in 2005, said, "There's no doubt that Mexicans, filled with dignity, willingness, and ability to work, are doing jobs that not even blacks want to do there in the United States."

APPLY YOUR KNOWLEDGE

What do you think? Are Fox's words indicative of racism or racial bias? Consider the equations below to help you decide:

Racism = Prejudice (+) Power (+) or (-) Intent
Racial Bias = Prejudice (+) or (-) Intent

My Analysis

Fox's statement created a huge uproar in the black community and was considered racist because of how his words were stated and the implications of the statement. The assumption hidden in his statement was that blacks are more likely to or more prone to perform grunt work, as well as the implication that in comparison to blacks, Mexicans have a stronger work ethic and more dignity. Fox's overall message was that the United States should not consider Mexicans as lowlier than blacks, but they should be looked at and treated with higher regard because Mexicans are at least willing to work harder than blacks, who are perceived to be at the bottom.

On what basis can Fox make his claim? Perhaps in his everyday life, he may have seen many hardworking Mexicans, but as I have stated before in this book, and will focus on specifically in chapter 7, it is problematic and reckless to believe that *your* personal experience can automatically be generalized to stand for *the* common experience of the world.

In line with the outrage expressed by the black community when Fox made his comment, I too believe his words were racist. His words were obviously prejudiced in favor of Mexicans. And whether intentionally or not, Fox successfully used his power and his platform to put black people at a disadvantage. One could argue too that his words probably led black workers to be overlooked as primary options for jobs, which would ultimately affect them economically and socially. Moreover, Fox's comment was essentially flawed because he made a blanket statement about *all* blacks and *all* Mexicans. No racial group is monolithic, so we run into trouble when we generalize. I will reiterate: it is always important to remember that there are always exceptions to what we think we know. There are always exceptions to our *personal* truths. Case in point: Ann Coulter articulated her personal truth that "our blacks (Republicans) are so much better." However, John Sununu and Rush Limbaugh beg to differ, since they publicly criticized their fellow black Republican Colin Powell because he voted for President Obama.

John Sununu and Rush Limbaugh

During the 2012 presidential campaign, John Sununu claimed that Colin Powell endorsed Barack Obama only because both men are black. Sununu said,

> [W]hen you take a look at Colin Powell, you have to wonder whether that's an endorsement based on issues or whether he's got a slightly different reason for preferring President Obama ... I think when you have somebody of your own race that you're proud of being president of the United States, I applaud Colin for standing with him.[7]

Rush Limbaugh made a similar claim in 2008. Limbaugh wrote in an e-mail to reporters,

> Secretary Powell says his endorsement is not about race ... OK, fine. I am now researching his past endorsements to see if I can find all the inexperienced, very liberal, white candidates he has endorsed. I'll let you know what I come up with.[8]

Colin Powell was clear on the reasons he decided to endorse Obama. Among them was his belief in Obama's sound ability to protect the United States from terrorism, saying his actions were "very, very solid." Powell also expressed his reservations about Mitt Romney's proposed policies, "especially with respect to dealing with our most significant issue—the economy."[9]

APPLY YOUR KNOWLEDGE

What do you think about the comments made by Sununu and Limbaugh? Are they racist or racially biased? Consider the equations below to help you decide:

Racism = Prejudice (+) Power (+) or (-) Intent
Racial Bias = Prejudice (+) or (-) Intent

My Analysis

So why not just take Powell at his word? Sununu and Limbaugh both displayed their racial biases (not racism) by insisting that the only reason Powell endorsed Obama was because he was black.

What happened to Republican solidarity and Coulter's suggestion that black Republicans are "impressively" superior to black liberals because they don't just "roll into" their positions as Republicans? This would mean that Colin Powell didn't just "roll into" his decision to vote for President Obama. And let's not forget that Colin Powell is a brilliant, retired four-star general and a former secretary of state who served under President George W. Bush. Given who he is, is it that much of a stretch to assume that Powell thought his decision through before he decided to publicly support Obama? Evidently, Limbaugh and Sununu were projecting their own biases onto Powell by suggesting that something as simple and superficial as skin color would prompt such a well-respected, historical figure in the US government to vote outside of his chosen political party.

Let's go with Sununu and Limbaugh's assertions for a moment. Let's agree that it was skin color that made Powell vote for President Obama and not his political acumen, his accomplishments, or anything more! If their claim is correct that Powell was moved by the opportunity to elect a black president as a way to overcome hundreds of years of racism, then why didn't Powell also support Herman Cain, Alan Keyes, Al Sharpton, Jesse Jackson, or other black leaders who have run for president in the past (regardless of their political affiliations)? Why not endorse them as a symbolic way of moving a black candidate past the primaries? The answer is simple: because Powell's support was not symbolic.

Despite their similar stances, the difference between Sununu and Limbaugh is that Limbaugh explicitly stated Powell's decision was based on race, whereas Sununu tried, albeit unsuccessfully, to veil his biases. After the housing crisis and the country's fall into a recession, it is not a surprise that Colin Powell voted as he did. Powell did not want to support the same policies that created the country's mess in the first place. Voting for Mitt Romney would have been antithetical to his sensibilities. The major problem with Limbaugh and Sununu's claims is that they are unsupported, specious theories that unfortunately were presented to the American public as truth.

As I repeatedly say in my workshops and seminars, it is important for all of us to bring forward and examine our unconscious and conscious racial assumptions and beliefs. And equally important, we must also examine the conscious and unconscious racial biases of others—especially those in positions of power to influence many.

Trayvon Martin

George Zimmerman shot an unarmed, defenseless, black male teenager whom he identified, judged, pursued, and killed. There are police tapes to corroborate what really happened, so why all the debate about whether or not it's a racial incident? Absolutely, unequivocally, it was race that led Zimmerman to stalk and kill Trayvon Martin. But was it racism?

APPLY YOUR KNOWLEDGE

What do you think about the Trayvon Martin case? Among other things, is Zimmerman guilty of racism or racial bias? Consider the two race equations again to help you decide.

Racism = Prejudice (+) Power (+) or (-) Intent
Racial Bias = Prejudice (+) or (-) Intent

My Analysis

I believe this case was trivialized and compromised by this question of whether or not race was a factor in the Trayvon Martin case. Without a doubt, racial bias was involved, but did Zimmerman's actions constitute racism? A 2013 article on CNN.com reported that "Zimmerman said he acted in self-defense [but] prosecutors say he ignored a police dispatcher's advice and was guilty of racial profiling."[10] Later in the article, it was stated that Zimmerman's lawyer, Mark O'Mara, denied it was racial profiling and insisted there was "absolutely no racism" because the FBI investigated the shooting and found there was none. I am curious to know, if his claim is true, how this investigation was conducted. What was the methodology used to evaluate and decide that "absolutely no racism" was present?

Here's my analysis. Let's simply refer back to the racism equation.

Racism = Prejudice (+) Power (+) or (-) Intent

Was there racial prejudice in this case? Yes. Was power used to alter the life of someone? Yes. Therefore, there was racism. How is a young teenager walking on a sidewalk with a drink and a bag of Skittles considered suspicious? Zimmerman was a neighborhood watchman and, most importantly, was in possession of a gun that gave him ultimate power over a defenseless, unarmed young teenager. Then he pursued Trayvon Martin, believing he had the *power* to control Martin because he had a gun. Zimmerman is guilty of racism. Swap Trayvon Martin with a white teenage male and it is highly unlikely the same terrible outcome would occur. Zimmerman said in the 911 call that there had been a series of neighborhood break-ins, so evidently he was on guard. This is probably why he claimed the person he saw "looked suspicious" and "up to no good." Martin's skin color was undoubtedly a part of Zimmerman's overall judgment about the situation.

On some level, I don't understand why there is even a question that racism was involved in the Trayvon Martin case. But when we return to what I have been saying about the confusion our society has in mistaking racial bias for racism, I am not surprised. Remember when we call every incident related to race "racism" and call every person who makes a racial gaffe a racist that the whole notion of racism—its heinous, disgraceful, and appalling nature—is grossly minimized and undermined. Regardless of race, we should all be outraged by what happened, simply because a preventable death occurred as a result of poor judgment, racial prejudice, and the power and intention to act on it. In short, it was racism. However, unfortunately, because we so often miscategorize incidents related to race, we don't see racism when it stares us in the face.

Another fascinating element of this case that received little to no attention is the fact that Zimmerman, a Hispanic man, singled out and racially profiled another racial minority, Trayvon Martin, who was black. There is an assumption that because someone is a minority, they should "know" better. As a result, they should not subject others to racial profiling or racial bias because they know what it feels like. But as you have already learned in this book, this idea does not hold together. To reiterate, it does not matter what one's race, ethnicity, gender, sexual orientation, age, or any other descriptor is; all people have racial bias. Whether it was done consciously or unconsciously, Zimmerman decided that Trayvon Martin was a criminal who was up to no good, and it seems clear this judgment was based on race, as was the subsequent incident that ended Trayvon's life.

Juan Williams

Another example of an incident involving a racial minority as the "culprit" is Juan Williams's comment. In 2010, Juan Williams had already been a longtime reporter and political analyst for National Public Radio (NPR) when he appeared on Bill O'Reilly's Fox program. Williams stated that, "Political correctness can lead to some kind of paralysis where you don't address reality."[11] He then declared that he was not a bigot before saying,

> [W]hen I get on the plane, I got to tell you, if I see people who are in Muslim garb and I think, you know, they are identifying themselves first and foremost as Muslims, I get worried. I get nervous.[12]

Williams, who is black, was subsequently fired from NPR.

APPLY YOUR KNOWLEDGE

What do you think about the comments of Juan Williams? Is it racism or racial bias? Consider the two race equations again to help you decide:

Racism = Prejudice (+) Power (+) or (-) Intent
Racial Bias = Prejudice (+) or (-) Intent

My Analysis

Juan Williams's comment is an example of bias, but in this case, it is ethnic bias. However, even though there isn't an equation to sum up disparaging remarks made about a particular ethnicity, I still analyze and categorize this incident as racism because race and ethnicity are so closely linked. In fact, if you recall a definition of racism I shared earlier, some scholars define racism as "unjustified negative treatment and subordination of members of a racial or ethnic group."[13] Also, just to help us understand and evaluate the gravity of Juan Williams's comment, let's substitute "black" or "Asian" or "Latino" for the word "Muslim" in his comment. Is it easier now to see why his comment was racist? And, if indeed Williams had made this comment about blacks or Asians or Latinos, without question there would have been more outrage from those communities.

That said, in a post-9/11 era, is it that farfetched for Williams or anyone not to consider the what-ifs while getting on a plane? I look at *everybody* when I get on a plane! The problem with Williams's comment is that he used his *power* on a public platform to share his irrational thinking—making a sweeping generalization about all Muslims being potential threats on airplanes. His words have the ingredients of racism: prejudice, power, and the intent to hurt the credibility of a particular group of people. Ironically, the underwear bomber was a black man, just like Williams. Again, we should never generalize because there are always exceptions to our thinking. Not all Muslims are terrorists or bad, and clearly not all terrorists *look* Muslim. Williams's response to seeing Muslims on a plane was substantively no different from George Zimmerman's cognitive response to seeing a young black man at night.

As we have seen thus far, generalizing from individual experiences is a remarkable feature of human rationality. The problem, as I have stated before, is when we do not consider exceptions to our personal theories. We should never believe that our thinking is the *only* way to think. There is always a full range of ways to interpret situations and to analyze events—especially those related to race or ethnicity. Case in point, let's return to the Trayvon Martin case.

Droves of people marched in their hoodies in support of the young teenager who was killed, while at the same time George Zimmerman collected money from citizens to support his case. One group clearly believed Trayvon Martin was a victim, while others believed Zimmerman was the victim who acted in self-defense. Even after Zimmerman's acquittal, the irony is that both groups still feel very strongly about their respective positions, and both probably believe the side they are supporting is the truth.

The Trayvon Martin case is a clear example of the type of chasm that can exist between two groups of peoples with differing opinions and versions of the truths about the same issue. However, one optimistic point I will add is that even though this case was about race, the chasm did not necessarily separate cleanly along racial lines. There were many nonblack people who were on the side of Trayvon Martin and his family because they looked at the case objectively. Moreover, due to the number of subsequent brushes with the law that Zimmerman has had since his acquittal, I'll bet he has lost some of his supporters.

Don Imus

In 2007, when radio personality Don Imus called the Rutgers University women's basketball team "nappy-headed hos," he was presumably trying to be funny. But in a subsequent appearance on *Keeping It Real with Al Sharpton*, host Al Sharpton called Imus racist.[14]

APPLY YOUR KNOWLEDGE

Do you agree with Al Sharpton? Was Imus's statement racist? Consider the two race equations again to help you decide:

Racism = Prejudice (+) Power (+) or (-) Intent
Racial Bias = Prejudice (+) or (-) Intent

My Analysis

If we consider again the racism equation, **Racism = Prejudice (+) Power (+) or (-) Intent**, it is clear that Sharpton was right. Imus glibly displayed his prejudices about the women's team—prejudices that were not only racist in nature but were also profoundly misogynistic. When you couple his comment with the public platform he has to disseminate information and the power to influence his listening audience and perceptions of black women, what he said was racist. Imus's comment also revealed some subconscious or unconscious biases, because even though there were eight black players and two white players on the team, he only honed in on the black players— presumably because the epithet is typically used to demean black women. It's not at all clear where the white players fit into Imus's portrayal of the team. However, prior to singling out the black players with the comment, Imus referred to the team as "rough." ("That's some rough girls from Rutgers. Man, they got tattoos and ...") It's not clear what connection he was trying to make between "rough women" and the racial epithet, but we can safely conclude that his comment was misogynistic and racially demeaning.

Did Don Imus just make a simple mistake displaying his biases, or was this simply a glimpse into how he views women of color or women in general? How did he get from young women playing basketball to calling them hos after they just finished playing in the NCAA Championship? Regardless of what he claims to think, I believe his intent was to demean and dehumanize the young women. Furthermore, in reference to the idea of intent, let's compare the Don Imus incident to that of Chris Matthews. Both incidents are considered racist, but should they be viewed the same? Should both "culprits" be reprimanded the same way? No. Chris Matthews's comment was unintentionally offensive, while Imus's intention was to demean. And why am I so sure about the intent of each? Because in determining a person's heart and intent, I think it is important to look at the number of times a person has made racial gaffes. Don Imus has a known history of racist conduct. By his own admission back in 1998, he said he hired one of his cohosts to do "nigger jokes."[15] Imus is a far cry from Chris Matthews and should not be lumped into the same category.

Rick Perry

In 2012, presidential candidate Rick Perry referred to fellow Republican Herman Cain as "brother" during a debate.[16] Referencing a presidential candidate in such a casual manner using racially colloquial terms is unusual.

APPLY YOUR KNOWLEDGE

What do you think about Governor Perry's comments? Is it racism or racial bias? Once again, consider the two race equations to help you decide:

Racism = Prejudice (+) Power (+) or (-) Intent
Racial Bias = Prejudice (+) or (-) Intent

My Analysis

Herman Cain was the only person of color at the forum, and he was the only one singled out and referred to as "brother" (or "sister"). This suggests to me that Rick Perry was unconsciously influenced by Herman Cain's race. Otherwise, Rick Perry would have referenced all of his fellow debaters as "brother" or "sister." So is this incident an example of racism or racial bias? There is clear racial prejudice in the incident, and prejudice is a part of both the racism and the racial bias equations. However, as you know, the distinguishing element in racism is power. Did Rick Perry have the power to negatively affect or influence Herman Cain's life? The answer is no. Rick Perry probably didn't even realize what he said, and I do not believe he intended to single out Cain as he did. Clearly, there were some unconscious biases operating in Perry's mind while he was relating to Cain, but I think what happened was normal.

As a black woman, I cannot tell you how many times I have been called "girlfriend" when meeting someone racially different for the first time because someone is uncomfortable and doesn't know how to interact with me. I do not take it personally because I know it is not about me but about the other person's issues. Therefore, when this happens, I pretty much ignore the colloquial greetings and speak proper English as I always do. This often sends the message to the person that they can relate to me just like anyone else. However, I am also aware that when I don't buy into colloquial jargon, this can make some people feel even more uncomfortable because my behavior is incongruent with their preconceived notions or stereotypes. This is fine. I don't really feel the need to make myself uncomfortable in order to make a stranger feel comfortable, especially if it is compromising my personal integrity.

Rush Limbaugh

During an episode of his radio show in 2011, Rush Limbaugh was commenting on a NASCAR crowd's negative response to an appearance made by First Lady Michelle Obama and the vice president's wife, Dr. Jill Biden. Limbaugh claimed that the crowd did not like, among other things, "paying millions of dollars" for vacations the first family had taken. "They understand it's a little bit of a waste," he said. "They understand it's a little bit of uppity-ism."[17] The word *uppity* means "presumptuous" or "arrogant." But we know this is not necessarily what Rush Limbaugh meant in its entirety. Historically, this word has been used by white people to describe black people who appeared to be putting on airs or who lived above what is assumed to be their natural station. In other words, when black people or other minorities are called "uppity," it means that they are trying to be something they are not—white.

We all know, however, that there are different classes of people within every race. This is why I find it comical when I hear the synonym for *uppity*, which is "acting white." There is inherent bias in the expression itself, "acting white," because the implication is that white people are a monolithic group. The implication is that all whites are of a particular class, and they are always higher than people of color. But we know there is diversity among all races of people.

APPLY YOUR KNOWLEDGE

What do you think about Limbaugh's "uppity" comment? Is it racism or racial bias? Consider the two race equations again to help you decide.

Racism = Prejudice (+) Power (+) or (-) Intent
Racial Bias = Prejudice (+) or (-) Intent

My Analysis

So was Rush Limbaugh's comment an example of racial bias alone or racism? This is probably a rhetorical question since many things Limbaugh says are racist. And this comment is no exception. With respect to prejudice, it is interesting that Limbaugh would call First Lady Michelle Obama "uppity." Mrs. Obama is a Harvard-educated lawyer whose husband was elected the president of the United States. Mrs. Obama is at the height of the social hierarchy, where she deserves to be because of her hard work, class, grace, and humility. She is the complete antithesis to the negative image that Limbaugh tried to portray on his show.

Evidently, when we consider the racism equation, we can conclude that Limbaugh's comment was racist because his comment was *prejudicial*, suggesting that Mrs. Obama will always be "at the bottom" of the social hierarchy simply because she is black. And Limbaugh used his *power* and public stage—his radio show— to influence the perceptions and opinions of many. Limbaugh's comment was made in the same vein as Ann Coulter's "our blacks are better" remark because they both referenced the invisible social hierarchy that has black people placed at the bottom. Additionally, with respect to *intent* in the equation, it is clear that Limbaugh intended to harm the reputation of First Lady Michelle Obama by perpetuating the stereotype that blacks are at the bottom regardless of what they achieve.

Furthermore, I would like to revisit the "acting white" conversation again, which is tantamount to racism. Even though today I can laugh at the expression because I recognize its absurdity, there was a time when it was very hurtful. Growing up, I was repeatedly accused of "acting white" and was called "white wash" and "Oreo" because my parents raised me to speak proper English and not to act stereotypically (i.e., unruly, disrespectfully, and inarticulately).

Ironically, in May 2013, I turned on CBS *This Morning* and watched Gayle King and Norah O'Donnell interview comedian and game-show host Wayne Brady. Rightfully so, Brady, a black man, was upset and challenged the words of Bill Maher, who suggested that Brady was not "black enough." I loved Brady's response. "I didn't know there were gradations to blackness."

I identified specifically with the exchange of experiences between Brady and King about being accused of "acting white" while growing up. This was also my experience. The two did not specify who or what race(s) of people accused them of "acting white," but in my case, it was both whites and blacks alike. Some of the whites didn't accept me because I was black, and some of the blacks didn't accept me because I spoke proper English and therefore was supposedly "acting white." Even today, as an adult, when I meet people for the first time and they hear me speak, some boldly ask if my husband is white because, apparently, since only white people articulate, a black woman who speaks well would have to be with a white, articulate man. Unfortunately, as I have repeatedly stated, all people, regardless of race, have racial biases, and clearly some can even regurgitate racist rhetoric. Moreover, when we consider the origins of white identity as described below, you will further understand why I classify this "uppity" comment (acting white) as racist.

European colonial powers established "White" as a legal concept after Bacon's Rebellion in 1676 to separate the indentured servants of European and African heritage who united against the colonial elite ... The creation of "White" meant giving privileges to some, while denying them to others with the justification of biological and social inferiority.[18]

When we hear someone being called "uppity" or "acting white," you now know why it is offensive.

Brad Paisley and LL Cool J

In 2013, country singer Brad Paisley released a song (featuring actor/rapper LL Cool J) bemoaning the history of racism that is often exemplified by the Confederate flag. To some Southerners, the flag is a symbol of regional pride, while to others it is a symbol of slavery and oppression. Apparently, Paisley was wearing a shirt with the Confederate flag on it, and someone took offense. His response was to write the song called "Accidental Racist." This song faced harsh criticism because of its underwhelming simplicity and the fact that the lyrics reflect embarrassingly obvious stereotypes. Consider, for example, the words "Caught between Southern pride and Southern bling/I'm proud of where I'm from, but not everything we've done."

APPLY YOUR KNOWLEDGE

What do you think about the song "Accidental Racist" and Brad Paisley wearing the Confederate flag on his shirt? Is it racism or racial bias? Consider the two race equations again to help you decide:

Racism = Prejudice (+) Power (+) or (-) Intent
Racial Bias = Prejudice (+) or (-) Intent

My Analysis

As much as this situation is offensive to some, I still do not believe Brad Paisley wearing the confederate flag on his shirt, or his song

"Accidental Racist," is racist. Of course, as I said, the Confederate flag is closely tied to a very dark period in US history for my people in particular, but obviously, it is not for others. I am not trying to condone what happened in the past, nor am I trying to promote the flag because it evokes such strongly negative emotions in black people like sadness, anger, and sometimes fear. This is the antithesis to the emotions it evokes in some white people like pride and heritage. As much as I don't care for the flag, I still believe it is a person's right to wear it.

All this said, however, given the fact that the flag is so offensive to so many people and the fact that it is representative of how badly black people were once treated in the United States, I believe people who wear the flag are insensitive. In this book, I have talked a lot about critical self-reflection and the importance of considering alternative perspectives than your own. Sure, one could argue that black people should just understand the perspectives of those who love the flag and who wear it as a symbol of Southern pride, but when we decide to look at this situation through eyes of compassion, empathy, sensitivity, and humanity, we immediately understand the wrongs of our ways. Why would anyone intentionally do something or say something that they know would hurt or harm another person? I understand the simplicity of my question, but this is a frustration of mine. We need to get back to the basics of human decency—respect for self and others, love, understanding, empathy, and patience.

Another huge one is accountability. I believe we all answer to a higher power that is greater than each of us, both individually and collectively. Even if you are an atheist or an agnostic and you don't necessarily believe you will have to answer to a higher power, this is your right. But we should all be paying close attention to our conscience because it serves as our internal regulators and navigators as we move through life and engage in behaviors that span the continuum of right and wrong. I do not profess to be perfect, nor am I suggesting that I don't make mistakes—I'm human! But my conscience and love for God keep me from intentionally doing anything that would hurt others.

Moreover, another word that I think we have lost from our vocabularies is *altruism*. We have become such a me-me-me culture. Everything must be handed to us, and *my* individual right is more important than the greater good. Many people believe they lose something when they make a sacrifice, but in fact, they gain so much more spiritually—beyond the superficial and the material—when they help others. This, in essence, is the crux of the health-care debate that astonishingly still persists long after the Supreme Court rightfully upheld The Patient Protection and Affordable Care Act, also known as "ObamaCare." From a *human* standpoint, why is it remotely acceptable for people to die simply because they don't have health care? We need to look beyond our individual beliefs and put ourselves in other people's shoes.

That said, let's return to the song "Accidental Racist." Putting ourselves in other people's shoes, I think, was a key message in Brad Paisley and LL Cool J's song. I applaud their courage for taking the chance to openly talk about the inherent tensions and internal conflicts many people feel when it comes to race. However, I would be remiss if I didn't discuss one other part of the song that pretty much exemplifies the confusion between racism and racial bias that led me to write this book. In the song it says,

If you don't judge my do-rag ... I won't judge your red flag ...
If you don't judge my gold chains ... I'll forget the iron chains.

These lyrics are problematic because, in essence, the artists are mixing apples and oranges. There is a sharp contrast between being judged because of a "do-rag" or "gold chains" (bias) and the "red flag" and "iron chains," which are representative of slavery and racism. Someone today deciding not to prematurely judge someone because of do-rags and gold chains cannot thereby erase hundreds of years of slavery. Again, I understand the intent of Paisley and Cool J, but they really missed the mark with these lyrics specifically. Do-rags and gold chains are superficial items that people choose to wear. The Confederate flag and the iron chains used to enslave black people will never be viewed independently of slavery and will always evoke negative emotions in black people. Unfortunately, LL Cool J's contributions were also mocked on *Saturday Night Live!* in such a way as to highlight the ridiculousness of the lyrics: "If you think that *NCIS* is good/Then I'll forget the Aryan Brotherhood." This is unfortunate. However, I still love LL Cool J. As a teenager, I listened to his music, and more than anything, I love what he stands for as a married man who is committed to his wife and family; he is a talented actor, and he is a hip-hop trailblazer. Many artists can learn from his example. At least he took a chance and stood up for something good, unlike many other artists who collect a paycheck by perpetuating racist and misogynistic messages in their music.

Nonetheless, the title "Accidental Racist" is interesting. I wonder, now that Brad Paisley knows how much that flag "hurts" people, if he still wears it. If so, then he cannot call himself an accidental racist anymore because then he will intentionally be sporting an emblem that he knows personifies racism and hurts people.

Nicki Minaj's Response to Steven Tyler's "Cornfield" Comment

Shortly after Steven Tyler's departure from the talent show *American Idol*, Nicki Minaj was hired as a judge. In an interview discussing the new judges, Steven Tyler made a disparaging comment about Minaj's judging competency when he said the following:

> You just have to give your opinion … These kids, they just got out of a car from the Midwest somewhere and they're in New York City, they're scared to death. If it was Bob Dylan, Nicki Minaj would have had him sent to the cornfield! Whereas, if it was Bob Dylan with us, we would have brought the best of him out, as we did with Phillip Phillips.[19]

Minaj responded on Twitter saying, "That's a racist comment."[20] She also suggested that Tyler's comment implied she wouldn't like

Bob Dylan because she is a black rapper and Dylan is a white folk singer.

APPLY YOUR KNOWLEDGE

What do you think about Minaj's response to Tyler's criticism? Was Steven Tyler's comment racist, or was it racial bias? Consider the two race equations again to help you decide.

Racism = Prejudice (+) Power (+) or (-) Intent
Racial Bias = Prejudice (+) or (-) Intent

My Analysis

Steven Tyler's comment was definitely prejudiced, because without knowing anything about Nicki Minaj other than the fact that she was a rapper, Tyler suggested that Minaj would not be able to recognize talent outside of her genre of music—hence the Bob Dylan comment. But was Tyler's comment racially prejudiced or biased? We don't know for sure, but given what I have said in this book about the inevitability of racial bias, it would be foolhardy to believe Tyler's comment was not made without some race in mind—at least subconsciously. However, was Tyler's comment racist? Definitely not. Take a look at the racism equation again. Steven Tyler prejudged Nicki Minaj, but Tyler's opinion of Nicki Minaj's judging ability clearly meant nothing to the *American Idol* executives because Minaj remained in her position as judge. The missing ingredient in this situation that would qualify it as racist is *power*; Steven Tyler had none to adversely affect Nicki Minaj in any way. More than anything, I think Tyler's comment was more about sour grapes because apparently he left the show involuntarily.

This is an example of how false accusations of racism shut down discussions and leave people having to defend themselves. If anything, I think Tyler's quote was more of a slight to Bob Dylan, suggesting he was from a cornfield! Nonetheless, in classic form, because we don't know what racism is and because someone cried "racism," even though it was not, the "racial offender" is forced to apologize or defend himself or herself. In this case, Steven Tyler defended himself in an interview with Canada's *eTalk*:

> I'm the last thing on this planet as far as being a racist. I don't know where she got that out of me saying, "I'm not sure how she would have judged Bob Dylan." I was just saying that if Bob Dylan came on the show, he would've been thrown off. Maybe I spoke out of turn, but a racist I'm not, Nicki.[21]

I agree with Tyler. When we allow these types of false accusations to go unchallenged, when "real" racism does happen, it is questioned, and there is a belief that a simple apology would just make things right. Donald Trump demanding to see President Obama's birth certificate and college transcripts is racist.[22] Are Donald Trump and Steven Tyler in the same category? I think not. The problem is that we continue to be desensitized to the moral power of legitimate accusations of racism when we allow illegitimate ones to stand as truth—dulling our powers of discernment. Again, it's like "The Boy Who Cried Wolf." We lose trust in the power of words when those words are not used carefully and conscientiously. Nicki Minaj accused Steven Tyler of racism, but it is she who made the racial gaffe.

Paula Deen

In 2013, over the course of a single month, celebrity chef and cooking show host Paula Deen was dropped from the Food Network, followed by Kmart, Sears, Walgreens, Home Depot, Target, QVC, and other major retailers who sold Deen's culinary products. Smithfield Foods also cut ties with Deen, who was the company's spokesperson, and Deen's name was also removed from several Caesars Entertainment restaurants. Additionally, even Random House canceled a five-book contract with Deen.[23] The Paula Deen brand, built over decades, died an almost instantaneous death. Why?

In June 2013, details of a deposition Paula Deen gave a month earlier in relation to a racial and sexual discrimination complaint launched by a former restaurant employee were revealed.[24] During the deposition, Deen, who owned the restaurant with her brother, admitted that she considered having an authentic Southern plantation-style wedding for her brother, replete with black waitstaff. She also admitted using racial slurs in the past but insisted that racial slurs were never an ordinary part of her life and that she hadn't uttered them in decades. All this despite the fact that Deen suggested the culture of the South while she was growing up largely condoned the use of racial slurs—almost as if it weren't offensive.

APPLY YOUR KNOWLEDGE

This is typically the point when I ask you to review the race equations and determine whether or not the person's behaviors constitute racism. However, the fact that Deen was at the center of a racial discrimination lawsuit is evidence that there was some legitimacy and validity to the claims made against her. Therefore, rather than trying to decipher whether her conduct constituted racism or racial bias, I focus here on the subject of intent in the racism equation and the punishment Deen received. Did Deen's conduct warrant her losing all of her endorsements and the instantaneous crumbling of her empire?

My Analysis

When I first hear about cases like this, I usually wait until I hear about all the facts before I make a judgment. So initially, I believed that Deen had just made a mistake and that she was sincerely apologetic for her conduct. I got the impression that Deen did not seem to recognize the power of her racist language, even during her deposition, because of her explanation of the South historically having a cavalier relationship with racial discrimination. The following quote from the deposition is an example of how clueless Paula Deen seemed.

[T]hat's just not a word that we use as time has gone on ... Things have changed since the '60s in the South. And my children and my brother object to that word being used in any cruel or mean behavior.[25]

One implication of her testimony is that the word *was* acceptable to use at one time, and in fact, to some degree, it still was okay if she said her children and brother object to using it in any cruel or mean way. When isn't the n-word used in a cruel or mean way? In my world, that word is always offensive, demeaning, and despicable. That word was uttered before, during, and after my black brothers were hanged from trees not too long ago. The word is unacceptable to use by anyone! So if Deen was suggesting that the n-word was used as a term of endearment in her establishment, that is not okay. This has come up as an issue while facilitating discussions with teachers. Teachers often ask what they think they should do when students in their classes cavalierly call each other the n-word even while greeting each other. I always respond to their questions with a question, and forgive me for being crude. I ask, "Would you allow your female students to walk around in your classroom calling each other 'cunt' as a term of endearment?" I ask this question rhetorically. The teachers immediately see the absurdity of their question once I substitute one offensive word for another. The use of the n-word is unacceptable in schools and in any workplace, including Paula Deen's.

All this said, however, to some degree I understand why Deen believed it was okay to use the n-word "affectionately" in her establishment. Unfortunately, people throw the n-word around like the word pal. And what is more confusing for many people is the fact that some black people themselves use the n-word as a term of endearment, which I think is blithering idiocy. Find another word! Find another word that is not so offensive or historically painful! Black people who use the n-word suffer from internalized racism. Here is the definition again:

The individual inculcation of the racist stereotypes,

values, images, and ideologies perpetuated by the White dominant society about one's racial group, leading to feelings of self-doubt, disgust, and disrespect for one's race and/or oneself.[26]

This definition describes the mind-set of the black male boss who was recently sued by a black female employee for use of the n-word. The boss repeatedly called the woman the n-word and she sued and won a judgment against her black boss and his nonprofit for more than a quarter-million dollars.[27] I agree with this verdict made by a New York federal jury. This word should not be used by anyone.

Nonetheless, there is one big caveat to this discussion that I must share because I have seen it come up over and over in public discussions. In particular, one situation that stands out involved Dr. Laura Schlessinger in 2010 when a black woman called into her show complaining that her white husband's friends would say racist things to her. Dr. Schlessinger was heavily criticized for repeatedly using the n-word. Shortly thereafter, Schlessinger announced that she would be leaving the radio clearly out of frustration. She commented, "I don't get it. If anybody without enough melanin says it, it's a horrible thing."[28]

Schlessinger was absolutely correct! As much as I despise the use of the n-word by anyone, it is especially off limits for white people because of its historical significance and the fact that it was used to reinforce the heinous degradation and treatment of black people. Yes. It is a double standard, but this is a consequence of a history that was not created by black people. My point is reinforced by another incident that happened in 2011 between Barbara Walters and Sherri Shepherd on *The View*. A heated discussion between Walters and Shepherd developed when Walters was discussing the name of the ranch leased by the family of then-Republican presidential candidate Rick Perry. The name of Perry's ranch included the n-word, and fellow Republican and black presidential candidate, Herman Cain, during a debate, noted this as grossly insensitive. Shepherd interrupted

Walters after she used the n-word a couple times and expressed her disapproval of the use of the word by Walters. Shepherd said, "It was different when Whoopi said it." Shepherd continued, "When white people say it, it brings up feelings in me." Barbara Walters was clearly taken aback and commented that she never knew Sherry felt that way and said that it was "amazing to me." Walters should have apologized then, but instead she became a little defensive and said she was just "reporting" the story.

If we hark back to Schlessinger's comment about not having enough melanin and couple it with Sherri Shepherd's reaction, you understand that even while "reporting" a story, white people should not use the word. This understandably is probably confusing for some who feel close to their black friends and who are aware that their black friends use it with their friends and family, as Shepherd admitted. However, even the closest and most meaningful interracial friendships do not negate the reality of systemic racism and racial bias that people of color deal with on a daily basis. Whites and people of color do not have a shared experience with life when we consider it in racial terms. Nonetheless, Shepherd excellently told Walters that if someone tells you that they don't like something, then out of respect you shouldn't say it. I have to commend Sherri Shepherd for speaking up, because Barbara Walters has a lot of power, and all too often I see people of color succumb to fear and don't speak up for what they believe in because they worry about being reprimanded or losing their jobs. It was refreshing to see the courage of both Walters and Shepherd to have a "real" conversation about such a difficult topic.

Interestingly, just as Barbara Walters didn't realize she was being offensive by using the n-word while discussing the Rick Perry ranch, I initially thought the same was true of Paula Deen not realizing she was saying and doing things without full awareness of how offensive it was. However, after watching a subsequent interview she had with Matt Lauer on the *Today Show*, I quickly changed my mind and no longer had sympathy for Deen; it was evident that indeed she knew exactly what she was doing.[29] I will come back to this point a little later, but here, you might be asking, "Why did you feel sorry for Deen in the first place?"

I initially felt sorry for Paula Deen because I know we all have experiences that teach us and make us who we are. So when I learned how she grew up in the South at a time when black people were in positions of servitude, and the fact that her great-grandfather owned slaves on his plantation and committed suicide when the Civil War ended and he lost all of his "workers," Deen's mentality was put into context for me. No, I am not trying to make an excuse for her behavior. I am simply offering a possible explanation because there is always a reason behind our actions. However, as adults, we cannot make excuses for our "bad" behavior, nor can we blame the past or our upbringing for our faults. Instead, we must take responsibility for our actions because by the time we reach adulthood, we should have learned how to be empathetic, altruistic, and considerate of other people.

This is why the interview with Matt Lauer changed my mind about Paula Deen. When an adult says, "I is what I is," as Deen uttered to Lauer,[30] this tells me that she is set in her ways and doesn't really care about the people she has hurt. Her declaration was just as careless as the comment she made about whites and blacks both being prejudiced in the South. While I agree with Deen's assertion, as I have stressed in this book that we all harbor racial prejudice regardless of race, Deen fails to understand that there is a fundamental difference between prejudging someone on the basis of race versus running an establishment that is uncomfortable and hostile toward employees because of race. This constitutes racism— and this is what she was accused of. This point brings me back to the central question I asked in this racial gaffe section about Paula Deen's punishment. Did Deen deserve to lose all of her endorsements?

In order to answer the aforementioned question, I have to return to the element of intent in my equation. The way I assess intent is by looking at the number of times a person has racially offended and whether or not they are sincerely apologetic once they have learned that what they have said or done is inappropriate or offensive. In Paula Deen's case, unquestionably there are multiple incidents and comments reported and documented in the media that support the idea that she was a repeat offender for some time.

Despite her primary socialization growing up in a home where she was apparently taught how to be racist, as an adult she had the opportunity to change that—namely, the full range of secondary socialization opportunities that have been afforded to her through her work and through her business. Her testimony revealed, however, that she continued to harbor racist attitudes. Apparently, Deen established a business empire and intentionally recreated a plantation-like work environment, continuing the legacy of her great-grandfather, who reportedly owned thirty slaves—the people she euphemistically labeled as "workers." According to the lawsuit that set off the media frenzy, Deen created a hostile work environment where her employees were subjected to racial slurs, including the n-word.[31]

Undoubtedly, if we consider the racism formula **Racism = Prejudice (+) Power (+) or (-) Intent**, there is no question that some of her comments were racist. I looked at the videotape of Deen calling her black friend on stage and commenting that he is "as black as the board." As awful and humiliating as it was for him, I don't believe her intent was to hurt him even though not everyone appreciates that type of humor. Paula Deen doesn't seem to understand that some behaviors aren't appropriate, even if they are presented as a joke. Remember, as I stated earlier in the book, racism can be masked by jokes. And bottom line: I do not believe in public humiliation. Deen used her power to make a grown black man walk up on stage to be insulted in front of cameras and a large group of people.

By that one act on camera, it is evident that Deen was in charge of her own empire and with the means to control, hire, and fire whomever she wanted. She created an environment that enabled her to feel comfortable being who she was and with the ability to say whatever she wanted without consequence—hence publicly disrespecting her employee. But I suspect that type of thing must have happened all the time at her establishment. If Deen said that so cavalierly on camera, I can only imagine what she says in the privacy of her own business and her home. Like the employee she called on stage to humiliate, even if Deen's employees were offended, they probably said nothing and put up with her comments and maltreatment because they relied on Deen for a paycheck and their livelihood. However, one person did not succumb to the power dynamic and came forward to file a complaint. And this person, to my surprise, happened to be white.

A Personal Lesson

When I first heard the story, I automatically assumed the person who filed the lawsuit against Paula Deen was black. Why? Because not only do people rarely stand up for what is right, but it is especially unusual for a white woman to be so offended by a racial slur reserved for black people that she would file a lawsuit against another white person. Recall the discussion of colorblindness in chapter 2. Colorblind racism teaches us that white people typically deny seeing color and are not necessarily the ones who would stand up for injustices like those alleged in the lawsuit against Paula Deen. But as I have stated over and over in this book, there are always exceptions to what we think we know. So this was an opportunity for me to engage in self-examination and really interrogate why I automatically assumed the woman suing her was black. This was a teachable moment for me, even as a person who specializes in this area of racial assumptions.

It is clear that there is no such thing as infallibility when it comes to race. What matters most is learning from the mistakes we make. Moreover, we have learned by Deen's example and the example of the black boss that we have to be careful about what we say because our words matter. Again, I do not believe *anyone* should use the n-word. I am hopeful that the recent verdict holding a black boss accountable for using it against a black employee encourages us *all* to rid our vocabularies of this word. Language evolves, and such a word going extinct would be a declaration of collective intolerance for all types of hate speech.

In sum, the goal of this chapter was not to create a laundry list of examples of racial gaffes. Instead, using the Poulton Race Equations, I have clarified my argument for the need to make a clear distinction between the concept of racism and the concept of racial bias. We need these tools to help us understand the complex world in which we live; otherwise, we will continue to have problems with our basic understanding of incidents related to race. This said, I am under no illusion that you might not agree with my analyses and maybe not even my distinction between racial bias and racism; this is fine. My primary goal is to make the point again that when incidents related to race happen in our society, we need to stop the brief, shallow, unintelligent, and uninformed responses to situations. Otherwise, we will not be able to get along with people who are different from us.

No problem can be solved from the same level of consciousness that created it.

—ALBERT EINSTEIN

CHAPTER SEVEN

Is It Always about Race?

Now that you've worked through examples of racial gaffes in the previous chapter—both your own views and my analyses—you know how to analyze incidents while looking through a racial lens. However, I would be remiss if I didn't also address the following questions: Is it always about race? Does race always stand on its own as the single factor that can influence the beliefs and reactions of individuals in different situations? The answer to both questions is no. In this chapter, I discuss the complex nature of race and racism as an intangible influence and how race also intersects with other factors like gender, class, and access to power to produce unpredictable behavioral outcomes.

Of course, it is difficult to quantify the percentage or amount of "race influence" in any given situation versus other factors, like gender or class. This is why, throughout this book, I have carefully used the phrases "incidents *related to* race" and not "incidents *because of* race." Yes, I have used critical race theory as the theoretical framework for this book, and thus race is believed to supersede all other factors that affect how we interact with one another, but this does not negate the fact that other issues might still be at play. In fact, some scholars suggest that race, class, and gender are *interlocking* categories of experience that affect *all* aspects of human life and simultaneously *structure* the experiences of *all* people in this society.[1] This intersection of race, class, and gender, or "positionality," is "a concept that acknowledges that we are all raced, classed, and gendered, and these identities are relational, complex, and fluid positions rather than essential qualities."[2] And consistent with the theme of this book, I would add one more descriptor: we are all raced, classed, gendered, and biased!

I made the point in chapter 1 that there are different ways racism and racial bias can be manifested. In fact, sometimes it is manifested with such subtlety that the recipient doesn't even realize what has happened until after the fact. Other times, the recipient does *know* what's going on but still carries the burden of "proving" what has happened because the culprit's behavior is not blatant or it is explained away. When we hear an NFL player screaming the n-word, as Riley Cooper did, we know unequivocally it is racism. However, at other times, racism is not so obvious. Let's analyze a recent incident involving Oprah Winfrey that is indicative of subtle racism.

Oprah in Zurich

As I'm sure you know, Oprah Winfrey is one of the richest and most recognizable people in the world. However, one day in the summer of 2013 when she walked into a luxury store in Zurich, Switzerland, apparently she was not. Oprah was interested in a handbag—a very expensive one, at more than thirty-eight thousand dollars. However, according to Oprah, the shop assistant "didn't want to offer me the opportunity to see the bag."[3] Oprah said the store clerk insisted that the bag was "too expensive," saying, "No, no, no, you want to see this one because that one will cost too much. You won't be able to afford that one."[4]

Following the incident, Oprah insisted she was denied the opportunity to see the bag because she was black, while the sales clerk strenuously denied Oprah's account by saying, "I simply told her that it was like the one I held in my hand, only much more expensive, and that I could show her similar bags."[5] The clerk also suggested that there was a misunderstanding based on language. "I spoke to Oprah Winfrey in English. My English is okay but not excellent, unfortunately."[6]

This is a perfect example of how a blatantly racist event can be trivialized. While it is clear on Oprah's end that she was treated as she was because of her skin color, on the other end the clerk "explained" her conduct and the situation by saying her English was not good. Remember when I said that we must pay attention to what's being said and to look for hidden meanings in text? This situation epitomizes why. If we accept that the clerk's English was not very good as the reason for the incident then the implication is that Oprah could not understand her clearly, and thus Oprah's take on the incident has to be wrong. This is how people use words to disguise racism. It is a common practice to call a racist incident a "misunderstanding" when the culprit involved tries to absolve him or herself from being held accountable for inexcusable conduct. It is a way to deflect the truth.

This scenario also underscores my point that unfortunately the onus always falls on the person of color to *prove* it is racism. Ironically, in a subsequent report about the incident, Oprah actually said that she made sure she dressed well before going to the store because she knew how people could be. Facetiously, perhaps she should have walked in with an entourage or with bodyguards in order to identify herself as a *legitimate*, prospective buyer of an expensive purse. The fact that Oprah, as a human being, walked into a store as a customer should have been enough to get basic respect. This scenario also highlights the importance of understanding the concept of positionality. When it comes to race, class, and gender, depending upon the context, one identity could be more or less important than the others. In this case, despite the fact that Oprah Winfrey is a brilliant businesswoman, the owner of her OWN television network (pun intended), and a billionaire, what only mattered on that day was the color of Oprah's skin and the assumptions the clerk made as a result of Winfrey's skin color. Just as critical race theory teaches us, race inevitably influences our behavior, and in this instance, race superseded every other factor. And how do I know this for sure? First, this scenario has happened to me several times. And, second, I will answer the question simply by asking another question: if Oprah walked into the store as a well-dressed white woman, would the clerk have behaved in the same manner? My answer is definitely not.

How Do We Know for Sure?

I just described in detail what happened with Oprah Winfrey in Zurich, provided my analysis of the situation, and shared that I too have experiential knowledge with this type of maltreatment. However, I am sure there are still skeptics who don't believe these incidents happen simply because of race. This is fine. It is fair to ask, "How do we know for sure that someone has treated us a certain way because of our skin color?" How do we know that it is not also because of other reasons? The answer is we don't know for sure. Race influence is intangible, just like gender bias, age discrimination, or class discrimination. As a woman, I was warned many years ago when I first started driving to never go to a mechanic on my own because I would be taken advantage of. It is commonly understood that in absence of a male figure, women are charged higher prices than men for the same services. And even though this is a collectively understood manifestation of gender discrimination, any woman would still be hard-pressed to prove what happened. Evidently, sexism is like racism because we don't necessarily see it in action until the effects are felt.

People are "positioned" differently according to race, class, and gender. Therefore, race, class, and gender should be seen as interactive systems and not just as separate features of experience.[7] For example, a person can be privileged by race but at the same time be disempowered by virtue of gender—as happens to white women. Also, one could say that black men are privileged because they are men, but this becomes a nonsensical thought when you consider their race, class, and gender together—unless the black men are athletes or entertainers, at which point they become *acceptable*. Considering positionality helps us explain the schizophrenic nature of how black men are perceived and treated in society. On one end, they are generally demonized and considered threats, but at the other end, this threat virtually disappears when we add money, class, and fame into the mix. Consequently, black men are *positioned* differently because of these added variables. Here's an example of how black men are treated in society when they are "unknown."

Out to Dinner

My family was recently out for dinner at a restaurant, and we were waiting for a table. I was already seated in the waiting area, but my husband, a black man, was standing in front of me until a space became available for him to sit down beside me. When the seat beside me became available, it also happened to be adjacent to a thirty-something white woman who quickly glanced at my husband and swiftly moved her purse. Her purse seemed to be fine on the couch beside her when the white male before my husband was seated beside her. This is an example of how a white woman, who more than likely has faced her own gender oppression in her life, was so influenced by my husband's skin color that she acted as though he were a criminal ready to steal her purse. Remember the experience of oppression does not necessarily keep us from potentially exhibiting behaviors that hurt others.

Considering Alternative Explanations

When we consider positionality theory while analyzing the aforementioned scenario, depending upon who one talks to, the possible explanations (other than race) for why the woman moved her purse are many. Maybe she was being courteous and wanted to give him more room? Maybe she was reacting to him as a male figure? Maybe, despite dining in the same restaurant, she considered him to be of a lower class and therefore desperate enough to potentially steal her purse? Or maybe she wanted to look at her purse at that very moment he was sitting down? There could be several explanations, but my husband and I believed unequivocally that the incident was related to race. Because of the glance she gave, the immediacy of her purse movement, and the fact that she had her purse sitting comfortably on the couch beside her when a white male stranger was seated before my husband, this tells us that this situation is race-related.

From a psychosocial perspective, of course, we will never know what prompted the woman to move her purse so swiftly.[8] We don't know what "mental models"[9] or taken-for-granted assumptions and expectations she had that supported her beliefs and actions in the situation.[10] However, there is no disputing the anger that I felt and, conversely, the surprisingly apathetic attitude of my husband when the incident occurred. My husband later shared during our conversation at dinner that that particular scenario has happened to him so many times in his life that he no longer reacts to it.

By sharing this scenario, I illustrate the point that for any given incident that a person of color believes is related to race, there are others who may not necessarily believe it is about race. However, it is important to validate the feelings of people of color whenever they believe they have experienced racism or discrimination, because people of color have firsthand experiential knowledge with racism and racial bias that whites do not. People of color face personal and institutional biases every day.[11]

Congruent with my position is that of adult educator, Stephen Brookfield, who is white.

He acknowledges his limitations of understanding the plight of black people. He writes,

> I cannot be an Africentric theorist whose being, identity, and practice spring from African values, sensibilities, and traditions ... I can have no real understanding of what this means. As a White person I have no experiential knowledge, visceral access to the philosophy born of struggle that comprises the central dimension of African American thought. My skin pigmentation, White privilege, and collusion in racism places me irrevocably and irretrievably outside the Africentric paradigm.[12]

While I agree with all of the author's sentiments regarding the inherent "limitations" of being white while trying to practice antiracist work, I also believe the work of workshop facilitator Jane Elliot has managed to give white people a glimpse of firsthand experience into the discrimination and poor treatment that people of color experience on a daily basis. Jane Elliot is the creator of the famous "blue-eyed/brown-eyed" experiment that was first done with elementary school students in the 1960s and was also showcased on *The Oprah Winfrey Show* some years ago. The following is a perfect description of the experiment's procedures and the reactions of individuals who participated in Elliot's extraordinary experiment:

> As Elliott arbitrarily divides up her workshop participants, putting collars on some to humiliate them, keeping them in hot crowded rooms without explanation, making them sit on the floor so they have to look up to her, giving them tests designed to cause them to fail, changing the rules at a whim—we watch the process of social construction before our eyes. People who came in strong and self-confident and accustomed to privilege are reduced to angry, confused, tearful, helpless individuals who lose much of their self-esteem and seem de-centered by workshop's end. Elliott notes this change and asks her blue-eyeds something like this: "If you have so much trouble accepting this kind of treatment for only a few hours, when you know it isn't even real, how do you think people of color feel during a lifetime of such treatment?"[13]

The inclusion of Jane Elliott's work is very important to this discussion because it is a lesson on how easy it is for an arbitrary attribute like race in this society to be regarded as inherently superior or inferior, good or bad, or worthy of reward or punishment simply because of its shade. In addition, the white individuals who were "positioned" differently for a short period of time during Elliott's experiments experienced a radical shift. "Instead of that homily of celebratory multiculturalism, we get a lesson in critical multiculturalism where white identity has the experience of living without empathy in a structure of oppression."[14]

The individuals who participated in Elliot's experiment know what it feels like to experience domination and oppression. However, racism and racial prejudice are not experienced by all of us, so this makes it difficult for some people to fully "get it," which is why, for example, the Museum of Tolerance (MOT) in Los Angeles, California, is not just a place where documents and artifacts are displayed. The museum also offers an interactive experience designed to "challenge people of all backgrounds to confront their most closely-held assumptions and assume responsibility for change."[15]

Upon entering the building, you are led to two large, double doors. Above each is a sign—one illuminated in neon green, the other in red with the words "Unprejudiced" on one and "Prejudiced" on the other. You can guess which color goes with which sign! On the unprejudiced doors is a notice that reads, "THINK ... Now, use the other door." If you decide to ignore the suggestion—or command, as it turns out—you will be disappointed. The "Unprejudiced" doors are locked. The only way into the interactive elements of the museum is through the "Prejudiced" doors. Given what I have said throughout this book, you shouldn't be surprised that I agree with the museum's approach; we are all prejudiced in one way or another—whether positively or negatively—even if we don't want to admit it. It is great that this museum challenges individuals to confront their prejudices.

Empathetic Listening

For those who have trouble believing that people of color experience prejudice and racism, essentially because they can't see it and have never personally experienced it themselves, I often analogize the unique experience of racism and racial prejudice to the experience of pregnancy. Unless you have had a baby, you will never know exactly what it is like to have a baby. Much like if you have never had the experience of living as a person of color, you could never really know what it is like. Even for a husband or a partner who stands beside his spouse for the duration of a pregnancy, watches her body change, sees her in pain, and puts his hand on her belly to feel the baby kick, he still could never have the same experience as the woman carrying the baby. He can, however, as much as possible, empathize with his partner and support her through the gestation period.

This is what people of color generally need from others when they suspect they have been treated unfairly: an empathetic ear and support, even if others don't fully understand it. This in essence is what I've been saying throughout this book: because you have not personally experienced something does not mean you can negate or invalidate the experiences of those who have. This is a big reason I have only shared real-life true experiences and scenarios in this book. True experiences cannot be refuted,[16] and they stay with people long after the day of the incidents.

Let's return to the incident involving the woman with her purse. This scenario also helps us understand the range of reactions people can have about the same situation. My response was anger, while my husband's response was apathy. This tells us that we cannot necessarily predict that members of the same racial group will respond to the same situation in the same manner—hence positionality theory. Other than race, there are many factors like age (he is older than I am), his gender, his experience, or even his personality (being "laidback") that could have made my husband's reaction to the situation so different from mine. Nonetheless, positionality theory certainly blurs our lines and upsets our categories when we are trying to understand our beliefs and reactions to different situations and how people are treated. Moreover, this scenario underscores the point that while analyzing race, class, and gender, we have to consider issues of power, privilege, and equity, as they shape different group experiences.[17]

Power, Privilege, and Perceptions

One scholar posits that "there is a power disparity between racial minorities and the white majority, between the poor and the wealthy, the uneducated and the educated, and women and men."[18] However, these categories are not always so clear-cut or predictable. For example, I already shared that Oprah Winfrey is a brilliant, powerful black woman and a billionaire, but ironically, she did not pursue a formal education. More evidence of these blurred categories are the numerous examples of racial gaffes I have shared in this book committed by *all* types of people regardless of race, class, gender, and age. It is important to understand that we cannot just look at people and determine who they are, their level of class, how they will react in any situation, or their access to power. It is important to remember that we all harbor racial biases, and we are all capable of exhibiting "behavioral patterns that perpetuate relations of domination."[19] In fact, there are general characteristics of a *dominant group*, which include having a self-image of superiority, competence, and being in control, entitled, correct, and unaware of hypocrisy and contradictions. In contrast, the *oppressed group* is described as having a self-image of inferiority, incompetence, and being controlled, not entitled, and having low self-esteem—but with the ability to see contradictions, irony, and hypocrisy.[20] Also,

> In whatever ways we have access to privilege, we have been carefully socialized to accept, protect, and maintain it. In whatever ways we are likely to be oppressed, we are socialized to accept it, while also working to protect ourselves and one another. This patterning [explains] why we duplicate the very relations we are trying to transform. As we become aware of the impact of domination on ourselves and others, we are appalled by how we have somehow participated in its persistence.[21]

I wonder if this is how Tyler the Creator feels. Is he appalled by the fact that as a black man, he created the 2013 Mountain Dew commercial that was dubbed by many as the most racist commercial ever? The premise of the commercial was a crazy goat that became obsessed with Mountain Dew. Specifically, in this first ad of a bizarre trilogy, the goat beats up a white female waitress for failing to bring sufficient quantities of Mountain Dew. In the second ad, the goat eludes police at a traffic stop. And the third ad was a masterful cacophony of images. It included a police lineup consisting of a group of black men and a goat, a severely beaten white woman hobbling on crutches, and a white detective, all coupled with an unfunny script voiced by Tyler the Creator, a rapper who is known for lyrics that glorify violence against women and homophobia.[22]

The commercial was disturbing on so many levels. In thirty seconds, it managed to reinforce the stereotype that black men are criminals and animals—hence the goat in the police lineup. It implied that black men are scary "gangstas" who beat white women, hence the visually bloodied woman. The goat further intimidated the white woman into not identifying him in the lineup by whispering in stereotypical "black" language: "Ya better not snitch on a playa," "Snitches get stitches," and "When I get outta here, I'm gonna do you up."

Also, bear in mind that all this is somehow intended to be related to soda with the inclusion of a buffoonish white detective who stands by ineffectually sipping a Mountain Dew. This dichotomous portrayal of a supportive and nonthreatening white man acting in defense of a battered white woman against black criminals was not lost.

Again, the supposedly creative force behind the spot—Tyler the Creator—is a black man himself. But if this is supposed to help anyone understand what the point of the three-series ad is, it fails. In one interview, even Tyler himself admitted he was surprised Mountain Dew went for the commercial since he came up with the idea only five minutes before the pitch meeting.[23] In another interview, Tyler also defended himself against his critics. "Weren't they 18 years old at some point, just having fun?" Further, Tyler's publicist said, "It was never Tyler's intention to offend ... He's known for pushing boundaries and challenging stereotypes through humor."[24] Unfortunately, he achieved the exact opposite of what he intended to do. "Socialized behavior does not instantly die when our intentions are to equalize intentions."[25]

Admittedly, I had no idea who Tyler the Creator was before this advertising fiasco. While I firmly believe in art and creativity of any kind, I must say that I know there is a fundamental difference between "pushing boundaries and challenging stereotypes" versus outright, stereotypical tomfoolery that is presented as creativity. This makes me think of the expression "Don't pee on me and tell me it's rain." Like many people, I found this commercial to be unequivocally offensive, racist, and beyond idiotic. I have to wonder, as so many others have asked, "Who was in the room when this commercial was pitched and approved?" I find it odd that given the layers of offensiveness in this commercial, no one stepped in to challenge the content either before or during its making.

The Mountain Dew debacle epitomizes and reinforces my saying, "Color does not mean consciousness." The commercial was racist, so if it came directly from the mind of Tyler the Creator then he probably must be influenced by internalized racism. Why else would he create such a horrible commercial that makes his own demographic (black men) look so bad in the eyes of the public? As a black man with unusual access to power, privilege, and influence, he used his position of power so poorly, which is disappointing. Moreover, the Mountain Dew executives involved in this commercial are also not without blame. They sought the advice of a "master lyricist" who has produced such winning verse as "rape a pregnant bitch and tell my friends I had a threesome."[26] Moreover, Pepsi Co, which owns Mountain Dew, also sponsored L'il Wayne's 2013 tour before dropping him shortly after the Tyler the Creator scandal. Apparently, Mountain Dew executives were disturbed by lyrics that compare a woman's vagina after sex to Emmett Till's face after he was beaten to death.[27]

Evidently, the executives should have been disturbed long before they sought the advice of Tyler the Creator and especially before, during, and after the Mountain Dew commercial was shared with the public. On some level, I suspect the executives probably believed that since a black man created the commercial, somehow the content was inherently "approved." Evidently not! Because a black person says or does something does not mean it will be widely accepted by other blacks. Remember no community is monolithic, including the black community. The commercial was dumb and offensive, and I have not met anyone, regardless of race, gender, age, etc., that didn't believe the commercial was crude and unintelligent. Evidently, this was the sentiment of the thinking public—hence the backlash.

Another disappointing situation involving a black man with extraordinary power and influence is Russell Simmons, who created a gut-wrenchingly horrible, disrespectful, and almost pornographic video depicting civil rights hero Harriet Tubman having sex with her slave owner. The video was so offensive, generating copious outrage from the black community, that Simmons had to eventually apology. Despite this major racial gaffe, I still like Russell Simmons because, to my knowledge, he has always been a positive figure. In fact, as a black girl growing up in Canada, where there were no black role models of any kind to show black kids what was possible to achieve in the arts, I grew up admiring his work. He was one of a few artists to show the way, including Run DMC, Queen Latifah, Boogie Down Productions, Chuck D., Eric B and Rakim, MC Lyte, and I've already talked about LL Cool J.

Again, what is the takeaway from this chapter? You cannot look at a person's superficial features and predetermine or anticipate his or her mind-set or type of behavior. Moreover, we also don't know who has access to power and nor can we assume how one will use it if they get it. Take each person as an individual because, like race, positionality also influences our social dynamics.

In the next chapter, I discuss my research and workshops in more detail, explaining how I encourage participants to explore and address their assumptions and biases of others.

In all affairs it's a healthy thing now and then to hang a question mark on the things you have long taken for granted.

—BERTRAND RUSSELL

CHAPTER EIGHT

CHECK Yourself!

In chapter 2, I discussed the importance of learning to think critically and what it means to engage in critical thinking. Ideally, as critical thinkers we want to

1. carefully assess the validity of both our own assumptions and those of others;
2. analyze and assess the source, nature, and consequences of our own and others' assumptions;
3. empathize and provide emotional support for others to engage in transformative learning;
4. learn to participate more fully and effectively in reflective discourse in order to assess the reasons for a belief or perspective;
5. anticipate the consequences of acting upon a transformed perspective and plan effective action;
6. develop the *disposition* to think critically; and
7. engage in cultural or social action to improve the conditions necessary to encourage adult learners to share these insights.[1]

While all of the aforementioned points are excellent goals for all of us to pursue, here in this chapter I focus on point number one, which is the importance of assessing the validity of our assumptions about others.

Assessing Our Assumptions

An assumption is what is taken as true without proof. Unfortunately, we often rely on our assumptions in order to facilitate deliberation or action. In the absence of verification, we may assume a restaurant is open and on that assumption get into the car on a rainy night to eat dinner. We may put a charge on our credit card on the assumption that we will still have income when it's time to pay the bill. Also, how often have you heard someone say or how often have you said in a discussion, "Okay, let's assume you're correct. If that's the case ..." We do this when we are attempting to consider an alternative perspective by reflecting on the ideas and arguments of another person. However, we should spend more time asking ourselves, "What assumptions am I making? Are any of my assumptions incorrect?" All too often we become fixated on what other people are doing or doing to us when we should be critically analyzing what we have done and how maybe we have contributed to any given situation. Especially when it comes to making assumptions about people on the basis of race, we should learn how to identify and investigate our assumptions. After all, if we're going to use assumptions as the foundations for deliberations and actions, we should have some robust ideas about what they are and whether or not they're worth having.

A perfect example of the link among assumptions, deliberation, and action is the August 2013 murder of a promising white baseball player from Australia, Christopher Lane, who was in the United States on a baseball scholarship. Three silly teenagers senselessly gunned Lane down. Their motive? "They were bored and had nothing to do."[2] In a subsequent piece I watched on CNN, anchor Don Lemon and his guests pondered the question as to whether or not the assailants should be charged with a hate crime because one of the shooters, a black teen, posted racist, antiwhite tweets on Twitter before the shooting. To me, the answer is simple.

Absolutely.

The racist postings on Twitter represent the mind-set of at least one of the assailants, and so it is not a stretch to assume that his thoughts informed his words and eventually his actions. You might recall my previous discussion on the difference between freedom of speech laws in Canada versus in the United States. Had this incident happened in Canada, there would be no question as to whether the incident should be categorized as a hate crime. Canadian law, and in particular the Human Rights Act, prohibits discrimination of any kind, and it forbids hate speech or other contemptuous messages, including on the Internet. Why? Because words lead to deeds, as we have seen in this senseless murder. And I have to say that if this situation were reversed and the victim was black, the incident would have been labeled "racist" just as it should be here. If we look at my racism equation again, **Racism = Prejudice (+) Power (+) or (-) Intent**, it is clearly a racist incident and should be deemed a hate crime.

Nonetheless, regardless of where this incident took place, we can all agree that it was a heinous, despicable act, and at the very least, it shows a correlation between thoughts and actions. This is why, in this chapter, I focus my attention on the need for us to check ourselves and work on our thoughts and assumptions, even if they don't lead to such extreme incidents. Especially with respect to race and the fact that we all have biases toward others that we grapple with all the time, it is important to recognize how closely linked our assumptions are to our biases, and to our beliefs.

The following passage, titled "The Airport," is an example of a real-life critical incident I share in my workshops while teaching adults how to explore and reflect on their assumptions and biases.

INSTRUCTIONS

Grab a piece of paper and a pen. Please read "The Airport" story below and answer the questions that follow. I encourage you to be cognizant of your initial thoughts, assumptions, and preconceived notions as you read and jot them down. Your *initial* thoughts, impressions, and preconceived notions represent what you ***really*** believe.

The Airport

A woman entered an airport lounge and smiled at "Person X" who was sitting in the section where she then sat down. With forty-five minutes to wait until her flight was ready to depart, the woman took her iPad out of her bag and started playing Words with Friends.

Person X, who was sitting directly in front of the woman a few feet away, stood up and walked toward the woman.

> "Would you mind watching my bags for a moment while I go to the restroom?" X politely asked.

> "Sure, I don't mind," the woman responded.

A few minutes later, Person X came back. However, X did not acknowledge the woman or say thank-you for watching the bags.

The woman briefly thought, *That's kind of rude*, but she shrugged it off and continued to play on her iPad.

A few more minutes passed. Then the woman noticed that Person X was visibly and nervously fidgeting around. Eventually, Person X stood up, grabbed the bags the woman watched earlier, and placed them in chairs directly adjacent to where the woman was sitting.

> Person X asked, "Do you mind if I sit down beside you for a second?"

> The woman said, "No, I don't mind at all."

> "You know," X said in the most sincere and gentle tone the woman had ever heard, "I believe God puts people in your path for a reason."

> "I totally agree," she responded, shifting in her seat to face X.

> Person X paused briefly and then continued. "I feel a connection to you, and I want to thank you."

"Thank me? For what?"

At that moment, Person X's eyes welled up with tears. "Do you know you are the first person to smile at me today?"

In response to the woman's stunned expression, X said, "When you walked in, you smiled at me."

On one end, she was pleased that she could be a person to offer a smile to a stranger. However, she was also horrified that it was four thirty in the afternoon and it was the first smile Person X had received all day.

"Really? I am very surprised," said the woman.

Person X just looked at the woman for a second and said, "Yesterday I was diagnosed with cancer."

"Oh, my!" the woman exclaimed. "I am so sorry to hear this." Then, with a concerned look on her face she asked, "Do you mind if I hold your hand for a moment?"

Person X did not verbalize the answer, but it was still clear that her request was okay.

The woman said, "I am really sorry to hear this. I want you to know that I understand what you are going through. I lost my father four years ago to cancer. My mother has cancer now, and I am on my way to see my uncle probably for the last time. He also has cancer."

They held hands for a short moment and cried together.

Person X then said, "Well, thank you. It was really nice to meet you."

Person X stood up, grabbed the bags, took a few steps away, and stopped. Person X looked back toward the woman for a few seconds, smiled, and then walked away.

The woman sat and wept for a while until she boarded her plane.

SELF-REFLECTION EXERCISE

Please answer the following questions:

1. What is the race of the woman?
2. What is the race of Person X?
3. Was Person X male or female?
4. What parts/clues in the scenario helped you decide the races of the individuals involved?
5. What parts/clues in the scenario helped you determine the gender of Person X?
6. Reflect on the assumptions you made while reading the scenario. Think about the reasons you made these assumptions.

Identities Revealed

The woman in this scenario is I, a black woman then in my thirties, and Person X is a white man who was probably in his late fifties to early sixties.

HOW DID YOU DO?

1. Did you guess the answers correctly?
2. Did you find any areas surprising?

Remember bias is *inevitable* so you should not be surprised if you answered the questions to "The Airport" scenario inaccurately. This is not about right or wrong. The mere purpose of this activity is to help you begin the process of bringing into your consciousness any assumptions or biases you might have that you wouldn't necessarily know are there.

FOLLOW-UP EXERCISE

Share and compare your results with your spouse and/or your friends. Did they have the same answers you did? Discuss your findings and share your initial assumptions and reactions to the scenario.

I shared this scenario as a way to get a taste of what it is like to tap into your unconscious and conscious assumptions and biases and how they might impact your overall judgment and behavior. What we should learn from "The Airport" story is the importance of treating others with respect even if we don't know them and even if they are "different" from us. It does not take much to say hello and connect with people at the human level rather than allow superficial, racial differences to dictate how and whom we interact with.

The CHECK

I use the acronym CHECK to sum up what we should do when meeting people for the first time. For each letter of the acronym explained below, I offer clear, practical, grounded behavioral suggestions on what you can do to keep your assumptions and biases in CHECK. Following these steps will help us all work toward a more peaceful coexistence between and among all races. I also say "among" because, remember, we can have prejudgments about people, even in our own race.

Consciously and continuously ask questions of yourself, "Why do I believe what I believe?"

Hold your tongue—you cannot listen if you are talking. Don't be quick to judge, especially out loud!

Evaluate each situation separately. Always consider the context of the situation and the players involved.

Critically reflect on what you say and what others say to you. Are there other possible ways to interpret what is said?

Kindness goes a long way. If you are in doubt about a situation or a person, just be pleasant. Smile or say hello!

<u>CHECK</u>: Description and Analysis

Consciously and continuously ask questions of yourself: "Why do I believe what I believe?" "What are my assumptions and truths?" "Where and how did I learn what I know?"

It is important for each of us to continually examine ourselves. We need to be honest with ourselves, and to do this requires humility. We have to admit that perhaps what we think we know is not the right way to think, which means we have to learn to be comfortable with the idea of being wrong. For example, our respective families raise us all, and sometimes the values and mores that have been entrenched in us as children do not necessarily serve us as adults. Through my work as a consultant, I have met many individuals who have shared their personal stories about being raised not to associate with certain types of people because their parents deemed them as bad. However, as adults, they have ended up working with people from that very group their parents told them to stay away from. This inevitably causes internal conflicts or cognitive dissonance, as was defined earlier as a state of disequilibrium. These individuals have internal conflict because they were raised to think one way via primary socialization, but then their experiences as adults (secondary socialization) have offered contradictory experiential knowledge.

So what is one to do when this happens—when new experiences do not reconcile with what they've known their whole lives? My best advice is to follow your gut and do what you think is right. Also, sometimes it's not even your choice. You might experience a disorienting dilemma that leaves you forever changed. However, I will caution you that sometimes when you undergo a change in perspective or approach to life and follow your own lead, others in your circle who expect you to be the same will not necessarily appreciate the changes. Consequently, friendships and family relationships might be threatened, and some may end. However, as long as you are doing what you think is right for you, the right people who really care about you will support you and stay in your life even if they don't agree with the changes. The following scenario exemplifies what I am talking about.

The White Supremacist

One day after I presented my workshop at a school district, a fellow teacher, a white female, stopped me in the hall. She told me she had a dilemma and wanted my advice. The teacher admitted that she used to be a white supremacist, but after working with children of color at a school in a high needs community, the experience changed her heart. In essence, she had a disorienting dilemma because the experience of teaching children of color made her unable to continue hating people of color. She fell in love with some of the kids. However, her change of heart and perspective created problems between her and her husband, who remained a white supremacist. The problem is that her husband did not have the same experience as the teacher. He did not have the same exposure or meaningful interactions with the children of color so he did not understand his wife's change in perspective. As a result, their marriage ended.

The teacher continued her story and asked my advice regarding her ex-mother-in-law, who was also a white supremacist. Unfortunately, when the grandmother would take the teacher's six-year-old child for a visit, the grandmother would say racist and disparaging things about people of color around the child. As a result, the child would come home and share the negative things she learned from her grandmother, and this would leave the teacher having to reeducate her child each time she came home from a visit at Grandma's house.

The teacher was not sure what to do because she wanted her child to see her paternal grandmother, but she also did not want her child to be *poisoned* with bigotry and racism. My advice to the teacher was straightforward. I told her she was responsible for what her child learns, and if she did not agree with what Grandma was saying, she would have to do one of two things: ask Grandma to curb what she says to her child (or she will have to stop sending the child for visits) or stop sending the child altogether.

In the next chapter, "Teaching Children about Race," I talk about the disservice that adults do to innocent children by burdening them with discriminatory baggage we have. However, before we teach children about race, we have to first understand it ourselves and grapple with it. This is why it is worthwhile to ask yourself, "Where did I learn what I know?" Clearly, in the scenario I just shared, the hatred and racism was passed down from the grandmother to her son, who ended up getting a divorce from the teacher I met because she had a change of heart. The marriage did not work because he was unwilling to change.

It is unfortunate because, as adults, it is our duty not to shrug our shoulders and say, "That's who I am," "This is how I was raised," or, in Paula Deen's words, "I is what I is." These types of definitive declarations don't allow a person room to grow, to move, or to learn from new experiences that come their way. A key principle of adult education is that we are all lifelong learners. Therefore, we should not be so rigid as to resist change because change is inevitable.

Hold your tongue. You cannot listen if you are talking. Don't be quick to judge, especially out loud!

This is a communication tactic that pretty much works in any situation you find yourself in. Especially in this context, holding your tongue allows you to pause for a moment and to really listen to others. If you listen closely to what someone says and how they say it, you will learn more than relying on your perceptions and prejudgments that are more than likely inaccurate. Holding your tongue is an effective tactic, as I have already demonstrated in this book. When I meet people for the first time, I obviously engage in conversation, but I do my best to be cognizant of my judgments and really listen to the other people in order to learn who they are and what their intentions are. This can't happen if I am not really listening. Ultimately, this is how I am able to differentiate between individuals who innocently ask me questions about my background or my family and those individuals who ask me questions in order to put me into a particular *category* or *box* in order to help them decide how to treat me.

We are all human, first and foremost, which means you don't have to figure out who someone is before you decide to treat them with respect. Basic decorum should be your first thought, regardless of someone's race, class, gender, sexual orientation, nationality, aptitude, or ability. Hold your tongue and choose behaviors that are demonstrative of openness and acceptance.

Evaluate each situation separately. Always consider the context of the situation and the players involved.

Another thing that distinguishes adults from children is our ability, if we are mature, to make distinctions, differentiate between things and people, and evaluate each situation on its own. For example, I was once in conversation with a man who had recently divorced from his first wife, who was of a different race. He was talking about the prospects of dating again and shared his preference for a new potential spouse. In the conversation, he shared that he would never date a woman of his own race (and never had), but he would be willing to marry another woman of the same race as his first wife.

Surprised, I said, "So how come you have never dated (and never will date) someone in your own race, and yet your first marriage failed with someone of a different race than yours, but you are willing to give someone outside your race a second chance before you are willing to give someone inside your race *one* chance?"

The man ended up sharing that he had been teased badly by women in his own race growing up, so he thought they were "all rude." I pointed out to him that he was taking one context that happened more than a decade earlier and was holding on to it and transferring it many years later. Things might have changed! I understood *where* his beliefs came from, but I also tried to explain to him that he was painting with broad strokes about people within his own race. Surely, between high school and more than a decade later, he would have met someone in his race, not necessarily to date, that would show him that not *all* women in his race were rude.

I am not suggesting at all that interracial dating or marriage is wrong or unacceptable. In fact, there are interracial relationships in my family, and as I shared earlier, I have biracial nieces and nephews whom I love dearly. What I am saying is that I see red flags when a person completely rejects people in his own race without even giving them an opportunity to show who they are as individuals. When a person outright rejects people from within his or her own race, this is a clear expression of self-hatred. As I have suggested all throughout this book, it is wrong to treat others, including people within your own race, as a monolithic group. We have to look at people as individuals and remember that even genetically no two people are alike. Therefore, we cannot assume that two people in one race or an entire race of people are the same. We should always be cognizant of our thoughts, words, and deeds and try hard not to transfer one context to another but instead evaluate each situation on its own.

Critically reflect on what you say and what others say to you. Are there other possible ways to interpret what is said?

It is important to listen to the words people say, but you should also pay attention to the intonation, the level of interest, and the level of respect or lack thereof. We should also pay attention to any hidden, obscured, or underlying messages from the communicator. What is really being said? What is omitted? Is there a hidden meaning? No, I am not advocating that you become suspicious of people. What I am asking you to do is think critically about what people say and not just take things at face value all the time. In this respect, the word *critical* is not to be understood in the common sense of the word like criticizing or being negative. In fact, "critical" means being skeptical, proposing alternatives, opening up complexity, not taking things for granted, and being self-reflective. Similarly,

> Critical reflection describes the process by which we become more skillful in argument analysis. In this tradition we act critically when we recognize logical fallacies, when we distinguish between bias and fact, opinion and evidence, judgment and valid inference, and when we become skilled at using different forms of reasoning (inductive, deductive, analogical, and so forth).[3]

Moreover, I also think it's important to listen to your intuition. If something doesn't *feel* right, there is a reason. Consider the scenario below.

Trophies on the Mantel

One day, one of my neighbors, a white lady, came by for a quick visit to my home. Around that time, my husband and I had just put a few of his trophies on the fireplace mantel. He'd won them for his outstanding work as a designer. My neighbor immediately noticed the trophies, walked over to the fireplace, and said, "Oh, these are nice. What are they for?"

I replied that they were awards my husband had won. She then paused for a weird moment, staring intensely at the trophies, and said, "Oh, that's great. Are they group awards?" The words she used and the way she asked the question let me know that there was no way she believed my husband, a black man, could have managed to win any of the awards on his own. When I told her, "No, they are not group awards," she was visibly surprised and said nothing more.

On the face of it, it looked like she was paying him a compliment by saying, "That's great." But she also delivered an insult at the same time. This is an example of why it is always important to not only listen to what people say but to also pay close attention to what they don't say while in conversation. This is necessary because I have learned that language is very powerful, and people do not always use it innocently or for positive purposes. This said, not surprisingly, even when people choose to be negative, they are usually still invested in preserving the positive perceptions that people have of them and that which reduces their anxiety.[4] In other words, when we are concerned that others may perceive us negatively, we are particularly careful about revealing anything associated with generating such a perception. However, in this case with my neighbor, I was able to read between the lines and figured out what she was thinking and what she meant. Consequently, she was not invited back to my home again.

You might be thinking how hypocritical it was of me not to invite her back to my home when I am preaching that we must be open to people. The answer is simple. I don't allow people with negative energy in my home. It is my space—a pure space that my husband and I have created and that we rely on to help us unwind, decompress, and purge ourselves of the negativities we experience from individuals we encounter in the outside world every day. We do not willingly invite such negativity into our home. This does not mean, however, that when I see my neighbor I am unkind.

> Kindness goes a long way. If you are in doubt about a situation or a person, just be pleasant. Smile or say hello!

"The Airport" story I shared earlier in this chapter is the best anecdote to illustrate this point of relying on kindness and a smile to ease situations. I walked into the airport lounge, and my eyes made four with the gentleman, so rather than just looking away and not acknowledging the brief connection, I chose to smile at him. And look what happened! That experience with a complete stranger is one that I will always cherish. It made me proud to be able to help someone, and without even trying to. My only regret is that I did not exchange information with the gentleman. I really would like to know how he is doing. Nevertheless, the point here is that people are put into our paths for a reason, so why not be pleasant and smile? Who knows? You might make a new friend or make someone's day!

What you help a child to love can be more important than what you help him to learn.

—African Proverb

CHAPTER NINE

Teaching Children about Race

Research has shown that children have healthier attitudes toward people from different races when their parents are proactive in discussing race and related topics.[1] What is meant by proactive? When parents choose to have general conversations about race with their children rather than being reactive—waiting for an incident to happen before the topic is addressed. This topic arose from my PhD research in which a thirty-seven-year-old woman under the pseudonym Angela shared a critical incident that happened when she was ten years old. Angela is a light-skinned black woman who attended a school that was majority white. The following is a description of the incident in Angela's words that took place when she returned to the changing room after physical education class:

> It [the picture] pointed out skin color and hair was like a big huge part of it and all the ways that they thought that I was different pointed out for everyone to see. So it was really traumatic and you know, it was the first time I realized that people viewed me differently. I didn't know that before but the real critical incident here is how my parents responded ... It wasn't until there were the negative effects of it like not wanting to go to school and behaving completely out of character that my parents really dealt with it ... So I think in two ways it affected me. First, I would have to always stand up for myself

because I didn't feel anyone was going to do it for me. And second, I took from my parents at ten ... that you are different and sometimes I read situations wrong because I have that underlying need to fit in. I learned that from my parents. But I'm aware of it now so I always ask, "Am I looking at this weird because of my need to fit in?" This is the instinct I have that comes from what my parents want for me rather than what I want for myself. Or am I really trying to see the best from people? So if someone says that someone treated me differently, I won't see it right away because I went so long, um, almost being told that that's not really what I'm seeing.

One key issue that we can point out from this scenario is that Angela's parents were very uncomfortable with the subject of race and chose not to address it in any way—even when incidents occurred. This, unfortunately, was a disservice to the ten-year-old child at that time, and the ripple effect was still felt by the thirty-seven-year-old woman decades later. Evidently, those types of experiences don't just "go away" with time. They stay with you, leaving indelible scars if they are not ever addressed. Angela's words were profound when she bravely shared that, because of that incident more than two decades ago and how it was not properly acknowledged or addressed, she learned from the experience that no one will stand up for her if something like that happens to her again. She also said as a result of the incident that she doesn't even realize what is going on when racial incidents happen to her or in front of her. She literally blocks the incidents out because she doesn't trust what she is seeing. Angela later thanked me for my research and called it a cathartic process, because she was holding onto that incident and the feelings surrounding it for more than two decades. She was grateful for the opportunity to address it and talk about it in a meaningful way after so many years.

My intent sharing this scenario is not to criticize Angela's parents, since I am sure they did the best they could with what they knew at the time. I shared this story to highlight yet another reason why we, as adults, should deal with this issue of race, racism, and racial bias. If we do not address our personal demons head on, we will likely pass on our hang-ups to our children, as I think was the case with Angela. This is not fair to a child. There is much hope for a better world if, ideally, we all do our personal work *before* we have kids so we don't pass along our issues to them. But even if the work begins today, this is better than the alternative, which is having adults poison the minds of young children.

It is always interesting, for example, when I take my girls to the park because I can tell just by how children behave whether or not they have been exposed to people of different races. I can also figure out pretty quickly which parents feel uneasy when their children play with my children, who are black. It saddens me when I see children who deliberately stay away from children of color because I know they have been *taught* to do so, whether directly or indirectly. Children pick up cues from their parents and learn how to behave. Those behaviors I just mentioned do not happen naturally. Children are not concerned about race the way adults are. They are concerned about their friends, their possessions, and their activities. We need to let children maintain their innocence for as long as possible rather than teaching them how to hate.

When I say "innocence," I do not mean keeping children in the dark and not talking about race. I am advocating that you consciously teach children about race at an age-appropriate level, which lays a foundation of understanding *before* things happen to them racially or before they do something to someone else. In essence, children need to be taught proactively about race in order for them to learn how to navigate through the world with a working compass.

Here's an analogy. Before you take your child to the beach, do you discuss water rules and boundaries? Do you tell children how far out in the water they can go? What about the use of sunscreen to protect them from the sun's rays? Of course you do! I am suggesting that it is equally important to establish boundaries and guidelines, expectations for behavior, and examples of appropriate and inappropriate language with children in order to protect them and others from the harms of racial incidents. Establishing these boundaries will probably also save you from embarrassment. Here are some questions to ponder:

1. Do your children know how you feel about race and racial diversity?
2. Do your children know what is acceptable rhetoric in your house? That is, are they allowed to say racial epithets in your house, even in jest?
3. Do you know what you would say and do if your child said something racially offensive?

If you answered no to even one of these questions, you have some work to do. At the publication of this book, my children were both under ten years old, and they knew exactly where I stand on these issues. Sure, you are probably thinking, *Well, you are an expert in this area, so it is easy for you.* But this is not necessarily true. My husband and I have struggled at times to have these conversations with our children. Much like the "birds and the bees" conversations, discussions on race are also not easy to have. Nor are they one-time endeavors. Race conversations should be ongoing and should get progressively more in depth as children get older. For example, not too long ago, our nine-year-old asked us what the "n-word" was because she heard people discussing the word when the movie *Django Unchained* hit theaters. My husband and I collectively decided that she didn't need to know what the "n-word" meant at nine years old and told her it was something we would explain to her when she got a little older. Yes, our daughter had already learned about history, including slavery, as well as the civil rights movement, but at that moment, we decided it was not necessary to break her innocence by sharing the ugliness of the "n-word."

Right or wrong, it was our decision to answer this question the way we did—just as you will make whatever decisions you feel are right for your children. Just say *something* to them about race! Open the dialogue, because keeping them in the dark, as we have learned from the critical incident involving ten-year-old Angela at her school, does not help. Children are cheated when they are not afforded the opportunity to openly talk about race. Children should be taught the basics about race, and they also need to know how their parents feel about the issue. I just hope and pray that these teachings are not ones of hatred and bigotry but about acceptance and love.

In my home, our children know that it is unacceptable to make fun of others or to make disparaging remarks about anyone because of race or for any other characteristic. Equally important, our children also know that it is unacceptable for anyone to say things of that nature to them. The following is another critical incident that emerged from my study in which a thirty-five-year-old white woman under the pseudonym Mary described something she did when she was thirteen years old that she admittedly was not proud of. The dialogue began with Mary speaking to other focus group members.

> Mary: I have my critical incidents, but I'm only going to share my second one because I am really and truly embarrassed and ashamed of myself so I'm not going to share it. Here I am twenty years later ...

After minimal encouragement, Mary shared the following.

> Mary: Okay, when I was thirteen years old ... Okay, I will share it. I have to get this out now. My friend Lydia and I were friends and we used to go trick or treating. We actually talked last week and every once in a while, things that I have done and ashamed of come flooding back at random times and I think, *Oh, gosh.* And there's a lot of them but we were talking about a Halloween costume. I hadn't thought about this for a long time.

> Anyway, I'm getting red just thinking about it because it's so awful. Anyway, we were talking about Halloween

and we were talking about moments of shame and I said, "When I was thirteen, do you remember ... and old enough to know better but clearly not thinking. I, aw, somebody had given me a sari and I dressed up like what I called a "Pakistani princess." And I went door to door in my neighborhood asking for Gandhi, you know like candy, like thinking that was quite hilarious.

George: Wow!

Mary: Yah, until I knocked on somebody's door and it was a pretty diverse neighborhood that I lived in and I just didn't think. I was young but should have known at thirteen. And I went around and an East Indian family opened the door. And I just ... In that moment ... It was obviously too late but I'm thinking, *I'm the biggest asshole that ever lived!* You know? What are you going to do? I don't think I apologized; I just took off! But I should have known better, and I'm sure I've done other things, but you know ... so insensitive.

Kate: But you were young and you didn't know better.

Mary: But I knew the minute they opened the door so I knew better. I obviously wasn't thinking about it but I knew. So when I was faced with it I knew.

Marilyn: This is just the point of view of an East Indian person. If they saw you standing there in a sari, they probably would think, *Oh my gosh, isn't that beautiful?* That would have been their perspective ... *Oh my gosh, isn't she beautiful, and she's wearing something from our culture.*

Mary: But I don't think I had intended initially to mock it, but I did when I found myself asking for Gandhi ... Anyway ...

Is it true? Should Mary have known better? Or should Mary just have been *taught* better? Again, this is not an exercise in "shaming" parents because we have hard jobs! However, at age thirteen, Mary should have known what was acceptable and what was unacceptable behavior, especially with respect to different cultures. Cognitively, only Mary knows what was going on in her head, but evidently coming face-to-face—literally—with people she was making fun of made her realize what she was doing was wrong. The experience stayed with her for over twenty years, and she was happy to finally address the guilt she felt about it.

What Can Parents Do?

So how do you begin to have these conversations about race with your child(ren)? Regardless of the approach you take, the most important thing is to be *honest* with yourself about your feelings and be honest when sharing them with your children. This honesty, coupled with a willingness to be open and not get defensive while talking and listening to your child, will go a long way. I have to caution you, however, that sometimes when you have these conversations, especially with older children, you might have to become the "learner" in the conversation and let your children educate you. Refreshingly, kids in this generation generally do not have the same hang-ups with race as their parents do. Thankfully, it appears that each generation is getting better with race relations. I have an eighteen-year-old niece who tells me all the time that she and her friends, who are all from very diverse ethnic and racial backgrounds, do not care about race. They are all friends, and that's all that matters.

So at what age should these conversations begin? Ideally, you would want to start having casual conversations about race and "differences" before your child is ready for school (age five or six) because inevitably they will encounter different types of people even beyond race. In fact, African American preschool boys could identify themselves as distinct individuals from other groups by age five. This finding laid the foundation for future work examining preschoolers' knowledge of the self with value judgments attached to their racial preferences.[2] For example, "people 'know' to which group they belong by the time they are three years old, although they may not understand the social implications of such group membership."[3] Also, a moral complication of racial identity comes early on. The "rightness of whiteness in the US culture affects children before the age of four, providing white youngsters with a false sense of superiority and encouraging self-hatred among third world youngsters."[4] Moreover, by age eight, children understand racial classification beyond simple physical features and characteristics, and by age ten, children recognize social stereotypes associated with different racial groups.[5] Given these statistics, it is no surprise that Angela experienced what she had at age ten. It is also why Mary, at thirteen years old, probably should have known better.

What about Older Children?

What if you are reading this book and you already have a teenager or a college student? Don't despair. It is not too late. Engage your children in open and honest discussions to see how they feel and what they know about the issue of race. But be prepared to hear the truth from your "older" children, who might tell you that they have learned some not-so-great things by hearing your words or by watching your actions. This is okay. The goal is *dialogue, not* shame, because no one is perfect.

I also encourage parents of older children to read this book with their children or share age-appropriate bits of information with their younger children. Much like the "birds and the bees" conversation, there is no right or wrong way to discuss race and racism. Just have the conversation and be open, because when you open up to your child and show a little vulnerability, it creates an opportunity to develop trust between parent and child, which ultimately leads to even more open, genuine dialogue that can continue over a lifetime. For example, do you remember when I mentioned the 1934 movie called *Imitation of Life*? Watching this movie is a family tradition.

My grandmother sat down and watched this movie with my mother and my two aunts when they were preteens. My mother watched the movie with my sister and me at about the same age. And when my girls are a little older, I too will sit down and watch the movie with them. Watching this movie is an excellent way to open up a conversation about race, because it wonderfully addresses the subject while also touching on topics of friendship, family, self-acceptance, and love. I am very fortunate and grateful to have grown up with parents who were not afraid to talk about the hard stuff in life. They knew I would inevitably encounter it, and they wanted me to be prepared. I know I am who I am today because of what they instilled in me at a very young age.

I am a living example of how it "works" to talk openly about race with children. Conversely, the following is an example of a missed opportunity for a parent to address the issue of race.

The Elevator

A colleague of mine, "Reya," told me about an experience that happened when she was about age four. Reya and her mother were in an elevator when an Asian woman got on at one of the floors and Reya just stared and stared at her. Finally, still looking at the Asian woman, Reya innocently put the tip of each of her index fingers at the outside corner of each eye and pulled back toward her hairline. Reya's mother noticed her daughter trying to imitate the Asian woman's eyes and, with a bit of embarrassment, pulled her daughter's hands away.

Reya is now in her forties, but she still remembers this incident vividly. Today, reflecting on the incident, Reya believes her mother was probably a little self-conscious and probably a little horrified by the idea that maybe the Asian woman believed she had taught her daughter to mimic Asian people. Reya doesn't recall if the Asian woman noticed what she was doing at that time, nor does she recall the woman saying anything. However, what Reya specifically recalls is the fact that her mother never said anything about the incident ever again.

Why not?

This scenario was a perfect opportunity to allow Reya the chance to articulate her feelings about "different" people and to ask questions. At the very least, Reya displayed that she was aware enough of her own appearance to notice a difference between herself and this other person. Moreover, it was a terrific opportunity for her mother to talk about the fact that there are lots of different types of people in the world and none are better than the other— only different. I think Reya was also old enough to be told that it was unacceptable to make fun of or to mimic someone who looks different. Even though, at the time, Reya probably would not have fully understood why her actions were inappropriate, as an "old-school" parent, I don't believe children always have to understand or have the capacity to understand everything you ask of them. Sometimes, they just have to understand that you are the parent and you know better, which means they should follow your directions and your lead. These are the beginnings of teaching children about ethical conduct, good character, moral judgment, and cooperation across differences of all kinds. However, even though parents are the first teachers, should the onus to teach race fall squarely on their shoulders? What about schools?

Race and Schools

Parents have the primary responsibility to teach their children about race and to articulate acceptable boundaries and behaviors. This is a very individual endeavor, and there is no one-size-fits-all approach. However, I think love and respect should be the underpinnings of all these discussions. Nonetheless, I think this topic should also be taught in schools and included in the curriculum. When I taught high school in a high-needs community in Toronto, I was fortunate to have a forward-thinking principal who believed in addressing the *-isms* of the world. Therefore, when I taught social science, I had the freedom to write and teach my own curriculum to my grade twelve classes. I taught students about racism, sexism, and classism and how businesses and organizations in particular dealt with these issues and employment equity laws in Canada. I also assigned a group project that required my students to make up a fictitious business, along with a business name, a mission statement, clearly articulated policies and procedures with respect to different types of discrimination, and consequences for breaching company policy. The students also had to create a brochure to be distributed to the class, highlighting all of the aforementioned requirements for the assignment. Each group also had to give an oral presentation to the class.

I created this assignment about fifteen years ago when I first started my teaching career. Back then my students thoroughly enjoyed the assignment, and today I am sure students would still benefit from this type of assignment because the issues are still relevant. However, I don't believe K–12 schools have even begun to address these issues in their classrooms in a meaningful way. Incorporating diverse authors into the curriculum is helpful to students of color in particular, because this teaches them that their experiences are relevant. However, at some point, students should be taught about the -*isms* they will eventually encounter. Too many kids are graduating from the K–12 system and are entering into the workforce or postsecondary institutions without awareness of these -*isms* that could affect them.

As you know, I have already discussed how race can play out in the workplace, affecting employee interactions and behaviors. However, do these racial dynamics exist in schools? Yes. Research has shown that teachers can also harbor racial biases toward students. This was my PhD research topic at the University of Georgia. And why is this important to know? Because even though the parent is the first teacher, children spend more time during the day with teachers than they do their parents in any given week. Therefore, since teachers are not infallible beings and are not necessarily free of bias, it is important to know how some teachers think and how they might negatively impact your child's learning environment and progress.

Teachers and Racial Bias

New and experienced teachers exhibit racial prejudice, which is sometimes called "invisibility bias."[6] These biases are also often reflective of unconscious and subtle forms of racism in the classroom, yet this issue is seldom investigated. It is also important to note that teacher bias has not only been tied to race. Students who are the recipients of bias and racism in the classroom are usually the marginalized, belittled, or violated segments of the population, namely students of color, poor students, female students, male students not typically "masculine," and students who are or are perceived to be otherwise abnormal. As a result, those students who are not white, American, male, hegemonic, masculine, heterosexual, and middle-class or wealthy are marginalized and harmed by various forms of oppressions in schools.[7] However, the subject of this book is race, and unfortunately, systematic racism occurs at all levels of education.[8] For example, take a moment and think about any school district(s) you have had the pleasure of experiencing. Did you know that the majority of school administrators and school board members, past and present, in the United States are white? Would this be true about the school district(s) you just recalled? It has also been posited that white educators experience a sense of racial superiority in schools, whether consciously or unconsciously, and this is "manifested in their assumption that they uniquely possess certain skills and knowledge necessary for 'appropriately' dealing with all students, parents, or even administrators and other teachers."[9] Moreover, most educators—even those of color—are supervised and evaluated by a white person. This structure of authority is the model that students experience and leads to perceptions of racial inferiority for students of color and racial superiority among white students.[10]

The status quo is also reinforced by what schools teach as much as it is by educator prejudices and hierarchies. A "hidden curriculum is operative at every level of the formal education system from nursery school to graduate school, even in higher educational settings where critical thinking skills are promulgated and valued, and emancipatory educational settings are developed and discussed."[11] For example, prejudicial theories like "Asian students are better at math," "Latino parents don't support their kids in school," or "Advanced placement classes are too difficult for black students"[12] are all examples of the hidden curriculum. These beliefs are not a surprise, however, when we acknowledge critical race theory (CRT), which again asserts that racism is everywhere, and therefore, racism and prejudice must occur in the classroom.[13]

Moreover, CRT also acknowledges the inextricable layers of racialized subordination based on gender, class, immigration status, surname, phenotype, accent, and sexuality.[14] Oppression is not always easy to recognize among educators, but it affects the expectations, assumptions, and treatment of the "Other."[15] Many educators have unquestioned assumptions about the attitudes and abilities of students of color and their families. Ultimately, it is institutionalized racism that allows these negative assumptions and stereotypes to persist unchallenged by those having positional power, including teachers of color.[16] If it is clear that all of us harbor prejudices (positive or negative) to some degree, then it is foolhardy to believe that all teachers are somehow immune to this influence.

Deficit Thinking and Teaching

Racism and bias are not free-floating forces that function independently of teachers. In fact, they are part of a conceptual framework called "deficit thinking" which is one of the most prevalent forms of contemporary racism in US schools. This sort of thinking essentially blames minority students and their families for poor academic performance. Why? Because the deficit thinker believes minority students do not have the knowledge or skills to succeed and their parents do not support or value education.[17] As a result, students of color must negotiate the psychological turmoil prompted by oppression and different status while simultaneously being viewed by the school system and the larger society as a problem.[18] It is evident that the psychological turmoil endured by students of color and the poor treatment they receive in the school system and beyond are largely influenced by negative stereotypes and other cognitive processes among educators that puts them at a disadvantage. Therefore, as the parent of a child of color, it is important for you to be actively involved in your child's education. In fact, as an educator, I would be remiss if I didn't say that *all* parents, regardless of race, should invest the time into their children's education. Getting your child up in the morning and just sending him or her to school is not enough. Schools are as good as parental input. It might feel like a job, but parents need to be on top of their children to make them apply themselves because, without accountability, there cannot be achievement. And this is important for *all* parents to do even though students of color, on average, have a more challenging time in school than their white counterparts. The ultimate goal for all students, regardless of the level education, should be to focus on getting good grades, recognize the "good" teachers, and remember that if you are a good person, things will always work out in your favor regardless of any obstacles that are in your way.

Race in the Workplace: There Is Hope

Throughout this book, I have shared many examples of racism in the workplace. However, the workplace can also offer numerous opportunities to cultivate and sustain meaningful relationships with people who are different from us. As I stated earlier, the world has become so diverse that it is almost impossible to live in a monolithic environment—unless you have intentionally created it. One question to ask yourself is whether or not you have done so. If your answer is no, you should still ask yourself if you've *unintentionally* homogenized your environment. Consider the following questions:

- Who do you choose to do business with?
- When you are at work, who do you eat lunch with?
- Who do you sit beside in meetings?
- Who do you talk to in meetings?

- With whom do you have meaningful conversations, and with whom do you have superficial exchanges—just enough to get the job done?

Practically every business, organization, and institution in the United States and beyond has some type of diversity policy in place. There are also opportunities for diversity training in order to promote harmony among and between different groups. However, unfortunately, the majority of these diversity-training opportunities offered at different establishments are not research-based, and they typically do not get to the heart of the issue, which is addressing our prejudices. At best, these training opportunities are superficial and so largely ineffectual. It has also been noted by academic scholars that substantive change is unlikely to be achieved in a single diversity-training workshop or endeavor.[19]

Optimistically, there are some workplace settings like in sports and entertainment that come to mind as examples of environments where genuine interracial friendships and relationships are cultivated. A perfect example is the television show *The Talk*. Two black women (Sheryl Underwood and Aisha Tyler), two white women (Sharon Osborne and Sara Gilbert), and one Asian woman (Julie Chen) meet daily to talk about a variety of issues. The group has a chemistry that cannot be pretended or rehearsed. They all seem to genuinely care for and like each other, and I think these genuine friendships have arisen because they "talk" to each other and share their beliefs on a regular basis. This is my philosophy when it comes to teaching people how to genuinely embrace diversity, which involves engaging in open and honest interracial and intercultural dialogue. Put simply, if you just talk to people, then there is less opportunity for prejudgments to take center stage and taint our interactions.

Similarly, the arena of sports is another workplace that models true diversity and the manifestation of genuine interracial friendships. Why? Because in agreement with Gordon Allport's contact hypothesis, belonging to a team that has a shared goal and again, the ongoing exposure and discussions with people who are different affords the opportunity to really get to know people beyond the superficial. As a former member of Canada's national track and field team and as a former NCAA Division I scholarship athlete, I had the opportunity to meet many different types of people. My track career ended almost fifteen years ago, but I still cherish many of my diverse friendships that were created through athletics. This is one reason why, every year, I enjoy watching the NFL Hall of Fame inductees talk about their time as athletes on a team, and how some call their ex-teammates "brother" even when they are racially different.

The arenas of sports and entertainment seem to transcend racial prejudice. This is probably because there are ongoing occasions for exposure to different types of people, which inevitably yields opportunities to formally and informally acknowledge and *work through* our assumptions and preconceived ideas. For example, I met one of my Indian girlfriends at work. Prior to meeting her, I did not know anything about Indian culture. She was also curious about the Caribbean, where my parents were from, so we made a point to have candid conversations about each other's cultures and our beliefs.

It is always helpful to have candid conversations with trusted individuals in order to learn more about us and about others. In addition, even though in a traditional workplace we probably have to spend more time creating opportunities to have genuine, ongoing exposure and conversations with others, unlike in sports and entertainment arenas, the workplace is the perfect setting to work on our racial issues. We spend so much time at work every day, so why not utilize the time effectively?

Ultimately, whether our ongoing contact and communication with others has come through the workplace or through our upbringing, it is obvious to me when I meet people for the first time where they fall on the continuum of what I call "racial comfort." Despite the fact that we all harbor racial biases, it is evident who has *worked through* their issues and who feels more comfortable interacting with people from different races. But let me stress that there isn't a final destination in this quest to manage our biases. We can never say that we finally have them under control, because it is an ongoing process. Every day, entering new environments and new contexts yields new and unique opportunities to revisit our assumptions and biases. Therefore, we have to continue to be self-aware, and when we offend, we need to apologize.

In the next chapter, I further this discussion about what we can do to manage ourselves and embrace diversity.

Love all, trust a few, do wrong to none.
—WILLIAM SHAKESPEARE, *ALL'S WELL THAT ENDS WELL*

CHAPTER TEN

DIVERSITY
Requires Effort and Commitment

This chapter highlights key behaviors and active thoughts that I believe people can adopt in order to sincerely embrace, demonstrate, and sustain diversity in their lives. The word *diversity* is listed as an acronym, and each letter is ascribed a specific action.

Decide to be open.

The way to embrace diversity is to be open—open to new ideas, new cultures, and the fact that, however difficult and psychologically uncomfortable it is to be wrong, it is better to learn than to live in ignorance. Clearly, openness is not something that just happens. Individuals have to make a conscious decision to be open-minded in order to welcome people into their lives who don't look like them. This often requires a person to step outside of herself/himself as s/he moves through the world every day. That's why you have to *decide* to be open.

Invite others into your circle of friends.

Is your world full of lookalikes? Who are your friends? Who do you invite over for dinner? Who is your best friend? Who is your dentist? Your doctor? Your neighbors? Our society has become increasingly more diverse, which means it is virtually impossible not to associate with different people as we go about our daily lives. Therefore, if your answers to the aforementioned questions reveal a world full of lookalikes, then it is important to recognize that, whether consciously or unconsciously, you have created a monolithic world to live in—in isolation from and contrary to the principles of diversity. Indeed, you may have created this world unconsciously, but it is still in opposition to your own principles of inclusion and openness.

View others through a lens of love.

Put simply, if you have the attitude and the mission to connect with people who are different, you will have an easier time if you lead with love. Love is an emotion that we all possess, crave, disseminate, and enjoy. In *Long Walk to Freedom: The Autobiography of Nelson Mandela*, Mandela said,

> No one is born hating another person because of the color of his skin, or his background, or his religion. People must learn to hate, and if they can learn to hate, they can be taught to love, for love comes more naturally to the human heart than its opposite.[1]

If we learn to look through a lens of love, our lives would be much better.

Enjoy differences in people.

This is the essence of diversity—placing value on "difference" and embracing variety. Therefore, if we have people in our lives who are "different," this requires us to have concrete skills in exercising patience, listening, empathy, conflict resolution, and self-reflection.

Respect yourself and others.

We are all human beings. Therefore, we all have the right to be treated nicely and fairly—regardless of any difference. This does not mean we merely tolerate people who do not look like us. I do not like the word *tolerance* when teaching about diversity. We "tolerate" a horrible smell when we walk into a public restroom; we "tolerate" the noise of a screaming child who throws a tantrum in the middle of the supermarket. We put up with or "tolerate" these episodes because we know they will eventually end or because we are somehow required to do so. But this is not the same as respecting or embracing others. Consequently, the goal of respecting ourselves, and others, is not to just get through what I call "episodes of exposure." We want to learn how to genuinely connect, create, and sustain respectful relationships with others.

Suspend your judgments.

As every critical thinker knows, suspending judgments is one of the most difficult skills to develop. After all, it is normal, common, and not necessarily always a bad thing when we have preconceived notions about others. Our brain naturally categorizes things, makes associations, and combines "like" experiences—helping us understand and make sense of the world. However, we get ourselves into trouble and have missed opportunities to connect when we treat people poorly or differently because we have attached inaccurate and sometimes unfair judgments to these associations.

Suspending judgment affords us the opportunity to exercise the sort of intellectual humility that builds a strong character. This is because suspending judgment reflects awareness that one does not have complete knowledge or at least one does not have sufficient knowledge to make a reasoned judgment. Therefore, as you move through the world, the goal is to put your preconceived notions and biases on hold for as long as you can. Be conscious of your thoughts, engage in self-talk, and be open to new experiences by suspending your judgments.

Integrity should be your point of reference.

If you strive to be an honest person and cultivate a decent character, then you will be committed to self-analysis and self-reflection.

What does this mean? You are willing to truthfully look at yourself and your actions, especially in moments of conflict or uneasiness with others. You will honestly ask yourself, "What was my part? How did I contribute to the situation?" The goal, however, is not to be perfect, because perfection is unattainable and a fallacy. The goal is for us to own our parts in difficult situations. We should consciously ask ourselves if our biases or preconceived notions got in the way of a situation. Did we misjudge? Did we overreact? Did we condescend? The quiet moments before we fall asleep at night often yield profound opportunities to reflect on our daily actions. If indeed we have discovered we made a mistake, apologize to the person if you can. If you cannot, make the commitment to treat the next person who comes along differently. Strive to reach the highest level of personal integrity.

Treat others the way you would like to be treated.

Recall the dictum above to respect yourself and others. When we recognize that we share in the same dignity as other human beings by virtue of our humanity, and when we realize that there are fundamental principles of good reasoning recognized worldwide, it becomes difficult to justify treating others differently or poorly based on the view that mere difference has something to do with value. It's simply untenable to believe that some human beings *as* human beings are less valuable than others.

The saying, "Truth is stranger than fiction" is well suited for this point. Truth is stranger than fiction because, as a result of our differing experiences, we all have our own personal truths or realities. Yes, even though personal experiences are irrefutable truths because they actually happened, we should still be cognizant of the fact that our truths are not necessarily *the* truths. Because something happened to us doesn't mean it will happen to someone else.

We have to remember that there are always exceptions to the truths we hold. For example, if you were once mugged by a big, broad-shouldered man, then naturally that experience would make you fearful of big, broad-shouldered men, and you would probably stay clear of them. However, someone without your experience would not necessarily understand your fear. In fact, a big, broad-shouldered man himself would likely be offended if you acted afraid of him; he might be a decent person who would never mug someone. Therefore, it is incumbent upon all of us to always consider the reality that our truths are not necessarily *the* truths—an idea broached in the dictum above to suspend judgment—which means we don't have license to write people off or treat them poorly because of a previous bad experience we've had with someone else.

It is important to hold your judgments in abeyance for a while and enter each situation as a clean slate. You would be amazed how much you learn if you deliberately look for exceptions to the truths you hold on to. Would you want someone to prejudge you and not give you a fair chance to show who you are? Treat others the way you would like to be treated.

You are in control of your actions.

The fundamental difference between adults and children is that adults are supposed to exercise self-control, and have the mental capacity and experience to understand and anticipate fully, all likely consequences of their actions. By adulthood, urges of impulsivity without thought, empathy, or regard for others is unacceptable. If we want to be on the straight path to practicing behaviors that promote diversity, we must take responsibility and be in control of our actions.

Final Thoughts

I hope I have convinced you, through my interpretations of scholarly research, cogent argumentation, and analyses of racial incidents, that there is a significant difference between racism and racial bias. An equally important goal was to convince you that it is important to explore, recognize, and critically reflect on your biases and assumptions of others, and I have even taught you how to do so. As you have learned, harboring racial bias is normal, and it is also possible to unintentionally commit acts of racism. However, if we *check* ourselves and learn to be cognizant of our racial biases, our actions, and our intentions, we will increase our chances of recognizing when our racial biases are in operation before they degenerate into racism.

As human beings, we are naturally social creatures who yearn for meaningful contact with each other. However, we continue to let this superficial issue separate us and divide us for no good reason. When we choose to exercise habitual, hegemonic, or hateful attitudes toward others, our prejudices are further entrenched. As a result, our worldview remains narrow, mean-spirited, and close-minded, which is the antithesis of truth and tranquility. In one of my favorite movies, *12 Angry Men*, Henry Fonda's character makes a profoundly true statement. "Prejudice always obscures the truth." I agree. If we work on managing our prejudices, our assumptions, and preconceived notions about others, we would be much better off individually and collectively as a nation.

I understand what I am asking you to do is a scary endeavor. It is human nature to be protective of our ways of thinking, and we can get defensive when our beliefs are challenged or called into question.

This is especially likely when we are forced to reevaluate what we have learned from our parents. However, we are adults now, so we know it is best to separate our beliefs from our emotions. It is also a good idea to separate our beliefs and our emotions from our sense of self-worth. It is dangerous to connect your sense of self-worth to your belief systems, because what happens when your beliefs are challenged or disproved? What do you have left? Have you ever had the experience of engaging in dialogue with someone and when you disagreed with his or her side, the person took it personally, reacted in anger, and blew things out of proportion? Or perhaps you might be one of these people? A person who reacts in this manner to simple discourse is someone who cannot separate his or her emotions and self-worth from their beliefs.

In these instances, I find it pointless to try to convince them of anything because they are unwilling to "see." These are the times when you leave it to critical incidents, disorienting dilemmas, or divine interventions to help individuals reconsider their positions. Only engage in dialogue with people who demonstrate a willingness to at least hear a different perspective. Otherwise, you are wasting your time.

Bottom line: if someone disagrees with you or asks you to reconsider your beliefs, it should not be taken as a personal attack. We need to get to a place where our identities are not threatened whenever our ideologies are called into question. Otherwise, our sense of self-worth will never be anchored, nor will it grow. It will instead continue to whimsically blow with the wind from side to side in accordance with whether or not others agree or disagree with our opinions. This is a life of unbalance. We should be secure enough in ourselves to consider the perspectives of others without feeling threatened and be willing to move and grow.

In 2008, the election of Barack Obama to the US presidency was historic and a symbolic of growth. And his reelection in 2012 confirmed again that whatever people think about race in this country, the country's citizenry has largely matured beyond willful ignorance and blind hatred. How this maturity has occurred is a complex story and one I have not tried to tell in these pages. Instead, I have attempted to look at today's United States and have analyzed its state of racial health. What I see is indeed heartening, but it is also disturbing.

For example, with technological advancements have come increasingly rapid and diverse ways in which people communicate: smartphones, Facebook, Twitter, Instagram, 24-7 news, Internet blogs, and so on. But these modes of communication have not necessarily brought us closer together; nor have they made us more reflective, more thoughtful, or wiser. Even though these devices have increased our opportunities for instant communication, they have not increased our chances for meaningful, authentic connections with others. Especially with respect to race, social media has enabled people to make hateful, racist remarks without accountability and often with anonymity. For example, in May 2013, a Cheerios commercial featuring an interracial couple and an adorable little girl generated so many hateful comments, including references to Nazis and racial genocide, that the comments section on YouTube had to be shut down.[1]

I have spent my entire adult life studying this topic, and I believe we are better than this. We are capable of making profound advancements in our ways of thinking about both ourselves and about others. We can choose to have more quality interactions with people from different racial and ethnic backgrounds. However, this is only possible if we are committed to thinking critically about our beliefs and our attitudes and being open to new teachings and experiences. We have seen, over the course of this book, exactly what can happen when we don't do this. And although it is not an easy feat, how rewarding will it be if we individually and collectively work on raising our levels of consciousness?

Discerning Eyes

If you agree with me that there is a significant difference between racism and racial bias, from now on you will undoubtedly view incidents when they happen with new, discerning eyes. You will pause before you automatically label an interaction that involves people from different races as a racial incident, and you will also use my equations (**Racial Bias = Prejudice (+) or (-) Intent** and **Racism = Prejudice (+) Power (+) or (-) Intent**) to help you evaluate an incident related to race *before* you decide that it is racist. Remember, *It's Not Always Racist ... but Sometimes It Is*. And now you know how to figure out which things are. Before rushing to judgment, you should take a moment when things happen and first determine exactly what happened; second, analyze the situation using my equations; and third, decide how or if the culprit(s) involved should be punished.

One of my hopes is, despite the work involved, that you are inspired to work on bettering yourself in this area of race of racism. We can all do better, and we can all be better! And most significant to our progress is the commitment to systematically take stock of our personal beliefs and attitudes so we can better understand our individual biases and whether or not we need to modify or eliminate them. Doing so will also aid us in learning how to *objectively* evaluate incidents related to race when they occur.

The time is right for us to get out of this racial rut. As the saying goes, "If not now, when? If not us, who?"[2] It is time to start the movement of clearing the confusion and reshaping how we think about racism. My ultimate goal of this book was to get a mature, thoughtful conversation going about race and racism and to get you onboard. We must believe not only that this is a worthy endeavor but also commit to being partners in it.

Notes

Preface

[1]   Cox, T. H., *Cultural Diversity in Organizations: Theory, Research, and Practice*, (1994). Berrett-Koehler Publishers.

[2]   Through my work and research, I have encountered some individuals who object to the label of "victim" because, for some, this word connotes a position of inferiority or helplessness. I use the term, however, as an all-encompassing way to describe the position of a person who has been on the receiving end of an incident related to race.

[3]   There are terms that I use in a specialized sense. When I do, the surrounding narrative provides the connotative context or the denotation. The appearance of quotation marks signals this special use.

Introduction

[1]   *Pocket Oxford Dictionary*, 11th ed., Oxford University Press, 2013.

[2]   Brown, R., Prejudice: Its social psychology, Oxford Press, 1995, 4.

[3]   *Developing New Perspectives on Race: An Innovative Multimedia Social Studies Curriculum in Race Relations for Secondary Level*, New Detroit Speakers Bureau.

[4]   http://www.anncoulter.com.

[5]   See, for example, Persell, Caroline Hodges, *Understanding Society: An Introduction to Sociology*, 3rd ed. (1990), Harper & Row Publishers, Inc.

[6]   http://abcnews.go.com/Politics/

president-obama-trayvon-martin/story?id=19715234 (July 19, 2013).

7 Twitter, 1:43 PM, 19 Jul 2013 and https://www.facebook.com/ToddStarnesFNC/posts/488008867940617.

8 Brown, ibid., 14.

9 Andersen, M. L. and Collins, ibid. H. *Race, Class, & Gender: An Anthology*, Thomson Wadsworth, 2007.

Chapter 1

1 http://www.foxnews.com/story/0,2933,131897,00.html.

2 I specifically address this question later in chapter 7, when I discuss the concept of positionality.

3 http://www.nytimes.com/2013/06/22/dining/paula-deen-is-a-no-show-on-today.html.

4 http://www.huffingtonpost.com/2012/11/28/steven-tyler-apologizes-nicki-minaj_n_2206591.html; http://idolator.com/7297932/nicki-minaj-steven-tyler-feud-twitter-drama.

5 http://www.huffingtonpost.com/2013/01/30/racist-super-bowl-ad-jamaica-volkswagen-commercial_n_2583710.html.

6 http://ABCNews.com, May 2, 2013.

7 http://townhall.com/columnists/anncoulter/2012/09/26/liberals_cant_break_200year_racism_habit/page/full.

8 http://obamareleaseyourrecords.blogspot.com/2012/07/trump-forces-hannity-to-talk-obamas.html.

9 http://mediamatters.org/research/2007/04/04/imus-called-womens-basketball-team-nappy-headed/138497.

10 http://tpmdc.talkingpointsmemo.com/2013/03/tea-party-event-on-racial-tolerance-turns-to-chaos-as-white-supremacists-arrive.php.

11 Tate, W.F., "Critical Race Theory and Education: History, Theory and Implications" (1997). *Review of Research in Education*, 22, 195–247.

12 Ibid.

13 Ladson-Billings, Gloria, "Just What Is Critical Race Theory and What's It Doing in a Nice Field Like Education?" (1998).

International Journal of Qualitative Studies in Education, 11:1, 7–24, 9.

14 See, for example, Yosso, Tara J., "Whose Culture Has Capital? A Critical Race Theory Discussion of Community Cultural Wealth" (2005). *Race, Ethnicity, and Education*, 8:1, 69–71, 70.

15 Fortney, N. D., Sept., 1977, "The Anthropological Concept of Race." *Journal of Black Studies*, 8:1, 35–54, p. 35.

16 Philip Roth's novel *The Human Stain*, which was made into a feature film, also deals with this topic.

17 Linnaeus, Carl, *Systema Naturae*, 2nd ed., 1740.

18 Helms, J. E., "The Conceptualization of Racial Identity and Other 'Racial' Constructs" (1994). *Human Diversity: Perspectives on People in Context*, ed. E. J. Tricket, R.J. Watts, and D. Birman, Jossey-Bass, 285–311, 299.

19 Ibid., 299.

20 Berger, Peter L., and Luckmann, Thomas, Anchor Press, 1967.

21 Ibid., 65.

22 Ibid., 130.

23 Ibid., 135.

24 Ibid., 131.

25 The significant others who mediate this world to him (the individual) modify it in the course of mediating it. They select the aspects of it in accordance with their own location in the social structure and by virtue of their individual, biographically rooted idiosyncrasies. The social world is "filtered" to the individual through this double selectivity. Thus, the lower-class child not only absorbs a lower-class perspective on the social world, he absorbs it in the idiosyncratic coloration given it by his parents (or whatever other individuals are in charge of his primary socialization (ibid., 131).

26 Forman, Tyrone, "Color-Blind Racism and Racial Indifference: The Role of Racial Apathy in Facilitating Enduring Inequalities," in Maria Krysan and Amanda Lewis (eds.),

The Changing Terrain of Race and Ethnicity (2004), 43–66, Russell Sage.

27 This is an example of what Berger and Luckmann (1966) call "secondary socialization," which is "any subsequent process [beyond primary socialization], that inducts an already socialized individual into new sectors of the objective world of his society" (130).

28 Ibid., 138.

29 Ibid., 138.

30 Singleton, Glenn, and Linton, Curtis, *Courageous Conversations about Race: A Field Guide for Achieving Equity in Schools* (2006), Corwin Press, 40.

31 Bell, L., "Theoretical Foundations for Social Justice Education" (1997). In M. Adams, L. Bell, and Griffin (eds.), *Teaching for Diversity and Social Justice*, 3–15, Routledge, 14.

32 Quoted in Singleton and Linton, ibid.

33 See, for example, Julian Weissglass, "Racism and the Achievement Gap," in *Education Week* (fall 2001). Weissglass defines racism as "[t]he systemic mistreatment of certain groups of people (often referred to as people of color) on the basis of skin color or other physical characteristics. This mistreatment is carried out by societal institutions, or by people who have been conditioned by the society to act, consciously or unconsciously, in harmful ways toward people of color."

34 Singleton and Linton, ibid., 39.

35 Singleton and Linton (2006), 40.

36 Ibid., 39.

37 Singleton and Linton, ibid.

Chapter 2

1 Singleton and Linton, ibid., 40.

2 I explain and analyze this claim further in chapter 6.

3 Hollway, W., and Jefferson, T., *Doing Qualitative Research*

Differently: Free Association, Narrative, and the Interview Method (2002). Sage Publications.

4   Kumashiro, K. K., *Troubling Education: Queer Activism and Antioppressive Pedagogy* (2002), Routledge Falmer.

5   Poulton, Dionne, "Exploring Factors That Inform Educators' Expressed Beliefs and Reactions to Incidents Related to Race," University of Georgia PhD dissertation (2011), 2, and relevant citations from this work.

6   See, for example, Poulton, ibid. (2011).

7   Lund, C. L., "Perpetuating Racism in the Field of Adult Education: A Process of Liberation for White European Descent Professors," (2005). Alaska Pacific University AERC Proceeding.

8   http://www.merriam-webster.com/dictionary/anti-semitism.

9   ABC.com, July 2, 2010.

10 http://abcnews.go.com/Entertainment/mel-gibsons-racial-slur-latest-rant/story?id=11071966#.UdLfiRbvwy4.

11 http://colorlines.com/archives/2013/09/watch_julie_chen_talk_about_racism_and_getting_eyelid_surgery.html.

12 Berbrier, M., "The Diverse Construction of Race and Ethnicity," 2008, 567–591. In J. A. Holstein and J. F. Gurium, *Handbook of Constructionist Research* (567–591), Guilford Press.

13 In his 1956 book, *When Prophecy Fails* (Wilder), Leon Festinger first discussed this topic of cognitive dissonance. Festinger subsequently published a book in 1957 called *A Theory of Cognitive Dissonance* (Stanford University Press), in which he fleshes out the theory.

14 Cox, T., *Cultural Diversity in Organizations: Theory, Research, and Practice* (1994). Berrett-Kohler, 118.

15 Brown, ibid., 11.

16 Kumashiro, ibid.

17 Poulton, ibid., 2011. See also Poulton, "Teaching Teachers How to Talk about Race: Increasing Comfort, Improving the

Dialogue" (2007). AERC African Diaspora Pre-conference proceedings.

[18] Utsey, S. O., Ponterotto, J. G., and Porter, J. S., "Prejudice and Racism, Year 2008—Still Going Strong: Research on Reducing Prejudice with Recommended Methodological Advances" (2008). *Journal of Counseling and Development*, 86, 339–347, 340.

[19] Wijeyesinghe, C. L., Griffin, P., and Love, B., "Racism Curriculum Design" (1997). In *Teaching for Diversity and Social Justice*, New York: Routledge, 82.

[20] Gordon, J., "Inadvertent Complicity: Colorblindness in Teacher Education" (2005). *Educational Studies*, 135–153.

[21] Ibid.

[22] Jervis, Kathe, "'How Come There Are No Brothers on That List?' Hearing the Hard Questions *All* Children Ask" (1996). *Harvard Educational Review*, 66, 546–576, 553.

[23] Thompson, A., "Color Talks: Whiteness and Off white" (1999). Educational Studies, 30, 141–160.

[24] Gordon, ibid.

[25] McIntosh, P., "White Privilege: Unpacking the Invisible Knapsack" (1989). *Peace and Freedom* (July/ August), 10–12; and Thompson, A., "Not the Color Purple: Black Feminist Lessons for Educational Caring" (1998). *Harvard Educational Review*, 68, 552–554.

[26] Wise, T., *Colorblind: The Rise of Post-Racial Politics and the Retreat from Racial Equity* (2010). City Lights Publishers.

[27] Mezirow, J., "Epistemology of Transformative Learning" (2003). Paper presented at the 8th International Transformative Learning Conference 2009, Hamilton, Bermuda (2003), 2.

[28] Poulton, ibid. (2003).

[29] http://theabd.org/Missing_Pieces_Women_and_Minorities_on_Fortune_500_Boards.pdf.

[30] "Rampant Discrimination against Whites in Atlanta, D.C. Labor Board Uncovered," Examiner.com, June 10, 2013.

[31] http://espn.go.com/espn/story/_/id/8747379/
espn-suspends-rob-parker-robert-griffin-iii-comments.

[32] Adair, M., Howell, S., and Adair, N., *The Subjective Side of Politics*. Tools for Change. (1988). Tools for Change, 10.

[33] Karen D. Pyke, *Sociological Perspectives*, Volume 53, Number 4, 2010, 553.

[34] Ibid.

[35] Brown, ibid.

[36] Ibid.

[37] See also Brown, ibid., 116.

[38] Ibid.

[39] Brown ibid., 89–90.

[40] Senge, M., *The Fifth Discipline: The Art and Practice of the Learning Organization* (1990). Doubleday.

[41] Mezirow, ibid.

[42] http://www.thedailybeast.com/articles/2013/06/24/george-zimmerman-trial-day-one-f-king-punks.html.

Chapter 3

[1] Merriam, S., and Brockett, R., *The Profession and Practice of Adult Education* (2007), Jossey-Bass, 156.

[2] Berger and Luckmann, ibid., 50.

[3] Caffarella, R. and Merriam, S. B., "Linking the Individual Learner to the Context of Adult Learning" (2000). In A. L. Wilson, and Hayes, E. R., *Handbook of Adult and Continuing Education* (55–70). Jossey-Bass, 59.

[4] Wilson, A. L., "The Promise of Situated Cognition" (1993). In S. B. Merriam (ed.), *An Update on Adult Education Theory*. New Directions for Adult and Continuing, No. 57. San Francisco: Jossey-Bass, 72.

[5] Merriam and Brockett, ibid.

[6] Caffarella and Merriam, ibid.

[7] Ibid., 55.

[8] Brookfield, A., *The Power of Critical Theory for Adult Teaching and Learning* (2003). McGraw-Hill.

[9] Mezirow, ibid., 1978.

[10] Mezirow, J., *Transformative Dimensions of Adult Learning* (1991). Jossey-Bass, 167.

[11] Mezirow, ibid. (2003), 1.

[12] Ibid., 4.

[13] Mezirow, ibid. (2003), 4.

[14] http://transcripts.cnn.com/TRANSCRIPTS/1307/19/se.01.html.

[15] Daloz, L.A., *Effective Teaching and Mentoring: Realizing the Transformational Power of Adult Learning Experiences* (1986). Jossey-Bass, 240.

[16] Ibid., 236.

[17] Ibid. (1990), 13.

[18] Senge ibid., 487.

[19] Daloz, ibid.

[20] Argyris, C., "Teaching Smart People How to Learn" (1991). *Harvard Business Review: Reflections*, 4 (2), 4–15.

[21] Ibid., 4.

[22] Argyris, C. and Shon, D., *Theory in Practice: Increasing Professional Effectiveness* (1974). Jossey-Bass.

[23] Senge, ibid., 487.

[24] Argyris and Shon, ibid.

[25] Argyris, C., *Inner Contradictions of Rigorous Research* (1980), Academic Press.

[26] Hart, M. U., "Liberation through Consciousness Raising" (1990). In J. Mezirow, *Fostering Critical Reflection in Adulthood: A Guide to Transformative and Emancipatory Learning* (47–73). San Francisco: Jossey-Bass, 55.

[27] Ruth, S., "A Serious Look at Consciousness-Raising" (1975). *Social Theory and Practice*, 2 (3), 289–300, 299.

[28] Taylor, E. W., "Building upon the Theoretical Debate: A Critical Review of the Empirical Studies of Mezirow's Transformative Learning Theory" (1997). *Adult Education Quarterly*, 48 (1), 34–59, 52.

[29] Pine and Hilliard, ibid.

Chapter 4

1 http://www.politico.com/blogs/michaelcalderone/0110/
   Matthews_I_forgot_he_was_black_tonight_for_an_hour.html.
   http://www.realclearpolitics.com/video/2012/10/13/ann_
   coulter_talks_race_and_racism_on_real_time_with_bill_
   maher.html.
2 Andersen and Collins, ibid. (1997 and 2007).

Chapter 5

1 http://www.pbs.org/tpt/slavery-by-another-name/themes/
   peonage/.
2 For an accessible summary, see, for example, http://www.
   princeton.edu/~achaney/tmve/wiki100k/docs/Ethnocentrism.
   html.
3 Allen, James, *Without Sanctuary: Lynching Photography in
   America* (2000). Twin Palms Publishers.
4 http://faculty.uml.edu/sgallagher/ThomasJefferson.htm.
5 Cox, ibid., 118.
6 Allport, ibid.
7 Helms, ibid., 291.
8 Ibid, 296.
9 Samuda, R.J., *Psychological Testing of American Minorities:
   Issues and Consequences* (1975). Harper & Row, 53.
10 http://www.ncbi.nlm.nih.gov/pmc/articles/PMC2882688/.
11 Wijeyesinghe, C. L., Griffin, P., and Love, B., "Racism
   Curriculum Design" (1997). In *Teaching for Diversity and
   Social Justice*, Routledge, 82.
12 Broadway musical conceived by Robert Lopez and Jeff Marx.
13 Devine, G., Plant, A. F., Amodio, D. M., Harmon-Jones, E.,
   and Vance, S. L., "The Regulation of Explicit and Implicit Race
   Bias: The Role of Motivations to Respond without Prejudice"
   (2002). *Journal of Personality and Social Psychology*, 82 (5),
   835–848, 835.
14 Hollway and Jefferson, ibid.

Chapter 6

[1] http://www.huffingtonpost.com/2011/11/01/ann-coulter-herman-cain-our-blacks_n_1069172.html.

[2] 01/14/13.

[3] http://americablog.com/2013/01/ann-coulter-murder-america-belgium.html.

[4] Luke, A., "Text and Discourse in Education: An Introduction to Critical Discourse Analysis" (1995–1996). *Review of Research in Education*, 21, 3–48, 13.

[5] Ibid.

[6] Ibid.

[7] http://www.nydailynews.com/news/politics/sununu-dismisses-powell-obama-endorsement-race-based-article-1.1192868.

[8] http://www.politico.com/blogs/jonathanmartin/1008/Limbaugh_Where_are_the_inexperienced_white_liberals_Powell_has_endorsed.html.

[9] *CBS This Morning* interview, 10/25/12.

[10] 02/27/13.

[11] http://www.cnn.com/2010/SHOWBIZ/10/22/juan.williams.controversy/index.html.

[12] http://www.cnn.com/2010/SHOWBIZ/10/22/juan.williams.controversy/index.html.

[13] Pine and Hilliard, ibid., 595.

[14] http://www.nytimes.com/2007/04/09/business/media/09imus_transcript.html?pagewanted=all.

[15] *60 Minutes*, 7/19/98.

[16] http://www.huffingtonpost.com/2011/10/20/rick-perry-herman-cain-brother_n_1021659.html.

[17] http://www.huffingtonpost.com/2011/11/21/rush-limbaugh-michelle-obama-uppity-ism_n_1105989.html.

[18] Adair and Howell, ibid., 17.

[19] http://www.cbsnews.com/8301-207_162-57556034/steven-tyler-to-nicki-minaj-im-not-racist/.

[20] Ibid.

[21] Ibid.

22 Ibid.

23 http://www.nytimes.com/2013/06/29/business/media/
publisher-drops-book-deal-with-tv-chef-paula-deen.html?_r=0.

24 http://www.cnn.com/interactive/2013/06/entertainment/deen-
deposition/index.html.

25 http://www.cnn.com/interactive/2013/06/entertainment/deen-
deposition/index.html.

26 Karen D. Pyke, *Sociological Perspectives*, Volume 53, Number
4, 2010, 553.

27 http://www.cnn.com/2013/09/03/us/
new-york-racial-slur-lawsuit.

28 http://voices.washingtonpost.com/livecoverage/2010/08/
dr_laura_schlessinger_apologiz.html?sid=ST2010082203285,
August 13, 2010.

29 http://www.usatoday.com/story/life/people/2013/06/26/
paula-deen-faces-matt-lauer-on-today/2458783/

30 www.youtube.com/watch?v=9PL02LMD8Gw.

31 See, for example, www.cnn.com/interactive/2013/06/
entertainment/deen-deposition/.

Chapter 7

1   Andersen, M. L. and Collins, ibid.

2   Martine, R. J., and Gunten, D. M., "Reflected Identities:
Applying Positionality and Multicultural Social
Reconstructionism in Teacher Education" (2002). *Journal of
Teacher Education*, 53 (1), 44–54, 46.

3   See, for example, http://www.dailymail.co.uk/
news/article-2391880/Oprahs-racist-handbag-
Swiss-store-owner-brands-star-sensitive.html
and http://www.reuters.com/article/2013/08/14/
entertainment-us-oprah-idU.S.BRE97C0NS20130814.

4   Ibid.

5   Ibid.

6   Ibid.

7   Andersen and Collins, ibid.

[8]   Berger & Luckmann, ibid., 50.

[9]   Senge, ibid.

[10] Mezirow, ibid. (2003).

[11] Weissglass, ibid.

[12] Brookfield, A., ibid., 157.

[13] Jay, G., "Whiteness Studies and the Multicultural Literature Classroom" (2005). *Journal of the Society for the Study of the Multi-Ethnic Literature of the United States,* 106.

[14] Ibid., 107.

[15] http://www.museumoftolerance.com/site/c.tmL6KfNVLtH/b.4866027/k.88E8/Our_History_and_Vision.htm.

[16] Brookfield, ibid. (1995).

[17] Andersen and Collins, ibid.

[18] Tisdell, E. J., "Interlocking Systems of Power, Privilege, and Oppression in Adult Higher Education Classes" (1993). *Adult Education Quarterly,* 43 (4), 203–226, 203.

[19] Adair, Howell, and Adair, ibid., 11.

[20] Ibid.

[21] Ibid., 13.

[22] http://music-mix.ew.com/2013/06/07/tyler-the-creator-australia-rant/.

[23] http://www.businessinsider.com/tyler-the-creator-and-mountain-dew-ad-2013-5.

[24] http://www.nytimes.com/2011/05/08/arts/music/tyler-the-creator-of-odd-future-and-goblin.html?pagewanted=all&_r=0.

[25] Adair, Howell, and Adair, ibid., 10.

[26] http://www.youtube.com/watch?v=hVECvG0IHnw.

[27] http://www.hollywoodreporter.com/news/emmett-tills-family-demands-apology-421739.

Chapter 8

[1]   Mezirow, ibid. (2003), 4.

[2]   http://espn.go.com/college-sports/story/_/id/9583091/baseball-player-killed-kids-were-bored.

[3]   Brookfield, ibid. (2000), 37.

[4]   Hollway and Jefferson, ibid.

Chapter 9

[1]   Hollway and Jefferson, ibid.
[2]   Clark, K. B., and Clark, M. K., "Racial Identification and Preference in Negro Children" (1947). In T. Newcomb & E. L. Harley (eds.), *Readings in Social Psychology* (602–611). Holt.
[3]   Katz, A., "Racism and Social Science: Towards a New Commitment." In A. Katz (ed.), *Towards the Elimination of Racism* (1976). Pergamon Press. See also Helms, ibid., 296.
[4]   Moore, R. B., "Racist Stereotyping in the English Language" (2007). In M. L. Andersen & H. Collins (6th ed.). *Race, Class, & Gender: An Anthology* (365–376). Thomson Wadsworth., 368.
[5]   Swanson, D. Cunningham, M., Youngblood II, J., and Spencer, M. B., "Racial Identity Development during Childhood" (2009). In H. A. Neville, B. M. Tynes, and S. O. Utsey, *Handbook of African American Psychology* (269–281), Sage.
[6]   Gollnick, D., and Chinn, P., *Multicultural Education in a Pluralistic Society*, 5th ed. (1998). Merrill/Prentice Hall.
[7]   Kumashiro, ibid., 36–37.
[8]   hooks, b., *Teaching to Transgress: Education as the Practice of Freedom* (1994). Routledge, 29.
[9]   Singleton and Linton, ibid., 43.
[10]   Singleton and Linton, ibid.
[11]   Tisdell, E. J., "Interlocking Systems of Power, Privilege, and Oppression in Adult Higher Education Classes" (1993). *Adult Education Quarterly*, 43 (4), 203–226, 203.
[12]   Henze, R., Katz, A., Norte, E., Sather, S., and Walker, E., *Leading for Diversity* (2002). Corwin Press, 42.
[13]   Tettegah, S., "The Racial Consciousness Attitudes of White Prospective Teachers and Their Perceptions of the Teachability of Students from Different Racial/Ethnic Backgrounds: Findings form a California Study" (1996). *Journal of Negro Education*, 65, 151–163.

[14] Yosso, ibid., 73.

[15] Kumashiro, ibid.

[16] Goodwin, A. L., "Making the Transition from Self to Other: What Do Preservice Teachers Really Think about Multicultural Education?" (1994). *Journal of Teacher Education, 45* (2), 119–130.

[17] Yosso, ibid.

[18] Singleton and Linton, ibid.

[19] Roberson, L., Kulik, C. T., and Pepper, M. B., "Designing Effective Diversity Training: Influence of Group Composition and Trainee Experience" (2001). *Journal of Organizational Behavior,* 22(8), 871–885; Rynes, S. and Rosen, B., "A Field Survey of Factors Affecting the Adoption and Perceived Success of Diversity Training," (1995). *Personnel Psychology,* 48(2), 247–271.

Chapter 10

[1] Mandela, N., *Long Walk to Freedom: The Autobiography of Nelson Mandela* (1994). Back Bay Books.

Final Thoughts

[1] huffingtonpost.com/2013/05/31/cheerios-commercial-racist-backlash_n_3363507.html.

[2] Hillel the Elder, *Pirkei Avot,* http://www.shechem.org/torah/avot.html.

About the Author

Jennifer Boxley Photography

D r. Dionne Wright Poulton has fifteen years of teaching experience in high schools and universities and as a diversity education consultant and speaker. She earned a PhD from the University of Georgia, a master's degree from San Francisco State University, a bachelor of education degree (teaching degree) from the University of Toronto, and a bachelor's degree from Rice University as an NCAA Division I track and field scholarship athlete.

Originally from Toronto, Canada, Dr. Poulton currently resides outside Atlanta, Georgia, with her husband and their two children.

PHILIPPE AUBERT DE GASPÉ

Ouvrages du même auteur

Psychologie de la mémoire, 2ᵉ éd., Montréal, Éditions du Lévrier, 1964, 264 pages.

Le Fort Saint-Jean, Montréal, Éditions du Lévrier, 1965, 96 pages.

The Unknown Fort, Montréal, Éditions du Lévrier, 1966, 104 pages.

Unsung Mission, Montréal, Institut de Pastorale, 1968, 176 pages.

Dictionnaire de la psychologie et des sciences connexes (français-anglais et anglais-français), Paris, Maloine S.A., 1972, 316 pages.

Collège militaire royal de Saint-Jean, Les premiers vingt ans, Saint-Jean, 1972, 44 pages.

Les Bataillons et le Dépôt du Royal 22ᵉ Régiment, 1945-1965, Québec, Régie du R. 22ᵉ R., 1975, 288 pages.

Les Défis du Fort Saint-Jean, Saint-Jean, Éditions du Richelieu, 1975, 188 pages.

La Seigneurie de Philippe Aubert de Gaspé, Saint-Jean-Port-Joli, Montréal, Fides, 1977, 166 pages.

La Psychologie au secours du consommateur, Montréal, Fides, 1978, 158 pages.

Histoire de la Base des Forces canadiennes Montréal, Saint-Hubert, CFB Montréal, 1981, 335 pages.

Le Régiment de la Chaudière, Lévis, Q.G. du Régiment de la Chaudière, 1983, 656 pages. (Coauteur: J. A. Ross).

Lady Stuart, Montréal, Éditions du Méridien, 1986, 128 pages.

Les Voltigeurs de Québec, premier régiment canadien-français, Québec, Q.G. des Voltigeurs de Québec, 1987, 528 pages.

Le Collège militaire royal de Saint-Jean, Montréal, Éditions du Méridien, 1989, 290 pages.

Jacques Castonguay

PHILIPPE AUBERT DE GASPÉ
Seigneur et homme de lettres

septentrion

Maquette de la couverture: Graphikel
Illustration de la couverture: Philippe Aubert de Gaspé
(Fusain de P. N. Hamel. Musée du Québec, photo Patrick Altman,
54203).

© Éditions du Septentrion
1300, av. Maguire
Sillery (Québec)
G1T 1Z3

Diffusion Dimedia
539, boul. Lebeau
Ville Saint-Laurent (Québec)
H4N 1S2

Dépôt légal: 1er trimestre 1991
Bibliothèque nationale du Québec

Données de catalogage avant publication (Canada)
Castonguay, Jacques, 1926-
Philippe Aubert de Gaspé: seigneur et homme de lettres
Comprend des références bibliographiques.
ISBN 2-921114-50-X

1. Aubert de Gaspé, Philippe, 1786-1871 – Biographie. 2. romanciers
canadiens-français — 19e siècle — Biographie 3. Romanciers
canadiens-français – Québec (Province) — Biographies I. Titre.

PS8401.U24Z58 1991   C843'.3   C91-096251
PS9401.U24Z58 1991
PQ3919.A72Z58 1991

Préface

L'histoire trame parfois de curieuses coïncidences. Le 29 mai 1838, lord Durham arrivait à Québec pour évaluer la situation, après la rébellion des patriotes. Quelque temps plus tard, il constatait que les Canadiens français, parmi d'autres misères, étaient un peuple «with no literature».

En ce même jour de printemps était incarcéré en la prison de Québec celui qui allait devenir le père de la littérature canadienne-française. Un quart de siècle plus tard, Philippe Aubert de Gaspé publiera *Les Anciens Canadiens*. C'était une éloquente riposte au fonctionnaire anglais. Voilà une œuvre à laquelle on peut toujours retourner: elle fait du bien à l'âme comme ces visites au hameau de l'enfance où le temps semble n'avoir pas vraiment passé.

Jusqu'à aujourd'hui, il n'existait aucune biographie élaborée de Philippe Aubert de Gaspé. Sa légende nous servait d'histoire.

Sa légende est belle et touchante mais je me réjouis d'avoir sous les yeux le manuscrit de sa première biographie. Pour l'auteur, ce fut un travail de passion. Monsieur Jacques Castonguay a d'abord rencontré le seigneur de notre littérature grâce à certains liens existant entre sa famille et celle de Philippe Aubert de Gaspé. Sans doute aussi, Jacques

Castonguay, jeune étudiant de Québec, a-t-il été intrigué par cette maison en pierre devant laquelle il passait souvent en se rendant au Séminaire de Québec. L'écrivain que l'on lisait et analysait en classe y avait vécu. Et un écrivain laisse toujours un peu de magie dans les lieux qu'il a habités.

Plus tard, monsieur Castonguay s'est même fait fermier à Saint-Jean-Port-Joli, le pays des de Gaspé et le site du fameux manoir incendié en 1759. Si je me rappelle bien nos conversations d'alors, il était plus intéressé par ses recherches sur l'auteur des *Anciens Canadiens* que par ses travaux d'irrigation. Je puis témoigner qu'il passait plus de temps chez les antiquaires et les notaires de la région que dans ses champs.

Au fil des ans, il a accumulé une documentation jusqu'ici insoupçonnée qui lui permet maintenant de suivre, dans ses entreprises, le seigneur de Saint-Jean-Port-Joli. Il a découvert des lettres qui expriment ses sentiments familiaux ou amicaux. Il a recueilli de nombreux témoignages de ses descendants.

À la lecture du texte de monsieur Jacques Castonguay, je me suis souvenu de certains jours où il apparaissait avec un certain sourire. Je savais alors qu'il allait m'annoncer: «J'ai trouvé quelque chose!» C'est avec ce sourire qu'il m'a annoncé avoir retracé le manuscrit original des *Anciens Canadiens*.

Cette biographie nous raconte une personne déchirée, torturée, pleine de contradictions, hésitante, généreuse, ambivalente: un homme, quoi! C'est par sa complexité qu'il est si attachant. C'est par elle que son œuvre encore aujourd'hui nous touche et durera.

ROCH CARRIER

Avant-propos

Nombreux sont les critiques littéraires qui se sont penchés sur *Les Anciens Canadiens* et les *Mémoires* de Philippe Aubert de Gaspé. Aussi ces deux ouvrages sont bien connus au pays et même jusqu'à un certain point à l'étranger. Il en est cependant autrement de la vie de cet illustre écrivain et grand seigneur. Seuls l'abbé Henri-Raymond Casgrain et le professeur Luc Lacourcière, à part naturellement Philippe Aubert de Gaspé lui-même, ont publié plus que quelques pages originales sur lui.

La notice nécrologique publiée par l'abbé Casgrain en 1871 fut rédigée à une époque où ce dernier souffrait de cécité et devait écrire, selon son propre témoignage, avec «le secours d'une plume étrangère». Pour cette raison, elle est faite presque exclusivement de souvenirs personnels et a fait l'objet de sérieuses réserves. Quant à la biographie écrite il y a une vingtaine d'années par Luc Lacourcière, elle est digne du chercheur et de l'écrivain sérieux qu'il était mais, comme elle devait paraître dans le *Dictionnaire biographique du Canada*, elle est forcément brève. Pour ce qui est des ouvrages de Philippe Aubert de Gaspé, on sait qu'ils constituent une importante source d'information sur la première moitié de sa vie, mais qu'ils sont très discrets, voire «silencieux», sur la seconde. Ces faits m'ont incité à poursuivre les travaux que j'ai entrepris il y a déjà plusieurs années sur les Aubert de Gaspé et à publier le présent ouvrage.

Ce volume n'a pas la prétention de donner une réponse définitive à toutes les questions qu'on peut encore se poser sur l'auteur du premier classique de la littérature canadienne. Il veut néanmoins apporter des précisions sur plusieurs points que ses premiers biographes, probablement faute de temps, d'espace ou de documents, ont traité parfois sommairement. Il m'est paru utile, par exemple, d'apporter des éclaircissements sur les faits entourant sa destitution comme shérif de la Ville de Québec et sur les longues procédures judiciaires qui s'y rattachent. Mais ce volume ne fait pas qu'apporter des précisions sur des événements connus. Il présente aussi un certain nombre de faits inédits qui projettent, croit-on, un éclairage nouveau sur sa personnalité. On n'était pas sans savoir, par exemple, que Philippe Aubert de Gaspé ne cessa pas complètement d'écrire après la publication des *Mémoires*. On a découvert depuis peu qu'à l'âge de quatre-vingt-trois ans, aux prises avec de sérieux problèmes de santé, il avait mis sur le métier un ouvrage comparable à ceux qu'il avait publiés en 1863 et 1866.

Plusieurs sources d'information importantes ont servi à la préparation de la présente biographie. Outres les *Mémoires* et *Les Anciens Canadiens*, j'ai consulté plusieurs sources manuscrites et imprimées conservées aux Archives nationales du Canada et dans les divers services d'archives des régions de Québec et de Montréal. Ne me limitant pas aux fonds conservés dans les grandes institutions, j'ai également examiné et compulsé des documents provenant des archives judiciaires, des greffes d'une quinzaine de notaires, des archives de plusieurs paroisses et aussi de quelques particuliers. À la suite de la publication de mes précédents travaux sur les Aubert de Gaspé, il m'a été donné de lier amitié avec plusieurs membres de cette grande famille. C'est ainsi qu'après avoir découvert les *Anciens Canadiens* grâce aux souvenirs qu'en conservait ma grand-mère paternelle, dont le père avait été le notaire de Philippe Aubert de Gaspé durant de nombreuses années, j'ai pu partager l'information orale et écrite de plusieurs de ses descendants, dont trois de ses arrière-petites-filles aujourd'hui décédées, Thérèse (Loulou) Fraser-Lizotte, Adèle Stuart et Laurette B. Perrault.

Les pages qui suivent et qui contiennent des textes inédits de Philippe Aubert de Gaspé, ainsi que des renseignements nouveaux sur ses activités de fonctionnaire, de seigneur et d'homme de lettres, s'adressent non seulement au grand public mais à tous ceux qu'intéressent de façon particulière l'histoire et la vie littéraire québécoises.

* * *

Il me reste à remercier tous ceux qui m'ont aidé et encouragé au cours de la préparation de cet ouvrage. La liste en est importante et il n'est pas facile de l'établir de façon exhaustive. Que ceux auxquels je suis redevable et dont les noms n'apparaissent pas ci-après trouvent ici une marque de ma plus sincère gratitude.

Aux noms des descendantes de Philippe Aubert de Gaspé mentionnées antérieurement, je voudrais ajouter ici ceux de mesdames Paule Vallée et Charlotte Perrault-Gadbois, et de monsieur Louis de la Chesnaye Audette, qui tous m'ont toujours réservé le meilleur accueil. Le personnel des Archives du Séminaire de Québec, dirigé par l'abbé Laurent Tailleur, a également des droits particuliers à ma reconnaissance. Il en est de même du personnel des Archives nationales du Québec où messieurs Renald Lessard et Jean-Paul de Beaumont m'ont toujours facilité la tâche. Il n'en est pas autrement du personnel des Archives nationales du Canada et des divisions des archives de l'Université Laval et de l'Université de Montréal.

Je voudrais également dire ici ma sincère gratitude au Dr Camille Gosselin, président de la Société québécoise d'histoire de la médecine, un ami dont les connaissances sur la ville de Québec m'ont été d'un précieux secours, ainsi qu'à messieurs Roch Carrier, recteur du Collège militaire royal de Saint-Jean, Gaston Deschênes, chef de la division de la recherche à la Bibliothèque de l'Assemblée nationale du Québec, et André Thibault, président de la Corporation Philippe-Aubert-de-Gaspé, qui n'ont jamais cessé de s'intéresser à mes travaux sur les seigneurs de Saint-Jean-Port-Joli.

Je désire enfin rendre témoignage à Marthe Beauchesne-Castonguay, mon épouse, qui a bien voulu faire la première lecture de mon manuscrit et le mettre sur disquette à l'intention de l'éditeur. Elle a grandement facilité mon travail.

CHAPITRE 1

De la Chesnaye et de Gaspé

(1655-1758)

Il n'y eut pas que des artisans et des laboureurs à braver les tempêtes, les glaces, les maladies et parfois même la mort, pour immigrer en Nouvelle-France au XVII\ siècle. Dans les cales infectes des petits voiliers reliant La Rochelle à Québec, on dénombrait aussi des notaires, des chirurgiens, des seigneurs, des religieux, des soldats et des commerçants. En fait, tous les métiers et toutes les professions de base y étaient représentés. C'est ainsi qu'on peut identifier à l'origine des familles fondatrices du Canada des personnes appartenant à toutes les classes de la société.

Le premier ancêtre canadien de l'illustre famille des Aubert de Gaspé appartenait quant à lui à la classe des commerçants. Né à Amiens le 12 février 1632, Charles Aubert de la Chesnaye s'embarqua pour le Nouveau Monde à l'âge de vingt-trois ans comme représentant d'un petit groupe de marchands de Rouen. Bien que «tout pauvre», comme il l'affirma lui-même, il acquit bien vite son autonomie et, s'intéressant à tout ce qui pouvait contribuer au développement du pays, devint le plus grand propriétaire foncier de son

Charles Aubert de la Chesnaye (1632-1702). (ANQ-Québec, coll. initiale.)

temps et le plus gros commerçant de la Nouvelle-France. Ses activités englobaient la traite des fourrures, l'exploitation agricole et forestière, la pêche, le transport maritime et l'importation de biens de toutes sortes dont avait besoin la colonie naissante.

La liste des terres et des seigneuries dont il fit l'achat ou qu'il se fit concéder est très longue, trop longue pour figurer ici. Ses intérêts ne se limitaient pas à la région de Québec: ils s'étendaient à l'Acadie, à la baie d'Hudson, au Labrador et à Terre-Neuve. Il suffit cependant de retenir ici qu'il acheta de Noël Langlois, 19 novembre 1686, la seigneurie de Port-Joly

Pierre Aubert de Gaspé (1676-1731).
(ASQ, photo W.B. Edwards Inc.
0297, p. 35.)

Ignace-Philippe Aubert de Gaspé
(1714-1787). (ASQ, photo W.B.
Edwards Inc. 0297, p. 35.)

que ses descendants exploitèrent durant près de deux siècles[1].

De la Chesnaye se maria à trois reprises: d'abord en 1664, avec Catherine-Gertrude Couillard, puis en 1668, quatre ans après le décès de sa première femme, avec Marie-Louise Juchereau de la Ferté et, enfin, un an et quelques mois après la mort de cette dernière, avec Marie-Angélique Denys de La Ronde. Anobli par Louis XVI en 1693 et nommé membre du Conseil souverain trois ans plus tard, il mourut à Québec le 20 septembre 1702.

Charles Aubert de la Chesnaye posséda de grands biens. Dépassé cependant par leur importance, il accumula aussi des dettes considérables. C'est ainsi qu'au moment du règlement de sa succession il fallut vendre tous les immeubles encore en sa possession. Son fils Pierre, quatrième des dix-huit enfants issus de ses trois mariages, sauva cependant du naufrage la seigneurie de Port-Joly en s'en portant acquéreur pour la somme de 705 livres, le 5 novembre 1709.

Né à La Rochelle en 1676, à l'occasion d'un voyage de ses parents en France, Pierre fut le continuateur de sa famille au Canada et l'arrière-grand-père de Philippe Aubert de

---

1. Le comte de Frontenac concéda la seigneurie de Port-Joly à Noël Langlois-dit-Traversy le 25 mai 1677.

Gaspé. Désireux de se distinguer de son père, comme on le faisait à l'occasion à l'époque, il prit le surnom de *de Gaspé*, désignation que conservèrent ses descendants[2].

Pierre Aubert de Gaspé passa les premières années de sa vie à Québec. N'ayant pas d'intérêt pour le commerce, parvenu à l'âge adulte, il alla vivre à la campagne et s'adonna presque exclusivement à l'agriculture. Il résida à la Grande-Anse (La Pocatière), sans doute sur le domaine qu'y possédait son père; il séjourna aussi à Port-Joly, sans vraiment y résider, semble-t-il, puis demeura plusieurs années à Saint-Antoine-de-Tilly, où son futur beau-père avait acheté en 1700 le fief du sieur de Villieu.

Pierre Aubert de Gaspé se maria lui aussi plus d'une fois. Le 19 décembre 1699, il épousa tout d'abord, à Québec, Jacqueline-Catherine, fille de Nicolas Juchereau de Saint-Denys et de Marie-Thérèse Giffard. De santé fragile, sa première femme n'eut pas d'enfants et mourut prématurément le 3 juin 1703. Il envisagea alors d'épouser sa cousine, Madeleine-Angélique LeGardeur de Tilly. Ce qui ne pouvait toutefois se faire sans une dispense de l'Église. Incapable de l'obtenir de l'évêque de Québec, il se laissa convaincre que le clergé français était plus libéral que le clergé canadien et alla chercher à l'étranger le document qu'on exigeait de lui. Son veuvage dura ainsi un peu plus de huit ans. Enfin, il réalisa son rêve à Beauport le 12 octobre 1711.

De son second mariage, Pierre Aubert de Gaspé eut huit enfants, dont cinq moururent en bas âge. Ignace-Philippe, né le 5 avril 1714, fut le seul garçon à atteindre l'âge adulte. Témoin des dissensions qui déchirèrent la France et l'Angleterre au XVIIIe siècle, il fit carrière dans les troupes de la marine. Ses états de service sont impressionnants[3]. Il parti-

---

2.   En prenant ce surnom, Pierre Aubert de Gaspé songeait sans doute à la seigneurie de Percé que Talon concéda conjointement à son père, à Pierre Denys de la Ronde et à Charles Bazire en 1702.
3.   Philippe Aubert de Gaspé, *Mémoires*, Québec, N.S. Hardy, 1885, pp. 136-137. Toutes les références aux *Mémoires* contenues dans le présent ouvrage renvoient à cette édition de 1885.

cipa d'abord à diverses expéditions contre les Renards, les Natchez et les Chicachas, puis combattit les Anglais en Acadie, dans la région des Grands Lacs, au lac Champlain et à Québec. Sur son itinéraire long de trente-trois ans figurent les noms de Michillimakinac, de la rivière Saint-Jean, des forts Nécessité, Niagara, Saint-Frédéric et George, et aussi de Carillon, de l'Île-aux-Noix et de Sainte-Foy. Sa conduite à Carillon lui valut les compliments du marquis de Montcalm qui était pourtant peu enclin à louanger les Canadiens.

Ignace-Philippe Aubert de Gaspé, quatrième seigneur de Port-Joly, épousa le 30 juin 1745 la sœur du célèbre Jumonville, Marie-Anne Coulon de Villiers. Son mariage à la cathédrale de Québec réunit tous les notables de la ville et ses principaux compagnons d'armes. Sur son contrat de mariage, passé quelques jours avant la cérémonie religieuse[4], apparaissent les signatures du gouverneur Beauharnois, de l'intendant Hocquart et de l'évêque de Québec, Mgr de Pontbriand. On voit aussi les noms de plusieurs officiers et de notables dont l'histoire conserve également le souvenir: Coulon de Villiers, de Boucherville, Debeaujeu, DeBoishébert, Legardeur, de Contrecœur, Duplessy, Delachesnaye, Delamartinière, Lagorgendière de Rigaud, Déchaillon, de Repentigny, Péan, Varin, Cugnet et quelques autres.

Dix enfants naquirent du mariage du capitaine de Gaspé à Marie-Anne Coulon de Villiers: cinq filles et cinq garçons. Des enfants mâles, seul Pierre-Ignace atteignit l'âge adulte. Appelé à succéder à son père, il passa la plus grande partie de sa vie sur la Côte-du-Sud. C'est de son mariage à Catherine Tarieu de Lanaudière que naîtra l'auteur des *Anciens Canadiens*[5].

---

4. ANQ-Q, greffe du notaire Jacques Pinguet, 26 juin 1745.
5. Pour plus d'informations sur la famille de Gaspé, on peut consulter Pierre-Georges Roy, *La famille Aubert de Gaspé*, Lévis, 1907, et Jacques Castonguay, *La Seigneurie de Philippe Aubert de Gaspé, Saint-Jean-Port-Joli*, Montréal, Fides, 1977.

LES ANCÊTRES DE PHILIPPE AUBERT DE GASPÉ

Charles AUBERT DE LA CHESNAYE
+ Marie-Louise Juchereau de la Ferté
‖
Pierre AUBERT DE GASPÉ
+ Marie-Angélique Legardeur de Tilly
‖
Ignace-Philippe AUBERT DE GASPÉ
+ Marie-Anne Coulon de Villiers
‖
Pierre-Ignace AUBERT DE GASPÉ
+ Catherine Tarieu de Lanaudière
‖
Philippe AUBERT DE GASPÉ
+ Suzanne Allison

Sur la rue du Parloir

(1758-1787)

Les jours qui suivirent la Conquête furent difficiles pour les Canadiens. Non seulement leur capitale avait été presque anéantie par les bombardements, mais les deux rives du Saint-Laurent, en aval de Québec, avaient été complètement dévastées. Ruines et désolation attendaient partout ceux qui, la guerre terminée, regagnaient leur foyer. La seigneurie de Port-Joly et les Aubert de Gaspé ne furent pas épargnés. L'auteur des *Anciens Canadiens*, substituant au nom de son grand-père celui du capitaine d'Haberville, l'affirme en ces termes:

> Lorsque le capitaine d'Haberville retourna dans sa seigneurie, il était complètement ruiné, n'ayant sauvé du naufrage que ses argenteries. Il ne songea même pas à réclamer de ses censitaires appauvris, les arrérages de rentes considérables qu'ils lui devaient, mais s'empressa plutôt de leur venir en aide en faisant reconstruire son moulin sur la rivière Trois-Saumons, qu'il habita plusieurs années avec sa famille,

Le collège et l'église des Jésuites (à droite, sur l'emplacement actuel de
l'Hôtel de ville) en 1761. La maison à l'extrême-gauche, avec le toit abîmé,
serait celle du capitaine de Gaspé. (Dessin de Richard Short.)

jusqu'à ce qu'il fut en moyen de construire un nouveau
manoir[1].

Pour Philippe Aubert de Gaspé, la destruction du
manoir et du moulin de son grand-père n'appartient pas à la
fiction. Les notes historiques contenues dans ses ouvrages
l'attestent[2]. L'historien Gaston Deschênes, auteur d'une
importante étude sur le sort réservé à la Côte-du-Sud en
1759, croit aussi, en s'appuyant sur le rapport de l'officier
commandant les troupes britanniques débarquées à Kamou-

1.   Philippe Aubert de Gaspé, *Les Anciens Canadiens*, Québec, Desbarats et
Derbishire, 1863, pp. 262-263. On peut lire également sur ce sujet les pages 202
à 207 et aussi dans les *Mémoires* la note I, page 52. Toutes les références aux
Anciens Canadiens contenues dans le présent ouvrage renvoient à l'édition de
1863.
2.   *Ibid.*, pp. 396, 397, 401 et 402.

raska, que la plupart des maisons du premier rang de Saint-Jean-Port-Joli, sinon toutes, furent alors incendiées[3].

Il semble bien que le capitaine de Gaspé eut beaucoup à souffrir de cette guerre. Fut-il «ruiné» pour autant, comme l'affirme l'auteur des *Anciens Canadiens*? On a peut-être raison d'en douter. Deux documents, l'un conservé dans le greffe du notaire Antoine-J. Saillant, l'autre dans celui du notaire Antoine Panet, attestent en effet qu'au moment de l'entrée des troupes britanniques dans Québec, et même quelques années après, Ignace-Philippe Aubert de Gaspé possédait encore une propriété fort respectable au coin des rues Buade et des Jardins, à quelques pas seulement de la cathédrale Notre-Dame et du Séminaire de Québec. Il la loua tout d'abord[4], puis la vendit en 1772 à un marchand de Québec pour l'importante «somme de huit mille livres[5].» Mais alors pourquoi, la paix revenue, choisit-il d'aller demeurer dans son moulin de la rivière Trois-Saumons? On est enclin à croire que la présence des troupes britanniques, dont les casernes se trouvaient à quelques pas de sa résidence de Québec, et peut-être aussi l'état dans lequel se trouvait cette dernière ne furent pas étrangers à cette décision. On sait en effet qu'elle fut bombardée durant le siège de la ville et «qu'une vieille fille du nom de Riopel» y fut tuée[6].

Le capitaine de Gaspé ne vécut pas seul le long de la rivière Trois-Saumons après la capitulation de Montréal en 1760. En plus de son épouse, il avait avec lui trois enfants, deux filles et un garçon. Ce dernier, baptisé sous le nom de Pierre-Ignace, avait vu le jour à Québec le 14 août 1758. Continuateur de la lignée des Aubert de Gaspé, il passa son

---

3.   Gaston Deschênes, *L'Année des Anglais, la Côte-du-Sud à l'heure de la Conquête*, Québec, Les Éditions du Septentrion, 1988, pp. 75 et 76.
4.   ANQ-Q, greffe du notaire Antoine-J. Saillant, n° 02032, 20 mars 1770. George Jenkins loua la moitié de la propriété du capitaine de Gaspé pour trois ans le 20 juin 1767 et de nouveau le 20 mars 1770.
5.   ANQ-Q, greffe du notaire A. Panet, 7 août 1772.
6.   *Journal du siège de Québec publié et annoté par Aegidius Fauteux*, bibliothécaire de Saint-Sulpice, Québec, 1922, pp. 37 et 95.

enfance à Saint-Jean-Port-Joli, puis étudia au Séminaire de Québec du 3 octobre 1769 à la capitulation de Montréal devant Montgomery, le 13 novembre 1775[7]. Fils de militaire, il était sur les remparts de Québec au moment de l'attaque des Américains le 31 décembre qui suivit. Devenu seigneur au décès de sa mère en 1789, il demeura dans la milice, fut promu colonel et commanda les divisions de Saint-Jean-Port-Joli et de Saint-Thomas (Montmagny). Enfin, appelé au Conseil législatif en 1812, il y siégea jusqu'à sa mort le 13 février 1823.

* * *

Plusieurs rues de Québec conservent le souvenir des Aubert de Gaspé. La rue du Parloir, qu'il ne faut pas confondre avec la rue conduisant au monastère des Ursulines, est du nombre. Située entre l'archevêché actuel et le presbytère de la paroisse Notre-Dame, elle comptait au XVIIIe siècle deux maisons qui connurent une certaine célébrité. La première avait été construite par le docteur Michel Sarrazin, un éminent médecin et naturaliste originaire de la Bourgogne qui exerça sa profession en Nouvelle-France à compter de 1685. Longue de soixante-trois pieds, cette maison de deux étages, qui contenait pas moins de quatorze pièces, s'élevait au sommet de la côte de la Montagne. La seconde, aussi impressionnante que la première, se trouvait à l'intérieur de la rue du Parloir. Construite par la veuve de Charles Perthuis, un riche négociant de Québec, elle avait à peu près les mêmes dimensions que celle de Michel Sarrazin.

Ces deux maisons changèrent plusieurs fois de propriétaires. Après la mort de madame Sarrazin en 1743 et le mariage de sa fille Louise-Charlotte trois ans plus tard, la première de ces demeures fut vendue aux enchères et acquise le 23 janvier 1748 par Charles-François Tarieu de Lanaudière. Ce dernier, qui avait épousé en premières noces

---

7.   ASQ, fichier des écoliers.

Geneviève des Champs de Boishébert, était le fils de la légendaire Madeleine de Verchères. Quant à la maison des Perthuis, elle fut vendue en 1754 à Joseph Lamarque sieur de Marin et à son épouse Charlotte Fleury de la Gorgendière. Dix ans plus tard, le chevalier de Lanaudière acheta aussi cette maison, devenant ainsi le propriétaire des deux résidences de la rue du Parloir.

À l'époque où la maison Sarrazin appartenait à la famille de Lanaudière, soit de 1748 à 1843, elle accueillit dans ses murs et ses salons les plus hauts dignitaires civils, militaires et religieux de la colonie. Bougainville, Bourlamaque, Roquemaure, les marquis de Vaudreuil et de Montcalm, les Villiers, les Baby, les Saint-Ours, les de Léry, les Aubert de Gaspé, les évêques de Pontbriand et Briand, et beaucoup d'autres, furent les hôtes des Tarieu de Lanaudière sur la rue du Parloir. Montcalm, entre autres, ne cachait pas à ses intimes le plaisir qu'il avait à fréquenter cette rue et les dames qui y résidaient. «Il est vrai, écrit le marquis à Bourlamaque en 1758, que de toutes parts il n'est question que de la beauté d'une dame du Parloir; je l'ai toujours trouvé aimable et plus d'esprit qu'on ne croit... Je suis très attaché, sans réserve, à toute la rue, et Marin a dû s'en apercevoir.» Un an plus tard, c'était au tour de Lévis de recevoir les confidences de Montcalm: «rien de nouveau, mon cher chevalier; les plaisirs à l'ordinaire; deux bals encore; ma vie accoutumée entre les maisons Pean et Lanaudière[8].»

Le chevalier de Lanaudière mourut, criblé d'infirmités, à l'Hôpital général de Québec, le 1er février 1776. Après son décès, sa deuxième femme, Marie-Catherine Lemoyne, et ses nombreux enfants continuèrent cependant à vivre sur la rue du Parloir. Ce qui laissa présager la célébration éventuelle de fastueux mariages.

Catherine fut la première des filles de madame de Lanaudière à contracter mariage. Elle épousa à Québec, le 28

---

8. Extraits de lettres cités par Henri Têtu, *Histoire du palais épiscopal de Québec*, Québec, Pruneau & Kirouac, 1896, pp. 121-122.

Pierre-Ignace Aubert de Gaspé (1758-1823).
(F. Daniel, *Histoire des grandes familles françaises du Canada*.)

janvier 1786, Pierre-Ignace Aubert de Gaspé, celui-là même qui abandonna ses études en 1775 pour s'opposer à l'envahisseur américain. Leur mariage scella l'union de deux grandes familles de noblesse française dont la vie fut indissociable de celle de la Nouvelle-France.

Un mois à peine s'était écoulé que les festivités et les réjouissances recommençaient sur la rue du Parloir. François Baby, homme d'affaires, officier de milice, fonctionnaire, homme politique, seigneur et propriétaire foncier, avait

Catherine Tarieu de Lanaudière (1767-1842).
(P. N. Hamel, 1879. Musée du Québec, photo Patrick Altman. 54205.)

décidé de mettre un terme à son célibat prolongé en épousant Marie-Anne, l'aînée des demoiselles de Lanaudière, de trente-deux ans sa cadette. La cérémonie religieuse, qui n'avait rien à envier à celle qui avait été célébrée un mois plus tôt, eut lieu le 27 février à la cathédrale de Québec. Le contrat de mariage passé sur la rue du Parloir porte la

Maison de la rue du Parloir où naquit Philippe Aubert de Gaspé
en 1786. (H. Têtu, *Histoire du palais épiscopal de Québec*.)

signature du lieutenant-gouverneur Henry Hope, de l'honorable Pierre Parent, de l'ancien évêque de Québec, Mgr Briand, de Jean-Baptiste LeComte Dupré, de dame Agathe Lemoyne de Longueuil. Les de Léry, de Saint-Ours, de Tonnancourt, d'Artigny et quelques autres étaient aussi présents et signèrent le document.

Moins d'un an après ces célébrations, le 30 octobre 1786, madame veuve de Lanaudière devenait grand-mère. L'auteur des *Anciens Canadiens* et des *Mémoires* a raconté l'événement en ces termes: «dans une maison de la ville de Québec, remplacée maintenant par le Palais épiscopal, un petit être chétif mais très vivace, puisqu'il tient toujours la plume à l'âge de soixante-dix-neuf ans, ouvrait les yeux à la lumière[9].» Il s'agit là, bien sûr, de la rue du Parloir et de la naissance de Philippe Aubert de Gaspé.

9. Philippe Aubert de Gaspé, *Mémoires*, N. S. Hardy, 1885, p. 11.

L'archevêché de Québec construit au milieu du XIXe siècle sur le site de la maison natale de Philippe Aubert de Gaspé. (Coll. de l'auteur.)

Le petit Philippe ne demeura que trois mois sous le toit de sa grand-mère maternelle. Pendant qu'à Québec il était dorloté, cajolé et caressé par ses tantes de Lanaudière, le manoir seigneurial de Saint-Jean-Port-Joli connaissait les affres de la mort. Malade, le capitaine de Gaspé, âgé de soixante-douze ans touchait à sa fin. Il s'éteignit le 26 février

1787 et, selon son désir, fut inhumé dans l'église paroissiale dont il avait précédemment donné le terrain[10].

Appelé à succéder à brève échéance au vieux soldat, Pierre-Ignace Aubert de Gaspé déménagea sa petite famille à Saint-Jean-Port-Joli au cours de l'hiver de 1787. Pour le jeune Philippe, la mort de son grand-père marquait le début d'un long séjour au manoir de ses parents. Il allait y passer presque toute son enfance.

---

10. Cette donation eut lieu le 14 novembre 1756 en présence du notaire Noël Dupont.

CHAPITRE 3

Premier séjour au manoir seigneurial
(1787-1795)

Selon l'auteur des *Anciens Canadiens*, le manoir qui accueillit sous la neige Pierre-Ignace Aubert de Gaspé, son épouse et leur fils Philippe, au cours de l'hiver de 1787, était plus modeste que celui qui existait avant la Conquête[1]. Construit probablement en plusieurs étapes et en s'inspirant de la maison monumentale que Charles Aubert de la Chesnaye possédait à la basse-ville de Québec au XVIIe siècle, il ne manquait pourtant pas d'intérêt. On considère qu'il présentait l'image idéale d'un manoir et que son plan, sa symétrie et ses proportions harmonieuses lui donnaient un aspect classique[2]. Il avait la forme d'un long rectangle aux extrémités duquel se trouvaient deux ailes ou avant-corps. Sa toiture assez fortement inclinée et recouverte de bardeaux était percée de plusieurs lucarnes, deux sur la façade et quatre à

---

1. *Mémoires*, p. 11. On a mis toutefois cette assertion en doute.
2. Ce sujet a été traité dans l'intéressante étude d'André Chouinard, *Le manoir Aubert de Gaspé*, La Pocatière, La Société historique de la Côte-du-Sud, 1986.

MANOIR DE Sᵗ. JEAN PORT-JOLI.

Gravure représentant l'arrière du manoir seigneurial des Aubert
de Gaspé construit après la Conquête. (ANQ-Québec, coll. initiale.)

l'arrière. Bien éclairé, il comptait aussi de nombreuses fenêtres. On en trouvait deux de chaque côté de la porte d'entrée
et cinq disposées symétriquement sur la façade de chacune
des deux ailes. Bien plus, une gravure ancienne montrant
l'arrière laisse voir sept autres fenêtres et une porte. Enfin,
entouré de plusieurs dépendances, dont un four à pain qui a
résisté à l'usure du temps, le manoir de Gaspé était situé sur
un domaine s'étendant jusqu'au fleuve, à proximité de la
route qui longe à cet endroit un promontoire couvert de
sapins[3].

---

3.   Il existe plusieurs photographies de la façade du manoir et une gravure
ancienne représentant l'arrière. Les observations qui précèdent proviennent
de ces documents.

Le jeune Philippe qui n'avait pas manqué d'affection sur la rue du Parloir n'en fut pas davantage privé au manoir seigneurial. Sa mère, qui depuis sa naissance l'entourait de soins et de tendresse, n'était pas seule au manoir à le cajoler et à le gâter. Deux autres femmes épiaient ses moindres gestes et cherchaient à répondre à ses besoins comme à ses caprices. Il y avait d'abord la tante Marie-Louise qui, après la mort du capitaine de Gaspé, avait suivi sa sœur au manoir. Plus jeune d'un an seulement que la mère de Philippe, elle allait en devenir son inséparable compagne[4]. À la suite de grands forfaits, raconte l'auteur des *Mémoires*, «ma mère me disait: «Va te coucher sans souper»; mais un instant après, ma tante ou une des servantes, portant un cabaret, entrait dans ma chambre en me disant de ne point faire de bruit, de crainte que ma mère s'aperçût que je prenais mon repas du soir comme le reste de la famille[5].» Philippe fut aussi l'objet de l'affection de sa grand-mère paternelle, devenue seigneuresse au moment du décès du grand-père de Gaspé. Lorsqu'il évoque cette période de sa vie, il se voit le soir sur ses genoux, jouant avec son chapelet et ses médailles, et empoignant son pince-nez. «Elle avait une grande paire de lunettes d'argent, qui lui pinçaient tellement le nez, que si j'eusse été assez fort, lorsque je les empoignais avec mes petites mains, j'aurais plutôt déraciné le nez de ma grand-mère qu'emporté les lunettes sans le nez[6].»

Philippe ne connut pas son grand-père maternel, Charles-François Tarieu de Lanaudière. Celui-ci mourut le 1er février 1776, une dizaine d'années avant la naissance de son petit-fils. Il en fut de même pour son grand-père paternel, Ignace-Philippe Aubert de Gaspé. Il mourut à Saint-Jean-Port-Joli alors que Philippe n'avait pas encore trois mois. Il ne connut pas davantage sa grand-mère maternelle, Marie-

---

4. Marie-Louise Tarieu de Lanaudière mourut le 4 avril 1842 et Catherine, sa sœur, neuf jours plus tard (*Le Canadien*, 15 avril 1842).
5. *Mémoires*, p. 70.
6. *Ibid.*, pp. 8 et 9.

Catherine Le Moyne de Longueuil, même s'il vit le jour dans sa demeure. Elle mourut le 15 avril 1788, un an et quelques mois après le départ des de Gaspé de la rue du Parloir. Philippe conservait cependant, on l'a dit, quelques souvenirs de sa grand-mère paternelle. Il n'eut pas pour autant le privilège de vivre longtemps en sa chaleureuse présence. Elle s'éteignit à son tour le 17 mars 1789. Bien qu'il n'eut alors que deux ans et cinq mois, le souvenir de cet événement demeura bien ancré dans sa mémoire. Septuagénaire avancé, il rappelait en ces termes le récit qu'il en fit à l'époque à sa mère:

> J'ai vu ici, un soir, repris-je, une personne morte couverte d'un drap blanc; sur une petite table, là (et je montrais la place), étaient deux cierges allumés; au milieu un crucifix, un gobelet d'eau et une petite branche de sapin. Mon père était agenouillé ici et il pleurait; vous étiez, vous aussi, à genoux; vous me teniez dans vos bras et vous me faisiez signe, en montrant mon père, de ne pas faire de bruit[7].

Marie-Anne Coulon de Villiers fut inhumée dans l'église de Saint-Jean-Port-Joli à côté du brave officier des troupes de la marine qu'avait été son mari.

* * *

Philippe eut une enfance heureuse dans le fief dont son père assuma la gestion à la mort de la grand-mère de Gaspé, en 1789. Il l'a écrit dans un passage qu'on ne saurait omettre de citer ici intégralement:

> Je trouvais la vie pleine de charme pendant mon enfance, ne m'occupant ni du passé ni encore moins de l'avenir. J'étais heureux. Que me fallait-il de plus! Je laissais bien, le soir, avec regret tous les objets qui m'avaient bien amusé; mais la certitude de les revoir le lendemain me consolait; aussi étais-je levé dès l'aurore pour reprendre les jouissances de la veille. Je me promenais seul, sur la brune, de long en large dans la cour du manoir, et je trouvais une jouissance infinie

---

7. *Ibid.*, p. 10.

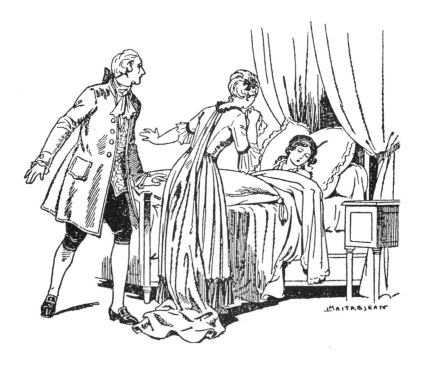

«Une malheureuse attaque de fièvre typhoïde, que j'eus à l'âge de sept ans,
me mit à deux doigts de la mort.» (Dessin de Maîtrejean, *Mémoires*,
Maison Alfred Mame & fils et Granger frères.)

à bâtir de petits châteaux en Espagne. Je donnais des noms
fantastiques aux arbres qui couronnent le beau promontoire
qui s'élève au sud du domaine seigneurial. Il suffisait que
leur forme m'offrit quelque ressemblance avec des êtres
vivants pour me les faire classer dans mon imagination.
C'était une galerie complète composée d'hommes, de femmes, d'enfants, d'animaux domestiques, de bêtes féroces et
d'oiseaux. Si la nuit était calme et belle, je n'éprouvais aucune
inquiétude sur le sort de ceux que j'aimais; mais, au contraire,
si le vent mugissait, si la pluie tombait à torrent, si le tonnerre
ébranlait le cap sur ses bases, je me prenais alors d'inquiétude
pour mes amis; il me semblait qu'ils se livraient entre eux un
grand combat et que les plus forts dévoraient les plus faibles.
J'étais heureux le lendemain de les trouver sains et saufs[8].

8.   *Ibid.*, p. 12.

À l'âge de sept ans, Philippe eut cependant la typhoïde et faillit en mourir. À l'idée que le docteur Frédéric Oliva pouvait le sauver, son père ordonna à son meunier et à un autre employé d'aller le chercher en toute hâte. Enfourchant leurs chevaux, ils coururent bride abattue jusqu'à Québec. Bientôt, le vieux médecin d'origine allemande fut au chevet du malade. Faisant ouvrir toutes les fenêtres, même si c'était l'hiver, contredisant en cela les prescriptions du médecin de campagne qui l'avait soigné jusque-là, le docteur Oliva lui sauva la vie. Et l'histoire veut que le seul à avoir souffert de la folle chevauchée qui avait permis d'amener le médecin à Saint-Jean-Port-Joli fut le meunier du seigneur de Gaspé: il demeura quinze jours sans pouvoir s'asseoir!

Une des sequelles de la typhoïde dont souffrit Philippe fut une diminution relativement importante de la prodigieuse mémoire qui avait été la sienne jusque-là. Il ne s'en plaignit pas trop cependant, puisqu'il conserva une rétention des faits exceptionnelle qui lui fut fort utile dans la rédaction de ses ouvrages.

La maladie et la mort en bas âge n'étaient pas des phénomènes inusités chez les Aubert de Gaspé, pas plus d'ailleurs que chez la plupart de leurs contemporains. Pierre Aubert de Gaspé, l'arrière-grand-père de Philippe, eut huit enfants et il en perdit quatre en très bas âge. Ignace-Philippe, son grand-père, en eut neuf et un seul d'entre eux atteignit la maturité. Les parents du jeune Philippe ne furent pas plus heureux. Des six enfants qui virent le jour au manoir seigneurial de Saint-Jean-Port-Joli, un seul atteignit l'âge adulte. Antoine-Frédéric, né le 10 août 1788, vécut onze jours; Charles-Guillaume, né le 10 août 1789, vécut huit jours; Ignace-Xavier, né le 30 juillet 1793, vécut onze jours et Marguerite, née au mois de juin 1798, vécut quelques mois seulement. Catherine, née en 1796, créa des espoirs chez ses parents, mais ce fut pour peu de temps. Elle mourut le 7 décembre 1803. Sa mère, raconte Philippe, eut tant de chagrin que personne n'osa plus prononcer son nom en sa pré-

Profil de Thomas Aubert de Gaspé (1790-1824), unique frère de l'auteur des *Anciens Canadiens*. (ASQ, photo W. B. Edwards Inc. 0297, p. 35.)

sence[9]. Antoine-Thomas fut donc le seul des enfants nés au manoir seigneurial à atteindre la maturité[10]. Bien qu'il eut trois ans de moins que son frère Philippe, il en devint le compagnon de jeu et d'espièglerie.

Comme tous les enfants de son âge, Philippe, à Saint-Jean-Port-Joli comme plus tard à Québec, aimait s'amuser et

9. *Les Anciens Canadiens*, p. 392.
10. Né le 21 décembre 1790, Antoine-Thomas épousa Marie-Louise Giasson au Sault Saint-Louis le 15 janvier 1816. Il eut cinq enfants et, âgé de 33 ans, mourut le 27 mai 1824.

parfois bruyamment. Les dommages faits, il se sauvait dehors pour éviter les corrections, courait sur la grève ou allait rejoindre aux champs les frères Chouinard et le père Castonguay, les faucheurs les plus redoutables de la paroisse. S'il est vrai que, dans ces circonstances, il craignait peu sa mère, qui mettait rarement, sinon jamais, ses menaces à exécution, il en était autrement du paternel. Le pire avertissement que pouvait lui faire sa mère était de lui dire qu'elle en parlerait à son père:

> «Je le dirai à ton père.» Ah! diable! voilà ce que je redoutais le plus. Il est vrai que mon père ne m'avait jamais donné un tapin, ce qui ne m'empêchait pas de le craindre comme le feu, même lorsque j'étais homme fait. Comment soutenir, en effet, son regard quand il était courroucé ou qu'il affectait de l'être? La vue de ces grands yeux noirs, qui lançaient alors des flammes et que peu d'hommes pouvaient soutenir, m'effrayait tellement que je me serais alors réfugié dans un trou de souris[11].

Pierre-Ignace Aubert de Gaspé, membre du Conseil législatif, juge de paix de Sa Majesté, colonel de milice, sut se faire respecter de tous. Perçu par son fils aîné comme «assez vindicatif» et «inspirant la crainte,» il n'était pas perçu autrement par ceux qui fréquentaient le château Saint-Louis, le Conseil, les salons et le mess des officiers. S'il est vrai qu'on redoutait son tempérament combatif et fougueux, on appréciait cependant la sagesse et la justesse de ses jugements. Loyal envers ses nouveaux maîtres, il ne renia pas pour autant les siens.

* * *

Durant son enfance à Saint-Jean-Port-Joli, Philippe fut témoin de quelques réceptions dont il conserva longtemps le souvenir. Comme «il y avait peu de société» à la campagne, l'arrivée des récollets au manoir «était considérée comme

---

11. *Mémoires*, p. 71.

une bonne fortune.» Madame de Gaspé, qui se disait être en riant «la mère supérieure de la maison», confiait ses «deux monstres» aux moines auxquels elle versait un petit verre de liqueur aux framboises, puis disparaissait pour vaquer aux soins de son ménage. Appuyée par Lisette, une cuisinière mulâtre pour qui l'art culinaire n'avait pas de secret, elle réapparaissait bientôt pour faire connaître le menu à ses convives qui, soit dit en passant, arrivaient toujours à l'heure des repas: «une soupe blanche au riz, navets, carottes et fines herbes, un pâté de morue sèche à l'huile d'olive, un plat de notre délicieuse truite du lac Trois-Saumons à la sauce robert, et pour couronner la soupe, devinez?... un plat d'œufs à la tripe[12].» Généralement une bouteille de vin vieux apparaissait aussi au dessert.

Les de Gaspé, qui s'étaient fait installer un imposant «tournebroche qui se montait comme une horloge» et dont le mécanisme se trouvait au grenier du manoir, donnaient aussi occasionnellement des réceptions plus élaborées. C'est ainsi que Philippe put voir à la table de ses parents quelques notables, des officiers, des ecclésiastiques et des seigneurs. Figuraient en tête de liste des invités les seigneurs Vincelot, Couillard et Casgrain, et les curés Verrault, Péras et Panet, respectivement de Saint-Roch, de Saint-Jean et de L'Islet[13].

* * *

La seigneurie de Saint-Jean-Port-Joli connut un développement important durant l'enfance de Philippe. Pendant que le grand voyer faisait tracer et ouvrir de nouveaux chemins au niveau des deuxième et troisième rangs, le seigneur encourageait ses censitaires à mettre leurs terres en valeur et

---

12. *Ibid.*, pp. 72 et 73. L'esclavage dans le Bas-Canada fut aboli en 1833. Les de Lanaudière et de Gaspé eurent des domestiques noirs, comme plusieurs familles de Québec. Louis fut à l'emploi du grand-père de Philippe et Lisette à l'emploi de son père.
13. Le seigneur Vincelot était de Cap-Saint-Ignace, le seigneur Couillard, de Saint-Thomas (Montmagny) et le seigneur Casgrain, de Rivière-Ouelle.

La rivière Trois-Saumons. À droite, le moulin banal des Aubert
de Gaspé au début du XIXe siècle, à gauche, la distillerie
des Harrower. (Bouchette, *The British Dominions*.)

en concédait de nouvelles. Les choses allaient si bien que,
non seulement le curé dut alors songer à agrandir son église
de trente pieds, mais le seigneur acheta un autre fief. C'est
ainsi qu'il acquit, les 23 juin et 23 septembre 1790, la seigneurie de l'Islet-à-la-Peau, une étendue de terre d'une «demye
lieue de front» (d'où le nom de «Demie-lieue» qui lui est
resté) et de «deux lieues de profondeur» située entre Saint-
Jean-Port-Joli et Saint-Roch-des-Aulnaies. Ce fief, qui avait
été concédé par le comte de Frontenac à Marie-Anne
Juchereau de Saint-Denys le 16 mars 1677, porta aussi les
noms de Réaume, d'Auteuil et surtout La Pocatière. En 1790,
il appartenait à des commerçants anglais et à Amable
Réaume, un résidant de l'Ancienne-Lorette[14].

---

14. William Goodall et ses associés qui résidaient à Londres possédaient en
1790 huit neuvièmes de ce fief et Amable Réaume un neuvième.

Le seigneur de Gaspé, qui ne détestait pas, semble-t-il, brasser des affaires, fit d'autres transactions immobilières à cette époque. À la mort de sa belle-mère, à Québec, le 16 avril 1788, les deux maisons dont cette dernière était propriétaire sur la rue du Parloir furent mises en vente. Tandis que François Baby se portait acquéreur de l'ancienne maison du docteur Sarrazin, située au sommet de la côte de la Montagne, là où Philippe avait vu le jour, Pierre-Ignace Aubert de Gaspé achetait pour la somme de vingt-cinq louis la maison voisine, construite par les Perthuis en 1728. La maison acquise par le seigneur de Gaspé demeura sa propriété jusqu'en 1806. Quant à la maison achetée par François Baby, elle devint à sa mort la propriété de sa femme et demeura ainsi entre les mains des Baby et des Tarieu de Lanaudière jusqu'au 7 mars 1843, date à laquelle l'archevêque de Québec, Mgr Signay, l'acquit pour la détruire et construire sur son site le palais épiscopal que réclamait le haut clergé de Québec[15].

Le 1er mai 1844, date fixée pour la prise de possession et la destruction de la maison Baby-Lanaudière, deux personnes s'y trouvaient encore: l'excentrique Marguerite Tarieu de Lanaudière, une des tantes de Philippe Aubert de Gaspé, et Josephte Baby, une de ses cousines. «Ce ne fut pas une petite affaire que de s'emparer de cette forteresse, car la garnison ne voulait pas se rendre et surtout ne voulait pas en sortir», raconte l'auteur de l'*Histoire du palais épiscopal de Québec*. «On comprend facilement l'embarras des nouveaux propriétaires, poursuit Mgr Têtu, qui d'un côté ne voulaient pas manquer de courtoisie envers ces dames, et d'un autre côté n'avaient aucunement l'envie de se plier à leurs caprices. Dans un conseil de guerre, il fut décidé de se rendre maître de la place en faisant attaquer par la base le côté le plus faible de la muraille et en le faisant tirer ensuite par le sommet de

---

15. En 1792, deux ans après avoir acheté L'Islet-à-la-Peau, Pierre-Ignace Aubert de Gaspé vend à François Baby, son beau-frère, sa part de la seigneurie de Saint-Pierre-les-Becquets, soit un huitième.

manière à le faire tomber tout d'une pièce. Le plan réussit à merveille. Au jour fixé et au moment où les demoiselles de Lanaudière et Baby se croyaient à l'abri de toute surprise, un craquement épouvantable ébranla la maison, le pignon s'écroula en entier dans la rue, rendant toute défense et un plus long séjour impossible[16].»

Le premier séjour de Philippe Aubert de Gaspé à Saint-Jean-Port-Joli dura environ neuf ans. Au cours de ces années, il vécut intensément. D'un «appétit vorace», il mangea beaucoup et dormit peu; d'une vitalité étonnante, il s'amusa ferme et joua des tours pendables; d'une véracité sans réserve, il ne chercha pas à échapper aux corrections bien méritées; d'une mémoire exceptionnelle, il apprit rapidement et emmagasina de nombreuses connaissances. En 1795, considérant qu'ils ne pouvaient faire davantage pour lui à Saint-Jean-Port-Joli, ses parents jugèrent que le temps était venu d'affronter la grande ville. Philippe ne manifesta aucune réticence. Québec lui plaisait. Il l'avait réalisé au cours des promenades que lui avaient fait faire ses parents désireux de montrer à leurs amis «leur petit animal rare». Ayant fait ses adieux à Thomas, son compagnon d'infortune, à Marie-Louise, sa tante préférée, à Lisette, son inestimable cuisinière, à Niger, le fidèle berger allemand, enfin à tous les êtres réels ou imaginaires avec lesquels il avait vécu à Saint-Jean-Port-Joli, il rejoignit la voiture qu'un domestique avait amenée à la porte du manoir. Pour le seigneur de Gaspé et son épouse qui allaient l'accompagner jusqu'à Québec, ce voyage ne ressemblait guère à celui qu'ils avaient fait ensemble au cours du dur hiver de 1787. Pourtant, ils éprouvaient des sentiments analogues, ceux qu'on ressent face à un lendemain incertain.

---

16. Têtu, *Histoire du palais épiscopal...*, pp. 154-156.

CHAPITRE 4

Un gamin formidable
à l'école de l'évêché

(1795-1798)

La *Gazette de Québec* du 19 novembre 1778 publia une petite annonce signée James Tanswell qui ne passa probablement pas inaperçu de ses lecteurs. Elle faisait connaître l'ouverture imminente d'une «Académie et École de Pension» sur la petite rue du Parloir, là même où Philippe Aubert de Gaspé vit le jour en 1786. Cette institution serait bilingue et mixte, bilingue en ce sens qu'elle accueillerait indistinctement des étudiants anglophones et francophones, et mixte en ce sens qu'elle serait accessible aux garçons comme aux filles, à la condition cependant que ces dernières soient regroupées pour leurs cours dans «un appartement séparé». Avec l'autorisation du gouverneur Haldimand, on y enseignerait «à lire, à écrire, l'Arithmétique dans toutes les parties, la méthode de tenir les Livres à l'Italienne, les langues anglaise, française, latine, grecque, la Géographie, les Globes et les autres parties des Mathématiques». À une époque où les enseignants n'étaient pas nombreux à Québec, tout particu-

AVERTISSEMENS.

ACADEMIE et ECOLE de PENSION.

AIANT eu une Permiffion et Commiffion fpéciale de Son Excellence le Général HALDIMAND, je prens la liberté d'informer le Public, que Lundi prochain 23 préfent je commencerai une Academie dans la rue du Parloir, près l'Evêché, où je ferai préparé à recevoir à des conditions raifonnables des jeúnes gens pour leur enfeigner à *Lire, Ecrire*, l'*Arithmetique* dans toutes fes parties, la methode de *tenir* les *Livres* à l'Italienne, les Langues *Angloife, Françoife, Latine* et *Grèque*, la *Géographie*, les *Globes* et autres parties des *Mathématiques.*

On veillera particulierement fur la conduite extérieure des Enfans, ainfi qu'à l'avancement de leur inftruction.

Pour la commodité de ceux qui ne pourront y venir dans la journée, je leur donnerai quelques heures le foir.

Ceux qui ont deffein de m'honorer de leurs ordres font priés de m'en avertir au plutôt poffible, car je n'en voudrois pas en prendre plus qu'il ne m'en faut pour m'acquitter de mes obligations.

N. B. J'inftruierai les Jeunes Demoifelles dans un appartement feparé.
JAs. TANSWELL

Quebec. 19 *Novembre,* 1778.

James Tanswell annonce l'ouverture de son école dans
la *Gazette de Québec* du 19 novembre 1878.

lièrement au sein de la population anglaise, cette nouvelle fut sans doute accueillie avec satisfaction.

Tanswell n'était pas un personnage ordinaire. Né en Angleterre vers 1744, il passa, selon son propre témoignage, les vingt premières années de sa vie dans les meilleures maisons d'enseignement de son pays, puis, en 1765, décida d'ouvrir une école à Londres. Sept ans plus tard, à l'invitation de gros commerçants de la Nouvelle-Écosse, on le retrouve à Halifax, où il fait de même. Enfin, en 1778, à l'invitation cette fois de citoyens de Québec, il s'établit d'abord sur la rue du Parloir, puis l'année suivante dans l'ancien évêché loué par le gouvernement le 1er août 1777. Tanswell s'engageait à veiller «particulièrement sur la conduite extérieure des Enfans, ainsi qu'à l'avancement de leur instruction». Aussi connut-il un certain succès à Québec: il dut déménager de nouveau en 1801 et engager, en plus de son fils, quelques adjoints.

Pierre-Ignace Aubert de Gaspé avait pris des dispositions avant d'amener Philippe à Québec en 1795[1].

---

1. Dans *Divers* (1893), une œuvre posthume, on lit que Philippe demeura près de cinq ans chez les Chôlette et y arriva au mois de novembre 1794.

L'Académie de James Tanswell ayant fait ses preuves, il avait décidé, comme l'avaient fait certains de ses compatriotes, de l'y inscrire. Comme la gestion de ses fiefs le retenait la plupart du temps à Saint-Jean-Port-Joli, il avait également fait le nécessaire pour lui trouver une pension convenable. Pour des raisons inconnues, mais qui pouvaient bien ne pas être étrangères au fait que Tanswell avait été secrétaire provincial de la franc-maçonnerie, il ignora l'établissement de ce dernier et opta pour une pension de famille, où deux de ses amis, Jean-Baptiste Couillard, seigneur de la Rivière-du-Sud, et Pascal Taché, seigneur de Kamouraska, envoyèrent également leurs fils[2].

La maison de pension choisie par le seigneur de Gaspé était plutôt sympathique. Elle était tenue par «deux vieilles filles», Catherine et Charlotte Chôlette, qui n'avaient pas l'étroitesse d'esprit qu'on prête trop souvent aux femmes d'un certain âge demeurées célibataires. Nées du mariage de Pierre Chôlette (Cholet) à Marie-Catherine Pelot dit Laflèche, elles avaient plusieurs frères et sœurs, dont Ives qui partageait leur gîte. Personnage «morne et bourru», ce dernier se montra néanmoins tolérant et généreux envers leur jeune pensionnaire. Et même s'il est vrai que ceux qui demeuraient chez les demoiselles Chôlette devaient réciter chaque jour en commun la prière du soir et le chapelet, personne ne pouvait se plaindre de manquer de liberté chez elles, tout particulièrement Philippe qui devint vite l'enfant gâté de la maison[3].

Ives Chôlette occupa beaucoup de place dans la vie du jeune Philippe. Le nombre de pages qui lui sont réservées dans les *Mémoires* en témoignent largement et méritent d'être lues intégralement. À lui seul, le passage qui suit illustre bien le genre de relations qui existait entre Philippe et celui que ce dernier appelait familièrement «mon vieux Ives»:

---

2.   Gaspard Couillard et Paschal Taché pensionnèrent avec Philippe à Québec.

3.   Philippe Aubert de Gaspé, qui conservait de bons souvenirs de son passage chez les Chôlette, parle longuement de cette famille dans les *Mémoires* (chapitre sixième) et dans *Divers* (La statue du général Wolfe).

Si j'étais aimé par Ives Chôlette, il n'avait pas lieu de se plaindre que je le négligeais: s'il descendait l'escalier pour aller à son ouvrage, je prenais un élan, je lui sautais comme un petit singe sur les épaules, et comme le tenace vieillard qui s'attachait si opiniâtrement à Sinbad le marin, je faisais une longue promenade dans les rues sur cette monture d'une nouvelle espèce. Quant à Chôlette, il était, je crois, heureux de me procurer cette promenade, tout en criant de temps à autre: Veux-tu descendre, méchant diable! Je vais te s...r à terre!» Mais s'il grondait d'un côté du visage, il riait de l'autre[4].

«Vivant dans une maison où j'étais si gâté», lit-on plus loin, «je devins bien vite maître absolu de toutes mes actions, et que je ne me fis pas faute d'en profiter». De James Tanswell qui s'engageait par ailleurs à «veiller sur la conduite extérieure des enfans» lorsqu'ils étaient à l'école, Philippe ne dit mot. Nommé en 1796 interprète à la Cour du banc du roi et à la Cour des sessions trimestrielles, l'instituteur avait sans doute d'autres chats à fouetter. Et c'est ainsi que les craintes éprouvées par le seigneur de Gaspé et son épouse au moment d'amener leur fils à Québec allaient se concrétiser. Philippe allait devenir, et c'est lui qui l'affirme, «un gamin formidable et des plus turbulents[5]».

Les six premiers mois à Québec ne furent pas des plus heureux. Ayant fait la connaissance du chef des gamins, Joseph Bezeau, surnommé Coq Bezeau, il fut bientôt présenté «à tous les polissons du quartier». Abusant de son naturel plutôt confiant, ces derniers s'amusèrent ferme à ses dépens. Tandis que Bezeau, sous prétexte de lui enseigner la boxe, lui bouchait les deux yeux, Justin McCarthy, «l'enfant le plus retors du pays», lui subtilisait habilement tout son argent. S'attachant à lui comme une sangsue, ce dernier réussit un jour à lui vendre «un costume complet d'évêque officiant pontificalement». Bien plus, lorsque Philippe se laissa convaincre qu'il devait porter ce déguisement pour prendre part

---

4. *Mémoires*, p. 139.
5. *Ibid.*, p. 157.

La porte Prescott. À droite, l'ancien palais épiscopal où était située
l'école de James Tanswell. (W. H. Bartlett, Musée du Québec,
photo Patrick Altman, G-66-133-E.)

à la procession de la Fête-Dieu, d'autres prirent un malin
plaisir à le réduire en charpie. Philippe raconte aussi dans ses
Mémoires comment, le deuxième dimanche après son arrivée
à Québec, on lui vola son argent à la cathédrale, sous prétexte de le donner à la quête pour acheter du pain bénit, et
comment, plus tard, une poignée d'espiègles tirèrent la
chaîne qui servait à sonner la cloche du couvent des Récollets
et le poussèrent rudement entre les jambes du frère portier.

Sa rencontre avec le sieur Lafleur, «le gamin le plus
redoutable de la cité lorsqu'il sortait de son élément naturel»,
n'est pas moins digne de mention. Petit animal amphibie,
«lorsqu'il n'était pas dans l'eau, on était certain de le voir
juché, comme un petit singe, sur les plus hautes manœuvres
des vaisseaux, dont il connaissait toutes les parties par leur
nom propre». En sa compagnie, Philippe apprit à affronter le
danger, à faire «enrager» les matelots, à nager plus habi-

lement et à échapper de justesse aux courants qui menaçaient de l'engloutir. «Fils de monsieur», à la peau «tendre comme un officier», en quelques mois il savait «hurler avec les loups et rendre coup de griffe pour coup de griffe[6]».

* * *

Le 6 septembre 1796, vers quatre heures de l'après-midi, Philippe se trouvait à l'école de l'ancien évêché et venait de recevoir quelques coups de baguette pour n'avoir pu conjuguer correctement un verbe français, quand sonna le tocsin et que les tambours battant la générale se firent entendre. Un instant plus tard, on accourait de partout: des professionnels, des fonctionnaires, des marchands, des ouvriers, mais aussi des membres du clergé, leur évêque en tête, des femmes et des enfants. Philippe qui avait laissé Tanswell à ses savantes considérations était naturellement du nombre. Observant au passage un récollet, un seau à la main, qui tentait d'éteindre une flammèche poussée par le vent sur le toit de son monastère, il continua vers ce qui semblait être le cœur du sinistre. Comme il n'avait pas plu depuis longtemps et que le vent était très fort, lui comme les autres avaient très peur! Rapidement, le feu, qui avait débuté dans une étable au coin de rues Saint-Louis et Sainte-Ursule, atteignit la maison du juge Monk. On se mit à craindre pour la résidence du gouverneur et le couvent des Ursulines.

Philippe est partout et emmagasine dans sa mémoire ce dont il est témoin. Chez le juge Monk, il est estomaqué de voir les pompiers improvisés «jeter par les fenêtres du premier et du second étage, les miroirs, les cabarets chargés de verreries et de précieuses porcelaines». Au couvent des Ursulines, il est plus surpris encore d'apprendre que l'évêque venait de donner «sa bénédiction au feu qui faisait déjà tant de ravages». Tout à coup, raconte Philippe, quelqu'un cria: «l'église des Récollets est en feu!» «Je ne fis qu'un saut; mais lorsque j'arrivai sur les lieux, le toit n'offrait plus déjà

6. *Ibid.*, pp. 187-219.

qu'une masse de flammes. Le couvent et les bâtisses adjacentes furent bien vite réduits en cendre[7].»

Ce jour-là brûlèrent à Québec une douzaine de maisons et plusieurs dépendances. Les pertes furent considérables, plus considérables encore qu'on ne l'avait imaginé. Ce sinistre signifiait aussi pour la colonie la dispersion des récollets et pour les Aubert de Gaspé, dont Philippe qui leur consacra plusieurs pages de ses *Mémoires*, la perte de grands amis.

---

7.   *Ibid.*, pp. 56-58.

CHAPITRE 5

Du Séminaire de Québec
à l'école anglo-protestante
(1798-1806)

«Je n'étais pas tout à fait un saint, et mon père que je craignais comme le feu était sévère en diable pour mes peccadilles»[1], remarque Philippe Aubert de Gaspé. Cette sévérité devait mettre un terme à ce qu'un de ses amis intimes appela «l'âge d'or de sa gaminerie[2]». Son père connaissait bien le Séminaire de Québec pour y avoir étudié durant six ans. Il connaissait le sérieux de l'enseignement qu'on y donnait et la formation qu'on cherchait à inculquer aux élèves. Il se souvenait des exercices religieux échelonnés au cours de la journée: prières du matin et du soir, messe, vêpres, salut du Saint-Sacrement, chapelets et lecture spirituelle. Il n'avait surtout pas oublié la discipline qui régnait dans cette institution par le moyen de règlements et de puni-

---

1. *Mémoires*, p. 203.
2. H. R. Casgrain, *P. A. de Gaspé et Francis Parkman*, Montréal, Librairie Beauchemin limitée, 1917, p. 26.

Le Séminaire de Québec. (ANQ-Québec, coll. initiale.)

tions sévères. Les châtiments auxquels s'exposaient les élèves les plus téméraires étaient connus de tous:

> le pensum, la férule, le fouet, manger à genoux au milieu du réfectoire, passer une partie de la récréation à genoux, la récréation toute entière sans bouger de sa place, être séparé des autres et renfermé pendant qu'ils vont à la promenade ou pendant les récréations ou pendant la journée entière, sans paraître ni au réfectoire, ni à la salle, ni même en classe suivant la grièveté des fautes[3].

Tout cela ne répugnait pas à la personnalité du seigneur et lui paraissait tout à fait acceptable, si ce n'est les punitions corporelles. À ses yeux, ce dont son fils avait grandement besoin, après les trois années qu'il venait de passer plus

---

3.   ASQ, Séminaire 95,25, dernière page, passage cité par Noël Baillargeon, *Le Séminaire de Québec de 1760 à 1800*, Québec, Les Presses de l'Université Laval, 1981, pp. 139 et 140.

souvent dans la rue que chez les demoiselles Chôlette et chez James Tanswell, c'était la formation qu'offrait le séminaire. Il est vrai que cette institution vénérable avait pour mission de préparer les enfants à l'état ecclésiastique et exigeait d'eux la docilité et des prédispositions à l'étude et à la dévotion, mais elle acceptait aussi les candidats ayant appris à écrire et à lire le français et le latin. On y trouvait d'ailleurs un certain nombre d'élèves anglo-protestants[4].

À la fin du mois de septembre 1798, un Philippe résigné franchit l'enceinte du Séminaire de Québec. Il était accompagné de ses deux amis de la pension Chôlette, Antoine Couillard et Paschal Taché, dont les parents avaient décidé de suivre l'exemple du seigneur de Gaspé. Pierre de Sales Laterrière, lui aussi fils de seigneur, faisait partie du groupe pour les mêmes motifs que Philippe. «Gamin redoutable comme moi, pendant son enfance, lit-on dans les *Mémoires*, son père, ainsi que le mien, se vit obligé de le mettre pensionnaire au Séminaire de Québec[5].»

La rentrée des nouveaux pour le début de l'année scolaire ne passait pas inaperçue. On peut les imaginer arrivant en voiture avec leurs parents, les cheveux fraîchement coupés et quelque peu poudrés, portant pour la première fois le «traditionnel capot bleu à nervures blanches». Ceux qui provenaient de familles à l'aise étaient généralement accompagnés d'un domestique auquel ils avaient confié le respectable trousseau que le règlement exigeait d'eux: pour le dortoir, un baudet, un matelas, un coussin, des draps, une ou deux couvertes, un ou deux peignes, des brosses et de la cire à souliers, un essuie-mains, une boîte de poudre, un petit bassin et un coffre; pour le réfectoire, un couteau, une fourchette, une cuillère et un gobelet; pour la salle d'étude, un cornet, des plumes, des cahiers et des livres de classe; pour les offices religieux, une robe ou soutane, un surplis, une barrette, un camail et un petit réchaud[6].

4. Noël Baillargeon, *Le Séminaire de Québec...*, p. 136.
5. *Mémoires*, p. 232
6. Noël Baillargeon, *op. cit.*, pp. 141-143.

Philippe commença ses études au séminaire en sixième année, tandis que ses amis Laterrière, Couillard et Taché, un peu plus jeunes que lui, en huitième. Au nombre des pensionnaires partageant le même réfectoire qu'eux, la même salle d'étude et la même cour de récréation se trouvaient plusieurs autres élèves dont Philippe conserva un impérissable souvenir. À l'âge de soixante-dix-neuf ans, leurs noms revenaient fréquemment sous sa plume: Louis-Joseph Papineau, dont il avait admiré au séminaire les talents d'orateur et suivi plus tard l'incroyable carrière politique; Pierre-Flavien Turgeon, qu'il avait vu accéder à la direction de l'archidiocèse de Québec; Joseph Painchaud, dont il avait apprécié sa vie durant la gaieté, le mordant, les qualités d'athlète et le dévouement; Rémi Vallières de Saint-Réal, qu'il disait être le plus doué des hommes qu'ait produit le Canada; Louis Plamondon, un compagnon de ses années folles, dont il n'oublia jamais l'esprit et les reparties; Louis Moquin, qui laissa à plusieurs le souvenir de l'avocat le plus brillant de son temps. Si Philippe ne sembla pas compter beaucoup d'amis parmi ses confrères anglophones du séminaire, il ne les ignorait pas pour autant. Les noms de Richard Cleary et James Maguire lui rappelaient de bons souvenirs; celui de Justin McCarthy de beaucoup moins bons cependant, même s'il crut devoir lui consacrer plusieurs paragraphes de ses *Mémoires*.

* * *

Qu'advint-il des espérances formées par le seigneur de Gaspé au moment d'inscrire son fils au séminaire? Philippe fut pensionnaire dans cette institution de 1798 à 1804. Durant cette période, il progressa sans ennui du point de vue scolaire, franchissant tous les échelons séparant la sixième année de la rhétorique. En classe quatre heures par jour, deux heures l'avant-midi et deux heures l'après-midi, il se fit remarquer par ses aptitudes intellectuelles, obtenant ses meilleurs résultats en thème latin. Sa dernière année comme pensionnaire fut particulièrement stimulante. Meilleur nageur du séminaire, avec son ami Joseph Painchaud[7], il partagea aussi avec lui le deuxième rang de sa classe. «Non tam autem diligentia quam dotibus» (non pas tant à cause de leur application qu'à cause de leurs talents), remarque leur professeur[8].

Une observation de son professeur de quatrième année, que ne vit sans doute pas son père, nous renseigne davantage. Évaluant la conduite de Philippe, il note, en latin lui aussi, «adonné à la dissipation et aux plaisanteries», remarque que n'aurait probablement pas contestée celui qui en était l'objet lorsqu'il rédigeait ses Mémoires à l'âge de soixante-dix-neuf ans. Toujours gai, joyeux, poli et courtois, Philippe changea bien peu, semble-t-il, au cours de son séjour au séminaire. «J'étais à peu près aussi gai, aussi fou, à l'âge de dix-sept ans qu'à douze», lit-on dans l'avant-dernier chapitre de son ouvrage[9].

Les initiatives personnelles n'avaient guère de place au séminaire. Le comportement à adopter au dortoir, au réfectoire, en classe et durant les récréations était prévu par le règlement. Il était interdit, par exemple, de porter les cheveux longs ou frisés, ou bien encore «poudrés d'une manière trop remarquable». Il était interdit de faire usage de tabac, d'eau-de-vie et d'armes à feu. Il était interdit de sortir de l'enceinte du séminaire, si ce n'est avec une permission expresse du directeur ou pour se rendre le jeudi à la métairie de La Canardière (Maizerets). Il était interdit de fréquenter les cabarets, les cafés, les salles de jeux ou les maisons de mauvaise réputation. Les obligations étaient également nombreuses. Les élèves étaient tenus, par exemple, de se laver chaque jour les mains, le visage et la bouche, de veiller à la propreté de leur lit et de leurs effets personnels, et d'adopter au réfectoire «les règles de la civilité et de la modestie». Gare à ceux qui étaient pris en faute. Ils devaient

---

7. Mémoires, p. 15.
8. ASQ, 103, n° 49.
9. Mémoires, p. 499.

La maison de La Canardière ou maison Maizerets.
Vue actuelle. (Coll. de l'auteur.)

«se découvrir sur le champ et profiter sans réplique de la reprimande qu'on leur fait», cite Noël Baillargeon, dans son excellent volume sur l'histoire du Séminaire de Québec[10].

Suivi par ses maîtres et sans doute aussi par son père qui passait l'hiver à Québec à cette époque,[11] Philippe ne dérogea probablement pas sérieusement au règlement durant ses six années de pensionnat. Élève hyperactif, il lui arriva encore cependant de se permettre quelques incartades plutôt mal vues à cette époque. L'interdiction de faire usage du tabac, et conséquemment «de pipes et de calumets», a de tout temps contrarié les étudiants. Philippe, qui se définissait comme «l'élève le plus turbulent du séminaire», ne fit pas exception à cette règle:

10. Baillargeon, *op. cit.*, pp. 139-144.
11. Pierre-Ignace Aubert de Gaspé, après la vente de sa maison de la rue du Parloir en 1806, habita la rue Saint-Georges, qui devint en 1876 la rue Hébert située entre les rues des Remparts et Sainte-Famille.

Le château Bellevue, maison de vacances du Séminaire située
à Saint-Joachim. Vue actuelle. (Coll. de l'auteur.)

Si nous n'avons pas fait brûler le séminaire, c'est que la
Providence veillait sur cette maison qui a rendu des services
si éminents à la jeunesse canadienne. L'usage de la pipe était
sévèrement interdit aux élèves; raison de plus pour nous en
donner la fantaisie. Un immense approvisionnement de bois
de chauffage couvrait alors le terrain sur lequel est situé le jeu
de paume actuel; il ne s'agissait que d'y pratiquer une
chambre au beau milieu pour être à l'abri de recherches les
plus minutieuses. Comme nous étions surveillés de bien près,
le travail fut long; mais à force de persévérance, un comité de
la pipe fut enfin organisé[12].

Heureusement pour Philippe et ses confrères, il y avait
à l'époque au séminaire «l'excellent M. Demers». «Nous
l'aimions tous comme s'il eut été notre père. Quelle bonté!
Quelle indulgence pour les fautes, pour les égarements de la
jeunesse[13]!»

12. *Mémoires*, p. 232.
13. *Ibid.*, p. 170.

* * *

Le séminaire autorisait rarement les élèves à passer les vacances d'été, qui ne commençaient que le 15 août, dans leur famille. Seules de graves raisons pouvaient les dispenser de séjourner au Petit-Cap, situé à Saint-Joachim, à quelques milles à l'est de Sainte-Anne-de-Beaupré. Philippe ne parut pas s'en plaindre. Son séjour à proximité du cap Tourmente lui a permis d'écrire ces paragraphes mémorables:

> Lorsque je reporte mes souvenirs sur les jours heureux de mon enfance, je me transporte souvent en esprit au château de Belle-Vue, dans la paroisse de Saint-Joachim, appartenant au séminaire de Québec. Le château, assis sur un promontoire qui domine une immense vallée rafraîchie par les eaux pures et limpides du fleuve Saint-Laurent, et couverte, pendant l'été, des plus riches moissons, des prairies les plus verdoyantes, offre déjà à la vue un des plus beaux sites du Canada, à part les scènes grandioses qui l'environnent de toutes parts. À l'ouest est l'île d'Orléans, qui semble surnager sur le prince des fleuves; vis-à-vis sont les vertes campagnes de la côte du sud, d'où surgissent les habitations blanchies à la chaux, qui semblent former un village continu aussi loin que la vue peut s'étendre. Au nord-est se déroulent les Laurentides, immense serpent vert, dont la tête gigantesque, le cap Tourmente, couvre, le soir, de ses grandes ombres les plus belles prairies qui s'étendent depuis sa base jusqu'au promontoire sur lequel est situé le château.
>
> Quand bien même les messieurs du séminaire de Québec eussent voulu choisir dans tout le Canada une résidence propre à délasser de leurs études, pendant leurs vacances, les élèves de leur maison d'éducation, ils auraient en vain cherché un autre asile champêtre où tout fût mieux réuni pour cet objet[14].

* * *

---

14. *Ibid.*, pp. 172 et 173.

Ce n'est pas sans une certaine tristesse que le 15 août 1804 Antoine Couillard, Joseph Painchaud et Pierre de Sales Laterrière prirent le chemin du Petit-Cap pour leurs vacances d'été. Ils savaient bien que le château Bellevue et son entourage n'avaient rien perdu de la beauté champêtre qui exerçait sur eux une irréductible séduction. Ce qu'ils appréhendaient, c'était la dissolution du groupe d'amis auquel ils étaient habitués depuis plusieurs années. S'ils acceptaient assez bien le départ inévitable des finissants auxquels appartenaient Louis-Joseph Papineau et Louis Plamondon, ils se résignaient mal à l'idée que même Philippe Aubert de Gaspé ne serait plus des leurs. Ainsi en avait décidé son père. Bien qu'il était très attaché à la langue française qu'il se faisait un devoir de défendre, même publiquement, il n'était pas moins convaincu de l'importance de maîtriser l'anglais. Tout en souhaitant voir son fils terminer sa philosophie au séminaire comme externe, il avait pris la décision de le mettre cette fois pensionnaire à l'école anglo-protestante dirigée par John Jackson[15].

Ce choix n'avait rien de très désagréable pour Philippe. Il allait ainsi apprendre rapidement l'anglais, qu'il disait ignorer alors totalement, et vivre sur la rue des Remparts dans une institution aux mœurs plus libérales qu'au séminaire. Seul étudiant canadien-français, il allait aussi, en raison de sa gaieté communicative, se faire de nombreux amis et passer «deux années heureuses dans ce pensionnat».

Durant son séjour dans cette école, qu'il qualifia d'excellente, Philippe se lia d'amitié avec le révérend Jackson, auquel il enseigna pour sa part le français. De lui et de son épouse, qui le traitèrent toujours avec égard et tendresse, il conserva un souvenir ému qu'il voulut aussi faire revivre dans ses *Mémoires*.

---

15. Philippe Aubert de Gaspé suggère à la page 499 de ses *Mémoires* (édition 1885) qu'il fit comme externe son cours de philosophie au séminaire de 1804 à 1806. Son nom ne figurant pas sur les listes de finissants de cette époque, un doute semble subsister quant à ce fait.

Étude en droit et mariage à Québec
(1806-1811)

Philippe Aubert de Gaspé réapparut occasionnellement à Saint-Jean-Port-Joli durant les vacances d'été lorsqu'il étudiait à Québec, en particulier avant et après ses années de pensionnat au séminaire. Il put constater que, durant ses absences prolongées, la paroisse où ses parents passaient la plus grande partie de leur temps[1] continuait à se développer. La population étant moins clairsemée au troisième rang, on travaillait à améliorer les chemins menant au cœur du village. Le lac Trois-Saumons où Philippe aimait pêcher semblait moins éloigné. Pour faciliter l'accès à l'église et au presbytère, on avait installé des «limandes» ou poteaux pour attacher les chevaux et Henry-Marie Duval-dit-Duponleau avait dû céder pour cela un lopin de terre. Tandis que le curé Jean-Baptiste Perras améliorait son église en faisant sculpter un retable par Jean et Florent Baillairgé, le marchand général

---

1. Pierre-Ignace Aubert de Gaspé vendit sa maison de la rue du Parloir à George Lengmore, qui l'habitait depuis un an, le 22 mars 1806.

Verreau augmentait la quantité et la variété de ses produits. Sur ses étagères figuraient maintenant des souliers d'orignal et des souliers «françois», des chapeaux en maroquin ou en paille, des châles rouges, jaunes ou noirs, des coiffes, des perruques, des bonnets, quelques paires de fausses manches, des bricoles et des ceintures, des mouchoirs de soie noire et des bas. Celles qui cousaient trouvaient aussi tout ce dont elles avaient besoin, entre autres des pièces de casimir, de *fléchine*, d'*indienne* et de *baptiste*. Il en était de même pour celles qui cuisinaient. Enfin, à côté des recueils de cantiques et des catéchismes, figuraient des calendriers, des jeux de cartes, du «papier à encre» et un «grément de bureau[2]».

Si, aux yeux de Philippe, le village de son enfance n'était plus tout à fait le même en 1806, aux yeux des habitants de Saint-Jean-Port-Joli le fils de leur seigneur avait lui aussi changé. Il semblait toujours aussi gai mais, comme il avait alors vingt ans et n'était plus un enfant, il était devenu pour eux «monsieur Philippe». D'une ascendance noble, «monsieur Philippe» avait l'avantage d'avoir fait de bonnes études, de parler couramment l'anglais et d'avoir un père ayant d'avantageuses relations à tous les niveaux de la hiérarchie civile, militaire et religieuse. Il pouvait ainsi espérer accéder rapidement à un poste de confiance dans l'administration. Il ne lui manquait en réalité qu'une profession et, tout comme l'avaient fait ou allaient le faire plusieurs de ses confrères et amis d'enfance, il choisit d'étudier le droit et de devenir avocat.

C'est ainsi qu'en 1806 on vit le colonel de milice et seigneur de Saint-Jean-Port-Joli frapper à la porte de Jonathan Sewell, procureur général du Bas-Canada. Fils d'un loyaliste éminent, Sewell était bien perçu par les anglophones de Québec qui appréciaient sa grande compétence en matière de droit et voyaient en lui un ardent défenseur des droits de la couronne. Quant à plusieurs Canadiens français, ils voyaient

2. Inventaire du magasin H. Verreau, 28 décembre 1811. Archives de l'auteur.

Le juge Jonathan Sewell auprès duquel Philippe Aubert de Gaspé
étudia le droit de 1806 à 1808. (ANQ-Québec, coll. initiale.)

surtout en lui un adversaire prônant l'anglicisation de leurs
enfants et l'affaiblissement de leur église. Ils lui faisaient en
particulier grief d'être à l'origine de projets de loi injustes et
d'être responsable d'arrestations et de condamnations
arbitraires. Quoi qu'il en soit, Sewell était respecté au sein de
sa profession et son cabinet jouissait alors d'un prestige
exceptionnel. Pour Pierre-Ignace Aubert de Gaspé, qui ne
cherchait pas à dissimuler ses sentiments royalistes et
connaissait bien Sewell, le maître dont son fils avait alors
besoin, c'était lui.

Dans ses *Mémoires*, Philippe relate en ces temes la première rencontre qu'il eut avec celui qui allait l'initier à
l'étude du droit:

Lorsque je signai le brevet d'usage en entrant dans son
bureau, mon père mit sur sa table un rouleau de cent guinées,
honoraires que M. le procureur du roi exigeait pour les cinq

La maison de Jonathan Sewell située sur la rue Saint-Louis.
Vue actuelle. (Coll. de l'auteur.)

années d'études de ses clercs. M. Sewell écrivit une quittance de cette somme au bas de l'acte et dit à mon père:

Accepter votre argent, monsieur, serait m'ôter le plaisir que j'ai de recevoir un jeune gentilhomme comme votre fils dans mon étude.

La gratitude n'a jamais été un fardeau pour moi, et je saisis avec plaisir cette occasion, la seule qui se présente de rendre justice aux éminentes qualités de mon ancien patron[3].

Jonathan Sewell dont la clientèle était nombreuse avait plusieurs clercs à son service. Philippe ne se retrouva donc pas seul dans son cabinet. Se liant d'amitié avec William Green et James Cartwright, il profita de ses études de droit pour parfaire ses connaissances de l'anglais. Il fut bientôt non seulement capable de traduire Walter Scott, mais aussi en mesure de goûter la lecture des poèmes et des pièces de théâtre de Shakespeare.

---

3. *Mémoires*, p. 226.

L'admiration qu'on avait pour Sewell provenait du fait qu'il excellait dans la théorie comme dans la pratique, qualité qu'il souhaitait retrouver chez ses élèves. C'est pourquoi il n'exigeait pas que du «griffonnage» de ses clercs, mais leur présence à la cour et l'étude de recueils de lois, de coutumes et de statuts divers. Philippe se retrouva d'ailleurs avec la *Coutume de Paris* sous le bras dès ses premières heures de travail[4].

Si l'on en croit les *Mémoires*, les délices que devait lui procurer sa profession furent lentes à venir. L'étude de la loi lui parut souvent «un collier de misère». C'est ainsi qu'il préféra maintes fois à ses livres la présence du capitaine Day, des lieutenants Butler et Loring, et du «jeune M. Burke que l'on appelait Château Burke, parce qu'il logeait chez le gouverneur Craig[5].» Il ne lui repugnait pas non plus de préférer à l'occasion le mess des officiers du 49e régiment au cabinet sévère du procureur général. Ce besoin inassouvi de divertissements ne l'empêcha pas toutefois d'apprécier son vieux maître qui s'y connaissait dans l'art de fermer les yeux sur les incartades de ses clercs:

> Malgré les reproches auxquels sa politique l'a exposé, M. Sewell n'en était pas moins, dans la vie sociale et privée, un des hommes les plus estimables que j'ai connus. Sans parler de sa charité envers les pauvres et d'autres qualités solides, il avait la courtoisie d'un Anglais de vieille souche[6].

* * *

Un événement imprévu devait cependant mettre un terme aux études de Philippe dans le cabinet de Jonathan Sewell. Nommé juge en chef du Bas-Canada le 22 août 1808, ce dernier, en raison de ses nouvelles fonctions, se vit en effet contraint de congédier tous ses clercs[7].

---

4.   *Ibid.*, pp. 305-308.
5.   *Ibid.*, p. 556.
6.   *Ibid.*, p. 226.
7.   Philippe Aubert de Gaspé parle ici de l'année 1809. Il est peu probable qu'il en fut ainsi puisque Sewell fut nommé juge en chef en 1808.

Le juge Olivier Perrault auprès duquel Philipe Aubert de Gaspé
étudia le droit de 1808 à 1811. (ANQ-Québec, coll. initiale.)

Olivier Perrault, auprès duquel Philippe termina sa cléricature, avait une certaine affinité avec Jonathan Sewell. Ses
études au Séminaire de Québec terminées, il étudia le droit
et fut reçu au barreau le 1er octobre 1799. Nommé avocat
général du Bas-Canada par celui qu'on appelait avec ironie
«the little King Craig», il se fit défenseur de l'ordre public et
donna son appui à la décision du gouverneur d'emprisonner
les principaux chefs du Parti canadien. Plus tard, à l'instar de
son collègue Sewell, il tenta sa chance en politique et fut
nommé membre, puis président du Conseil législatif. Il
habita, à compter de 1819, la célèbre maison Kent, située au
25, rue Saint-Louis, où fut signée en 1759 la capitulation de
Québec.

* * *

Le capitaine Thomas Allison. (Coll. privée.)

Les bonnes relations qu'entretenait Philippe avec les anglophones et les officiers britanniques de la garnison de Québec eurent à cette époque une certaine incidence sur sa vie publique et privée. Ne se contentant pas de défendre ces officiers contre ceux qui avaient tendance à les juger trop sévèrement, il sembla aussi s'intéresser davantage à la milice, suivant en cela l'exemple de son père qui, durant plus de trente ans, fut actif dans la milice de la Côte-du-Sud[8]. Lieutenant dans la première division de la Ville de Québec en 1809, il fut promu capitaine au premier bataillon de cette ville en 1812, puis nommé juge avocat à l'état-major de la milice du Bas-Canada.

---

8. Des documents attestent que Pierre-Ignace Aubert de Gaspé était major «de toutes les milices de la partie Sud de la Rivière Saint-Laurent» en 1790, lieutenant-colonel pour l'état-major des milices de la paroisse Saint-Thomas en 1798 et colonel commandant les divisions de Saint-Thomas ou de Saint-Jean-Port-Joli jusqu'à sa mort en 1823.

L'avancement au sein de la milice n'était pas un fait négligeable; il était cependant relativement peu important par rapport à ce qui attendait Philippe à la fin de ses années de cléricature chez Olivier Perrault, lorsqu'il épousa Susanne, la fille du capitaine Thomas Allison.

Né à Forcett Park, dans le comté de York, en Écosse, le 26 juin 1757, Allison était capitaine au 5e régiment d'infanterie lorsqu'il épousa, à Détroit, Thérèse Duperron Baby, une fille issue d'une grande famille de l'ouest du Haut-Canada[9]. Lorsque les Allison arrivèrent à Québec en 1798, ils avaient deux enfants en bas âge, Susanne et Thomas. Thomas mourut à l'âge de treize ans, le 25 novembre 1809. Quant à Susanne, qui n'avait que quinze ans à la mort de son frère, élégante et d'une grande beauté, elle était vue comme un des meilleurs partis de la société anglophone de Québec. Ce qui n'avait pas échappé à l'attention de Philippe et de ses amis.

En 1810, le capitaine Allison se faisait à son tour remarquer des Québécois, mais pour des motifs bien différents. Pendant que Philippe courtisait sa fille, les événements se précipitaient sur la scène politique. Non content de chercher à intimider les électeurs et de proroger «à répétition» la Chambre dont les initiatives lui déplaisaient souverainement, le gouverneur Craig décidait, suivant en cela l'avis de Sewell et du Conseil exécutif dont faisait partie François Baby, de porter un grand coup au journal *Le Canadien* soupçonné de trahison. Le 17 mars 1810, la troupe saisissait ce journal, arrêtait Charles Lefrançois, son imprimeur, et le jetait en prison. Quelques jours plus tard, toujours en raison de soupçons de «pratiques séditieuses», Pierre Bédard, Jean-Thomas Taschereau et François Blanchet, tous membres de l'Assemblée dissoute, étaient à leur tour mis en état d'arrestation. Cette saisie, «ma foi, il faut l'avouer», écrira plus tard Philippe Aubert de Gaspé, fut exécutée par un piquet de soldats commandé par un juge de paix qui était nul autre

---

9.   Pierre-Georges Roy, *À travers les Mémoires de Philippe Aubert de Gaspé*, Montréal, G. Ducharme, 1943, pp. 201 et 202.

Signatures apparaissant sur le contrat de mariage de Philippe Aubert de Gaspé et de Susanne Allison. (Greffe du notaire Joseph Planté, 23 septembre 1811.)

que le capitaine Thomas Allison. Commentant cet événement, l'auteur des *Mémoires* ajoutera:

> Je jette, aujourd'hui, le gant au torie le plus farouche, pourvu qu'il ait quelque teinture de la constitution anglaise, et je veux passer pour le plus sot individu du Canada, s'il peut me montrer une phrase, une seul phrase dans ce journal qui put motiver les rigueurs de l'oligarchie sous l'administration de Craig[10].

Cette condamnation implicite de Craig et de Sewell, corroborée d'ailleurs par le jugement du procureur de Sa Majesté en Angleterre[11], témoigne du sens critique de M. de Gaspé. Malgré ses nombreux amis anglophones, il prit plus d'une fois la défense de ses compatriotes d'origine française.

Philippe ne sembla pas tenir rigueur à Thomas Allison de la saisie du *Canadien*, sachant que ce dernier ne faisait

---

10. *Mémoires*, p. 345.
11. Lionel Groulx, *Histoire du Canada français*, Montréal et Paris, Fides, 1967, tome 2, p. 121.

Susanne Allison. (ASQ, photo W. B. Edwards Inc. 0297, p. 35.)

qu'exécuter des ordres, et il continua à fréquenter sa fille unique. Admis au barreau le 15 août 1811, il se retrouva sous son toit, le 23 septembre de la même année, pour signer en sa présence, et en la présence de ses propres parents et de quelques amis, un contrat de mariage le liant à sa fille Susanne. S'engageant à faire célébrer le plus tôt possible leur union «en face de notre mère la Sainte Église», il dota sa future épouse «d'une somme de mille livres [...] au cas qu'au jour du décès du dit Sieur futur Époux il y ait des enfants vivants ou à naître du futur mariage[12]».

Deux jours plus tard, le 25 septembre 1811, Philippe, âgé de vingt-quatre ans, épousait à la cathédrale de Québec «la plus belle d'entre les belles», celle qui allait, selon son témoignage, partager ses joies et ses douleurs[13]. Ayant peu ou pas

---

12. ANQ-Q, greffe du notaire Joseph Planté, n° 5795, 23 septembre 1811. La future épouse a signé Susanne et non Suzanne.
13. *Mémoires*, p. 356.

Philippe Aubert de Gaspé. (Fusain de P. N. Hamel, coll. Musée du Québec)

de sympathie pour les Canadiens français ou l'Église catholique, le capitaine Allison s'abstint d'assister au mariage de sa fille[14]. Nous savons cependant qu'il donna à son gendre «un cheval très violent et d'une vitesse extrême» que les charretiers appelaient «le diable du capitaine Allison[15]». L'histoire ne dit pas s'il s'en trouva pour lui prêter une intention malveillante!

14. L'acte de mariage conservé aux Archives nationales du Québec semble confirmer cette opinion de madame Laurette B. Perrault, arrière-petite-fille de Charlotte Elmire Aubert de Gaspé, les noms et les signatures du capitaine Allison et de son épouse qui apparaissent sur le contrat de mariage ne figurant pas sur cet acte.
15. *Mémoires*, pp. 534 et 536.

Avocat, homme d'affaires et shérif

(1811-1822)

Admis au barreau en 1811, Philippe Aubert de Gaspé s'adonna à la pratique du droit quelque temps. C'est à la cour de circuit de Kamouraska, qui siégeait durant l'été, qu'il fit ses «premières armes», en compagnie de trois confrères du Séminaire de Québec qui avaient terminé leurs études de droit à la même époque: Rémi Vallières de Saint-Réal, Jacques Leblond et Louis Plamondon. La tournée de Kamouraska était tout un événement pour les habitants de l'endroit et des villages environnants. Les demandeurs et les défenseurs étant nombreux et la période des audiences relativement courte, les auberges étaient bondées et on devait monter des tentes à proximité de la cour[1]. Tandis que les avocats venus de Québec plaidaient les uns contre les autres, en présence d'un juge de la Cour du banc du roi, également de Québec, les clients dont les causes avaient été entendues se réunissaient pour célébrer leur victoire ou noyer leur peine.

---

1. *Mémoires*, pp. 259 et 260. Dans les *Anciens Canadiens*, pp. 384 et 385, Aubert de Gaspé écrit que quatre cents causes étaient alors entendues en deux jours.

La rue Saint-Louis et le Palais de justice construit sur le site du monastère
des Récollets entre 1801 et 1804. (Aquarelle de James P. Cockburn, 1830.
Archives nationales du Canada, 12532.)

La tournée de Kamouraska, qui avait l'avantage d'approfondir les liens d'amitié entre les jeunes avocats, fournissait aussi à Philippe l'occasion de revoir Paschal Taché avec qui il avait logé chez les demoiselles Chôlette. Au cours des veillées qu'il passait en sa compagnie, au manoir seigneurial de l'endroit, on évoquait sans doute le bon souvenir des «deux vieilles filles», en particulier celui de Charlotte décédée au cours de l'hiver de 1812, de leur frère Yves qui, malgré son mauvais caractère, n'était plus célibataire, et d'un autre pensionnaire chez les Chôlette, Antoine Couillard. Reçu médecin en 1811, ce dernier était seigneur de la Rivière-du-Sud depuis 1808[2].

Le travail à Kamouraska terminé, suivait une course à travers les villages menant à Saint-Jean-Port-Joli et, de là, à la

2.   Antoine Couillard fut autorisé à pratiquer la médecine le 12 juin 1811 et Paschal Taché le notariat en 1809.

Maison située à l'intersection des rues Saint-Louis et des Jardins qu'habita Philippe Aubert de Gaspé de 1815 à 1824. (ANQ-Québec, coll. initiale.)

Pointe-Lévis. Tiré à vive allure par le cheval fringant du capitaine Allison, le cabriolet de Philippe atteignait bientôt le manoir seigneurial des Trois-Saumons et, le lendemain, Québec où les activités nombreuses attendaient les jeunes avocats.

L'auteur des *Mémoires* est discret au sujet de sa pratique du droit à Québec. On sait néanmoins qu'au cours de la décennie qui suivit la fin de ses études il prit une part active à la vie de ses concitoyens. Tout semblait l'intéresser et tous s'intéressaient à lui. Ses origines, son statut social, son apparente aisance financière, ses relations sociales et son dynamisme en faisaient un être auquel on aimait spontanément s'associer. Aussi croyait-il compter de nombreux amis...

On sait qu'en 1811, peu avant la guerre qui opposa l'Angleterre aux États-Unis, son oncle Xavier-Roch Tarieu de Lanaudière fut nommé adjudant général adjoint de la milice pour le Bas-Canada. L'année suivante, promu capitaine, Philippe fut appelé à remplir les fonctions de juge avocat à l'état-major du Bas-Canada. Mais la milice ne fut qu'une activité parmi bien d'autres. Les lettres, les loisirs, les sports, les finances et l'administration sont autant de domaines qui suscitèrent chez lui beaucoup d'intérêt et pour lesquels il n'hésita pas à se dépenser, la plupart du temps avec succès.

En 1808 et 1809, sous le patronage de Jonathan Sewell, son premier professeur de droit, il fonda avec quelques amis la première société littéraire de Québec, association dont il assuma quelque temps la vice-présidence. Cette initiative apparut plus tard comme un indice pouvant laisser présager ses futurs succès dans le monde des lettres. Le 6 février 1813, il faisait par ailleurs son entrée dans l'administration gouvernementale en succédant à son oncle Tarieu de Lanaudière comme traducteur et secrétaire de la Province du Bas-Canada, responsabilité qu'il avait déjà assumée de façon temporaire. Il habita quelque temps un appartement d'une maison de trois étages située du côté nord de la rue Saint-Louis, presque au coin de la rue Sainte-Ursule[3]. Puis, le 3 mai 1815, suivant l'exemple de son oncle, il fit l'acquisition, pour la somme de 1200 louis, de la maison que Xavier-Roch Tarieu de Lanaudière avait léguée à sa sœur Marguerite et à son frère Antoine-Ovide[4]. Située sur le côté sud-ouest de la rue

---

3. C. Cameron et J. Trudel, *Québec au temps de James Pattison Cockburn*, Québec, Éditions Garneau, 1976, p. 82.
4. ANQ-Q, greffe du notaire Joseph Planté, 3 mai 1815.

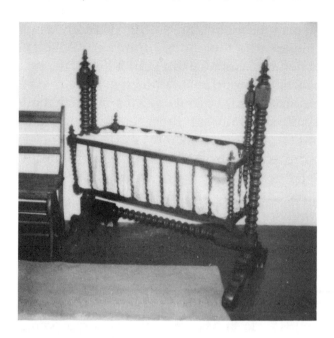

Berceau qui aurait servi aux treize enfants de Philippe Aubert de Gapé.
Il est conservé au manoir de Rivière-du-Loup. (Coll. privée.)

Desjardins, au coin de la rue Saint-Louis, cette maison à un
étage, surmontée d'un toit à pente raide recouvrant un double grenier, abrita l'auteur des *Anciens Canadiens* et sa famille
durant neuf ans environ. Selon le recensement de 1818, le
jeune avocat et son épouse avaient avec eux, cette année-là,
quatre enfants, soit Suzanne, Philippe, Adélaïde et Elmire,
nés respectivement en 1812, 1814, 1815 et 1817, et huit adul-
tes, dont sept domestiques.

Ensemble à Kamouraska, Vallières de Saint-Réal, Plamondon et de Gaspé se retrouvèrent aussi ensemble à
Québec, non seulement pour plaider mais pour faire des
affaires. Le 8 septembre 1815, l'année même où Philippe se
porta acquéreur de la maison de la rue Saint-Louis, les trois
amis, conscients que le faubourg Saint-Jean allait connaître
un développement important, achetèrent des Ursulines deux
grands terrains. Séparés l'un de l'autre par la rue Sainte-
Claire, ils comprenaient dix-huit emplacements de quarante

pieds sur soixante et quelques autres de moins grande super-
ficie. Ils payèrent le tout 10 262 livres et dix sols, les rentes
annuelles non incluses[5]. Ce qui était à l'époque, on le devine,
une transaction importante. Philippe Aubert de Gaspé se
porta aussi acquéreur ce jour-là, sans la participation de ses
collègues, d'un terrain subdivisé en huit emplacements de
quatre-vingts pieds sur soixante, et deux emplacements de
trente-quatre pieds sur soixante. Situé aux limites des rues
Saint-Olivier et Sainte-Claire, ce terrain qui appartenait aussi
aux Ursulines lui fut vendu pour la somme de 5000 livres, les
rentes annuelles non comprises[6]. Vallières de Saint-Réal fit
de même, achetant un terrain de deux cent vingt-neuf pieds
de front sur la rue Saint-Olivier[7]. On verra que Philippe ne
conserva pas bien longtemps ce terrain.

Deux ans plus tard, Philippe investissait de nouveau
dans l'immobilier en faisant cette fois l'acquisition, le 23
décembre 1817, de la Maison des Bains que venait à peine
d'ouvrir un de ses collègues, Robert Christie, sur la rue Saint-
Charles (aujourd'hui rue Saint-Vallier). Déménagé dans une
maison plus grande, mais située à proximité de la première,
l'établissement offrait, en 1818, six chambres avec bain, le
gîte et le couvert pour quelques personnes et, à compter de
1819, un jeu de paume. De plus, trois ans plus tard, il possédait aussi des bains d'eau salée de Kamouraska[8]. On sait
enfin qu'au mois de juin 1819 il devint un des nombreux
propriétaires du pont qu'on s'apprêtait à bâtir à Sainte-Marie
de Beauce[9], et acheta de ses oncles et tantes de Lanaudière la
moitié d'une ferme située à Saint-Vallier (seigneurie de la
Durantaye)[10].

---

5.   *Ibid.*, n° 6757, 8 septembre 1815.
6.   *Ibid.*, n° 6769, 8 septembre 1815.
7.   *Ibid.*, n° 6760, 8 septembre 1815.
8.   Voir sur ce sujet l'intéressant article de Rénald Lessard, «Les premiers
bains publics de Québec 1817-1823», dans *Cap-aux-Diamants*, vol. 1, n° 2 (été
1985), pp. 43 et 44.
9.   ANQ-Q, greffe du notaire Joseph Planté, n° 7759, 17 juin 1819. Il acheta
un centième de ce pont et des revenus à venir.
10.   Greffe du notaire Ant. A. Parent, 8 juin 1819.

L'intérêt que porta indirectement ou directement Philippe à la vie de ses concitoyens ne se limita pas à ces activités professionnelles et autres. En 1815, il contribua aussi à la fondation du Jockey Club, une entreprise qui durant de nombreuses années présenta à Québec des courses de chevaux. En 1816-1817, son nom figurait sur la liste des directeurs des Assemblées de Québec, une association majoritairement anglophone organisant des soirées récréatives[11]. Le 8 octobre 1818, il était nommé trésorier du comité chargé d'élever un monument à la mémoire de la princesse Charlotte, épouse de George III[12]. Enfin, au cours de cette même année, tout en continuant à apporter sa contribution à la Société du feu de Québec, il était élu directeur de la Banque de Québec, une institution dont il avait été un des fondateurs[13].

Mais l'événement le plus important de cette époque fut sans contredit sa nomination, par le gouverneur général, au poste de shérif du district de Québec, le 9 mai 1816. Joseph-François Perrault, qui venait de fonder la Société d'éducation du district de Québec, et le capitaine Thomas Allison, son beau-père, lui facilitèrent l'accès à ce poste en lui servant de caution. Philippe Aubert de Gaspé, qui n'avait que vingt-neuf ans, dut alors cesser de pratiquer comme avocat pour se mettre au service des tribunaux et des juges. Habitué qu'il était à s'adonner à des activités comportant une certaine satisfaction sur le plan humain, il se vit ainsi contraint à vaquer durant de longues et nombreuses heures à des activités plutôt prosaïques: signification de brefs d'assignation, exécution de jugements comportant la saisie et la vente d'immeubles, transcription et enregistrement de titres et d'actes de vente, paiement des sommes prélevées dans l'exé-

---

11. *Gazette de Québec*, 12 décembre 1816.
12. *Gazette de Québec*, 8 octobre 1818. Sophie Charlotte, fille de Charles-Louis de Mecklembourg-Strelitz, épousa George III en 1761. De leur union naquirent douze enfants.
13. *Gazette de Québec*, 12 février et 18 septembre 1818.

Bureau du Secrétaire Provincial,
Québec, 14 novembre 1822.
Il a plu à son Excellence le Gouverneur-en-chef nommer
William Smith Sewell, écuyer, schérif du district de Québec,
a la place de Philippe Aubert de Gaspé, écuyer.

QUEBEC:
JEUDI, 14 NOVEMBRE 1822.

William Smith Sewell succède à Philippe Aubert de Gaspé
comme shérif (*Gazette de Québec*, 14 novembre 1822).

cution de ses fonctions, tenue de livres de comptes, recrutement de huissiers, etc. L'histoire conserve, il est vrai, le souvenir du jour où, en tant que shérif, il eut l'honneur d'annoncer en grande pompe l'avènement du roi George IV[14], mais de tels événements étaient naturellement plutôt rares.

Philippe exerça les fonctions de shérif durant six ans et demi. Le 14 novembre 1822, la veille du décès de son beau-père[15], il fut remplacé par William Smith Sewell, le fils du juge en chef Jonathan Sewell. Son départ à l'âge de trente-six ans, s'il était prévisible dans les milieux judiciaires, surprit plusieurs de ses concitoyens. La *Gazette de Québec*, qui ne publia ce jour-là qu'un communiqué de quelques lignes émanant du bureau du Secrétaire provincial, laissa la plupart de ses lecteurs perplexes. Que s'était-il passé? Les événements qui suivirent devaient, sinon répondre de façon entièrement satisfaisante à cette question, à tout le moins projeter un peu de lumière sur ce qui était en réalité une destitution pure et simple.

14. Le 24 mai 1820.
15. Le capitaine Thomas Allison mourut le 15 novembre 1822.

CHAPITRE 8

Sous la main de fer du malheur
(1822-1838)

L'année 1822 marqua pour Philippe Aubert de Gaspé le début d'une période difficile de son existence. Pendant qu'il réunissait ses effets personnels et quittait son bureau de la cour de justice de Québec, où il avait travaillé un peu plus de six ans comme shérif, son père livrait sur la scène politique son dernier combat.

La grande question à l'ordre du jour cette année-là était un projet de loi déposé sans consultation préalable à la Chambre des Communes de Londres préconisant l'union du Bas et du Haut-Canada. Bien que les Canadiens français représentaient à cette époque les trois cinquièmes de la population des deux provinces réunies, le projet leur donnait seulement quarante sièges sur cent vingt à la Chambre d'Assemblée. Bien plus, il prévoyait qu'à l'avenir les lois seraient rédigées en anglais seulement et qu'après une période de quinze ans les débats seraient eux aussi tenus uniquement en anglais. Aux yeux des marchands britanniques de Montréal, qui jouèrent un rôle de premier plan

Maquette du manoir des Aubert de Gaspé. (ANQ-Québec, coll. initiale.)

dans ce dossier, la Constitution de 1791 nuisait au commerce et rendait irréalisable l'idée de faire du Bas-Canada une province britannique.

Les opposants à ce projet furent nombreux. Il s'en trouva dans les deux provinces. La presque totalité des Canadiens français firent naturellement front commun contre lui, jugeant qu'il allait faire renaître, s'il était approuvé, les dissensions occasionnées par les différences de langue, de lois, d'institutions et d'intérêts. À Montréal comme à Québec, on organisa des assemblées de protestation au cours desquelles on forma des comités et approuva des résolutions, dont une à l'intention du gouvernement de Londres contre tout changement à la Constitution. Le comité de Québec, présidé par Louis-Antoine de Salaberry, comptait des anglophones et des francophones, parmi lesquels se trouvaient Pierre-Ignace Aubert de Gaspé, le père de Philippe, Andrew Stuart, Rémi

Four à pain du manoir seigneurial avant sa restauration par
la Corporation Philippe-Aubert-de-Gaspé. (Photo A. Toussaint.)

Vallières de Saint-Réal, John Neilson, Louis Turgeon,
Edward Bowen et quelques autres.

La tempête passée, Londres ayant décidé de faire
marche arrière, Pierre-Ignace Aubert de Gaspé s'était retiré à
son manoir de Trois-Saumons pour y passer l'hiver, fatigué
par les intrigues des marchands montréalais et déçu par
l'évolution imprévue de la carrière de son fils. Toujours
attentif aux devoirs que lui imposaient ses charges de conseiller législatif, de colonel de milice et de seigneur, il ne
laissait pas présager sa fin prochaine. Aussi, ce n'est pas sans
surprise et sans peine que les Québécois apprirent, en lisant
leur journal le 17 février 1823, que Pierre-Ignace Aubert de
Gaspé, âgé de soixante-quatre ans, était mort quatre jours
plus tôt et avait été inhumé l'avant-veille dans l'église
paroissiale de Saint-Jean-Port-Joli[1].

_____

1. *La Gazette de Québec*, 17 février 1823.

Affecté par les événements entourant sa destitution, Philippe ressentit aussi douloureusement le départ de son père. Le souvenir de ce qu'il avait fait pour le préparer à assumer d'importantes responsabilités au sein de l'administration gouvernementale ajoutait à son affliction. Ses créanciers eurent moins de difficulté à contenir leur peine, la mort du seigneur faisant miroiter à leurs yeux la possibilité d'un héritage dont ils se voyaient déjà les bénéficiaires. Astucieux, Pierre-Ignace Aubert de Gaspé avait tout prévu, y compris les difficultés financières de Philippe. Le 1er décembre 1820, devant le notaire Simon Fraser, il annula le testament qu'il avait fait en 1807 en présence du notaire Félix Têtu et ne légua à Philippe que l'usufruit des deux tiers de ses biens, l'autre tiers allant à son fils Thomas. En instituant par ailleurs les enfants de Philippe ses légataires universels, le seigneur sauva ainsi du «naufrage» ses fiefs, son manoir, ses moulins et son domaine[2].

* * *

On a cherché à expliquer de diverses façons la destitution de Philippe Aubert de Gaspé comme shérif. Les uns ont parlé de son insouciance ou de son imprévoyance, les autres de sa trop grande confiance en de faux amis ou du manque de surveillance de ses fonctionnaires. On a même cru voir une relation entre son cas et celui du receveur général John Caldwell qui, après avoir utilisé à des fins personnelles l'argent dont il était le dépositaire, se trouva incapable de payer les dépenses gouvernementales prévues pour l'année 1822. Démis de ses fonctions l'année suivante, il fut condamné en 1825 à payer une somme d'un peu plus de 96 000 livres[3]. L'auteur des *Anciens Canadiens*, désireux

---

2.   ANQ-Q, greffe du notaire Félix Têtu, 18 mars 1807, et greffe du notaire Simon Fraser, 1er décembre 1820. Philippe et son frère Thomas n'héritèrent de l'usufruit des biens de leur père qu'après la mort de leur mère, Catherine Tarieu de Lanaudière.

3.   *BRH*, vol. 2, 1896, p. 75.

d'expliquer lui-même sa disgrâce, aborde ce sujet dans le dixième chapitre de son ouvrage en donnant la parole à M. d'Egmont. On y lit entre autres les lignes qui suivent:

> J'obtins une place de haute confiance dans les bureaux. Avec mes dispositions c'était courir à ma perte. [...] Mes affaires privées étaient tellement mêlées avec celles de mon bureau que je fus assez longtemps sans m'apercevoir de leur état alarmant. Lorsque je découvris la vérité, après un examen de mes comptes, je fus frappé comme d'un coup de foudre. Non seulement j'étais ruiné, mais aussi sous le poids d'une défalcation considérable[4].

Si l'on en croit ce passage, il faut conclure que Philippe Aubert de Gaspé n'était pas doué pour l'administration. Aujourd'hui, on sait que cette autocritique était juste. L'histoire a montré qu'il avait de grands talents, mais pour autre chose que l'administration publique.

Sa destitution marqua en fait le début d'une période de dix-neuf ans d'épreuves. On peut de nos jours en établir assez facilement la genèse. Ceux qui, le 14 novembre 1822, s'interrogeaient sur la cause de son départ subit n'eurent pas à attendre bien longtemps pour trouver un début d'explication. Le 23 février suivant, deux requêtes déposées et lues à l'Assemblée législative faisaient état de sommes d'argent dues et non payées par le shérif ayant causé des pertes considérables. La Chambre décida de confier ces requêtes à un comité de cinq membres «pour en examiner le contenu et en faire rapport avec toute la diligence convenable[5]». Faisant diligence, le comité en question prit trois ans pour accomplir sa tâche! Durant ce temps filtra cependant de l'information additionnelle dans le rapport du président du Comité du Conseil exécutif pour l'audition des comptes publics, cou-

---

4. *Les Anciens Canadiens*, pp. 170 et 171.
5. *Journaux de la Chambre d'Assemblée du Bas-Canada, Depuis le 10e. Janvier jusqu'au 22e. Mars 1823*, pp. 154 et 155. La somme totale réclamée par les neuf pétitionnaires qui signaient la deuxième requête, dont la *Gazette de Québec*, s'élevait à 3556 livres, 17 shillings et 8 pence.

Joseph-François Perrault (1753-1844). Il se porta caution pour Philippe Aubert de Gaspé en 1816. (ANQ-Québec, coll. initiale.)

vrant la période allant du 11 octobre 1821 au 12 octobre 1822. William Bacheler Coltman, dont la sympathie pour le mouvement en faveur de l'union du Haut et du Bas-Canada était bien connue, y affirmait que le Bureau d'audition n'avait pu admettre le compte du shérif en raison de son «état si imparfait», ajoutant que ce dernier avait été trouvé coupable de concussion pour un montant considérable[6].

Le rapport du comité chargé d'étudier les requêtes du mois de février 1823 fut finalement déposé et lu à l'Assem-

6. *Journaux de la Chambre d'Assemblée de la province du Bas-Canada*, volume XXXIIIe, Quatrième session du onzième parlement provincial, Appendice O.

blée législative le 17 mars 1826. Il recommandait «qu'il soit voté par la Chambre une Humble Adresse à Son Excellence le Gouverneur en Chef, le priant de bien vouloir ordonner aux Officiers en Loi de la Couronne de procéder, ainsi qu'il appartiendra en droit et en justice, contre le dit Philippe Aubert de Gaspé et ses Cautions, afin que les deniers qu'il doit comme Shérif puissent être assurés pour répondre aux Demandes légitimes de tous ceux qui en ont[7]». Cette recommandation présentée au gouverneur le 22 mars fut acceptée par lui le jour même.

Il fallut cependant attendre jusqu'en 1830 pour voir l'antipathique procureur général James Stuart engager une poursuite dans cette affaire contre une des cautions du shérif, Joseph-François Perrault, un personnage très en vue à l'époque en raison de ses réalisations dans le monde de l'éducation, des affaires et de la politique. À la demande de l'Assemblée législative, Stuart, un adversaire farouche du Parti patriote, fut démis de ses fonctions l'année suivante. Comme il se devait, les procédures furent longues. Commencées le 1er février 1830, elles se prolongèrent jusqu'au 20 juin 1834, date à laquelle Perrault fut condamné à payer à la Couronne 1169 livres et 14 shillings.

Quelques mois plus tard, le 1er octobre, Joseph-François Perrault déposait, tel que convenu s'il était trouvé coupable, une demande en garantie contre Philippe Aubert de Gaspé et son épouse, dont le père, Thomas Allison, avait bien voulu se porter caution pour son gendre au moment de sa nomination comme shérif. Le 16 octobre 1834, Susanne Allison était condamnée à payer 937 livres, 7 shillings et un penny[8], et l'ex-shérif, 1974 livres et 4 shillings, soit 7896,80 dollars, plus les

---

7. *Journaux de la Chambre d'Assemblée du Bas-Canada, Depuis le 21e Janvier jusqu'au 29e. Mars 1826*, p. 292. Il fut question de cette affaire en Chambre à cinq reprises en 1826: les 31 janvier, 4 février, 17, 21 et 23 mars.

8. Susanne Allison, sans être riche, n'était pas démunie. Sa mère, qui avait hérité des biens du capitaine Allison le 15 novembre 1822, lui a légué tout son avoir le 27 mars 1839.

intérêts sur la somme de 1169 livres et 14 shillings que Jean-François Perrault devait verser pour lui à la Couronne. Ces montants représentaient une somme d'argent très importante au début du XIXe siècle.

* * *

Abandonné de ses «faux amis» et menacé par de vrais ennemis, Philippe trouva refuge à Saint-Jean-Port-Joli à la fin de l'année 1823 ou au début de l'année suivante[9]. Représenté à Québec par son gendre William Power, auquel il avait confié la défense de ses intérêts, il tenta de retrouver la paix et la sérénité perdues dans le décor pastoral du manoir où il avait passé son enfance. On a raconté qu'il «avait creusé le sol sous la partie est de sa demeure et qu'il s'y terrait» tant il redoutait l'arrivée de visiteurs importuns[10]. Son père étant décédé, il était le seul homme, outre les domestiques, à habiter le manoir seigneurial à cette époque. En revanche, on y trouvait plusieurs femmes: d'abord sa mère qui, à titre d'usufruitière, gérait les fiefs de Port-Joly et de la Demi-lieue, puis son épouse Susanne, sa tante Marie-Louise et aussi, après le décès du capitaine Allison, sa belle-mère Thérèse Baby. On y trouvait aussi, du moins au début, les sept enfants que Philippe et son épouse avaient avec eux au moment de quitter la rue Saint-Louis: Suzanne, Philippe-Ignace, Adélaïde, Elmire, Zélie, Thomas et Édouard.

Vivant dans une constante inquiétude, sachant que ses «amis» n'allaient rien faire pour lui, même s'il n'était pas impossible qu'on en vienne à l'emprisonner, Philippe trouva dans son tempérament naturellement bon et confiant les ressources nécessaires à sa survie. Entouré de ses enfants qui inconsciemment lui procuraient des distractions, il les

---

9.   Dans ses *Mémoires*, de Gaspé écrit qu'il est arrivé à Saint-Jean à l'âge de trente-sept ans et qu'il y demeura alors quatorze ans. Si on prend à la lettre ces données, on peut dater son arrivée au manoir à la fin de 1823 ou au début de 1824, puisqu'il naquit le 30 octobre 1786 et fut incarcéré le 29 mai 1838.
10.   Gérard Ouellet, *Ma Paroisse, Saint-Jean Port-Joly*, Québec, Les éditions des piliers, 1946, p. 81.

Suzanne Aubert de Gaspé
(1812-1882). (Coll. privée.)

William Power.
(Coll. privée.)

accompagnait dans leurs promenades à la rivière Port-Joly
ou au moulin banal de Trois-Saumons. Il lui arrivait aussi de
s'intéresser aux travaux des champs et du potager. Et,
lorsque les jours devenaient trop sombres, il allait trouver
son vieux compagnon, Romain Chouinard, qui, par ses con-
tes, réussissait à le dérider. Marchant en sa compagnie à travers les champs, les bois et les montagnes, il gagnait le lac
Trois-Saumons où la pêche et la chasse l'aidaient à oublier les
événements pénibles qui, à Québec, préoccupaient les hommes de loi. Il lui arrivait également de faire des excursions à
la batture aux loups marins et à la Roche-à-Veillon, où le
gibier et les légendes parvenaient aussi à lui procurer
d'agréables heures de répit.

Le soir venu, toute la maisonnée était réunie pour le
souper. Compte tenu des circonstances, le repas était plutôt
simple et frugal. On acceptait volontiers de remettre à un
lendemain qui paraissait éloigné les entrées délicates, les
mets recherchés et les vins fins qui, à l'époque du seigneur

Adélaïde Aubert de Gaspé (1815-1895). (F. Daniel, *Histoire des grandes familles françaises du Canada.*)

George-René Saveuse de Beaujeu, seigneur et conseiller législatif. (Coll. privée.)

Pierre-Ignace, se trouvaient occasionnellement sur la table. Quelques fêtes et deux mariages vinrent, il est vrai, briser la monotonie qui semblait parfois vouloir s'installer. Le mariage de Suzanne, l'aînée des filles, à William Power, le 15 décembre 1829, fut célébré malgré tout dans la joie. Le 20 septembre 1832, ce fut autour d'Adélaïde de se marier. Elle unit sa vie à une célébrité de la région de Montréal, Georges René Saveuse, comte de Beaujeu, seigneur de Soulanges, de la Nouvelle-Longueuil et d'autres lieux.

Les naissances qui, dans plusieurs familles, n'étaient pas nécessairement des occasions de réjouissance, en raison du nombre élevé de décès en très bas âge, furent invariablement heureuses dans la famille de Philippe. Pendant que les plus âgés des enfants quittaient le foyer, chacun son tour, d'autres aussi nombreux venaient prendre leur place. Zoé (1825), Azéline (1827), Atala (1829), Alfred-Patrice (1831), Anaïs (1834) et Philomène (1837) virent tous le jour à Saint-Jean-

Port-Joli durant cette période de réclusion de leur père. Il se trouvait rarement au manoir à cette époque moins d'une vingtaine de personnes, les domestiques compris.

Les études au Séminaire de Québec et chez le révérend John Jackson avaient préparé Philippe à vivre au milieu de sa famille, loin de la ville. La lecture contribua elle aussi à l'empêcher de sombrer dans une irrémédiable mélancolie. En été, lorsque la température le permettait, il passait de longues heures à lire le long du fleuve ou dans le jardin faisant face au manoir. Au nombre de ses auteurs préférés figuraient Walter Scott, Victor Hugo, Charles Nodier, Eugène Sue, Honoré de Balzac, La Mennais et Edward Bulwer. L'hiver venu, cette activité occupait presque tout son temps. À la tombée de la nuit, une fois les enfants couchés, il acceptait bien de jouer un peu aux cartes, mais il se replongeait bientôt dans ses livres pendant que les dames assises sur les fauteuils ou les canapés du salon recommençaient à coudre ou à raccommoder le linge qu'elles destinaient aux pauvres de la paroisse[11].

Philippe, qui s'était initié à la traduction à l'école de John Jackson et qui avait exercé cette profession lorsqu'il était secrétaire et traducteur de la province du Bas-Canada, profita aussi, croit-on, du temps dont il disposait alors pour traduire les œuvres de Walter Scott[12]. L'arrivée impromptue de son fils Philippe, au cours du mois de février 1836, modifia quelque peu, semble-t-il, la routine de l'ex-shérif. Correspondant parlementaire de deux journaux de Québec, le jeune de Gaspé, dont la Chambre n'appréciait pas le comportement, avait dû fuir la ville avec Napoléon Aubin pour éviter d'être emprisonné une seconde fois. Renonçant à sa carrière de journaliste, du moins temporairement, il conçut alors le projet d'un roman s'inspirant «des faits et des personnages observés à Saint-Jean-Port-Joli». Écrit par Aubert de Gaspé fils, mais non sans l'aide d'Aubert de Gaspé père, il parut au

---

11. H.-R. Casgrain, *Philippe Aubert de Gaspé*, Québec, 1871, p. 57.
12. *Ibid.*, p. 17.

mois de septembre 1837. Intitulé *L'Influence d'un livre*, il fut accueilli plutôt froidement par la critique et devint rapidement l'objet d'une polémique. Néanmoins, en raison de son intérêt sociologique et littéraire, il connut de nombreuses éditions et rééditions. Il peut être considéré comme le premier roman canadien.

* * *

Condamné à payer 1974 livres et 4 shillings au mois d'octobre 1834, Philippe Aubert de Gaspé, qui ne gagnait que 100 livres par an, se vit dans l'impossibilité de se libérer de cette obligation. La maison de la rue Saint-Louis avait été vendue dès le 5 septembre 1816[13], même s'il continua à l'habiter par la suite, de même que, depuis le 15 décembre 1823, la Maison des Bains qu'il possédait sur la rue Saint-Paul[14]. Quant aux terrains du faubourg Saint-Jean dont il avait fait l'acquisition des Ursulines en 1815, ils avaient été cédés à Louis Plamondon le 18 janvier 1817, en échange d'un terrain situé sur la rue Saint-Louis et d'une somme de deux cents livres[15].

Durant ce temps, on commençait cependant à s'impatienter à Québec. À l'instigation de Joseph-François Perrault, le shérif William Smith Sewell fit saisir et mettre en vente, au mois de décembre 1834, la moitié de la seigneurie de Saint-Jean-Port-Joli et du domaine seigneurial, de même que la moitié du moulin banal et des dépendances[16]. Cette décision, de Sewell, qui avait négligé de prendre connaissance des documents juridiques relatifs à ces immeubles, stupéfia les Aubert de Gaspé, tout particulièrement les enfants de Philippe qui en avaient hérité en 1823. Utilisant les services de William Power et de son associé, Félix Fortier, tous s'oppo-

---

13. ANQ-Q, greffe du notaire Joseph Planté, n° 7083, 5 septembre 1816.
14. Rénald Lessard, «Les premiers bains publics de Québec 1817-1823», dans *Cap-aux-Diamants*, vol. 1, n° 2 (été 1985), p. 44.
15. ANQ-Q, greffe du notaire Joseph Planté, n° 7187, 18 janvier 1817.
16. ANQ-Q, T11-301, n° 940.

sèrent à cette vente, et gagnèrent leur cause, y compris Catherine Tarieu de Lanaudière qui détenait l'usufruit de ces biens sa vie durant. Il en fut de même de Louise Giasson, la veuve de Thomas Aubert de Gaspé, et d'Ann Thompson, la veuve de Robert Harrower, qui avaient également des droits sur ces immeubles[17].

Malgré ses réussites en affaires et son exceptionnelle contribution à «l'éducation du peuple canadien», Joseph-François Perrault connut d'importants revers de fortune à la fin de sa vie. Dans une lettre du 8 février 1839, il expliquait à ses «chers grands et petits-enfants» que sa ruine résultait, du moins partiellement, des difficultés financières de l'ex-shérif et du dernier testament de son père, Pierre-Ignace Aubert de Gaspé. «Pour tranquilliser vos angoisses et rétablir l'ordre et la confiance qui doivent régner dans la famille», écrivait Perrault, «je vous donne ici un précis des causes qui ont amené la saisie-exécution de mes biens meubles et immeubles. Le jugement que le gouvernement a obtenu contre M. de Gaspé, ci-devant shérif de ce district, et contre moi, sa caution, a été le commencement de ma ruine [...]. Le manque de la tenue de la cour d'appel pour juger de la validité ou l'invalidité du testament de M. de Gaspé, père, qui, voyant le délabrement des affaires de son fils, l'a en quelque sorte déshérité en faisant une substitution en faveur de ses petits enfants, privant les créanciers de ce dernier de leurs biens nobles de ce dernier, a couronné l'œuvre pour le moment et m'a mis hors d'état de payer mes créanciers[18]». Il est vrai que Pierre-Ignace Aubert de Gaspé fit une substitution dans son testament rédigé un peu plus de deux ans avant sa mort et qu'il légua alors ses biens à ses petits-enfants, laissant la jouissance de ceux-ci à son épouse, puis à ses deux fils. Il est toutefois inexact d'affirmer que le sei-

---

17. *Ibid.*
18. Lettre citée par P.-B. Casgrain, dans *La vie de Joseph-François Perrault surnommé le père de l'éducation du peuple canadien*, Québec, C. Darveau, 1898, pp. 158 et 159. Casgrain a préféré écrire «M. de G....» et non «M. de Gaspé».

gneur de Gaspé déshérita alors son fils Philippe. Dans son premier testament (1807), M. de Gaspé léguait tous ses biens sans exception à son épouse, Catherine Tarieu de Lanaudière, et non à ses enfants.

Pressé de verser une somme d'argent qu'il ne possédait pas, Philippe Aubert de Gaspé tenta, le 28 mai 1836, de se prévaloir des dispositions de la loi relative aux débiteurs insolvables (loi 6 Guillaume IV, ch. 4) et offrit de céder tous ses biens à la Couronne. Ce qu'accepta le tribunal de première instance, mais que rejeta cinq mois plus tard la Cour d'appel, alléguant que ces dispositions ne s'appliquaient pas aux débiteurs de la Couronne. Sans recours, l'ex-shérif n'avait plus qu'à attendre l'ordre de son incarcération, situation qui lui parut intolérable, rappelle le texte des *Anciens Canadiens*:

> Peut-on imaginer un supplice plus cruel que celui infligé à un homme, entouré d'une nombreuse famille, qui la voit pendant dix-huit mois, trembler au moindre bruit qu'elle entend, frémir à la vue de tout étranger qu'elle croit toujours porteur de l'ordre d'incarcération contre ce qu'elle a de plus cher! Ce qui m'étonne c'est que nous n'ayons pas succombé sous cette masse d'atroces souffrances[19]!

Ce martyre prit fin le 29 mai 1838, date à laquelle Philippe Aubert de Gaspé, résigné, franchissait l'enceinte de la prison de Québec avec William Smith Sewell qui avait procédé à son arrestation. Dans le registre des détenus de cette prison, on peut lire, inscrit à la suite de son nom, qu'il avait été incarcéré en raison d'une somme de 1714 livres, 7 shillings et 7 pence due à la Reine[20]. Durant ce temps, John Caldwell, trouvé coupable d'une défalcation beaucoup plus importante que celle de Philippe Aubert de Gaspé et démis de ses fonctions de receveur général à la même époque que

---

19. *Les Anciens Canadiens*, p. 177.
20. *Register of Prisoners Committed to the Common goal of the City and District of Quebec*, p. 12.

l'ex-shérif, n'était pas incommodé dans ses mouvements et demeurait membre du Conseil législatif. En 1840, deux ans avant sa mort, ce dernier devait encore à la Reine quelque 78 675 livres[21]. Philippe Aubert de Gaspé s'est plaint de l'ingratitude de ses amis dans ces circonstances. On imagine bien que ce ne fut pas le cas de l'ex-receveur général.

---

21. *DBC*, vol. VII, p. 148.

CHAPITRE 9

Séparé de sa famille
par la largeur d'une rue
(1838-1841)

L'année 1838 fut marquée par la seconde rébellion des patriotes, celle qui eut lieu au nord-ouest de Montréal, et aussi par des représailles consécutives aux événements de l'année précédente, en particulier les combats de Saint-Denis, de Saint-Charles et de Saint-Eustache. Tandis qu'à Londres on suspendait la constitution du Bas-Canada, au pays, on continuait les recherches et les poursuites entreprises l'année précédente pour neutraliser ceux qu'on croyait être les responsables de ces soulèvements. Si la rébellion armée eut lieu dans la région de Montréal seulement, le mouvement amorcé à la Chambre d'Assemblée s'étendit aussi à la région de Québec. Ainsi en fut-il des représailles et de la chasse aux présumés responsables.

Le chef de police de Québec, Thomas Ainslie Young, «réprimandé par le gouvernement pour avoir détourné des fonds lorsqu'il était shérif[1]», et son assistant Robert Symes,

---

1. *DBC*, vol. VIII, p. 1071.

rivalisant de zèle et croyant voir des «menées séditieuses» ou des «pratiques traîtresses» non seulement dans la ville et ses environs mais loin à l'extérieur, procédaient à de nombreuses arrestations. Saint-Michel-de-Bellechasse, Saint-Joseph-de-Beauce, Sainte-Marguerite-de-Beauce, La Malbaie, Saint-Thomas (Montmagny), Sainte-Anne-de-la-Pocatière étaient autant de paroisses figurant sur la liste noire des policiers. Incarcéré le 29 mai 1838, le jour même où lord Durham, nommé gouverneur général, mit pied à terre à Québec, Philippe Aubert de Gaspé n'eut donc pas que des brigands, des déserteurs et des misérables comme compagnons de geôle, mais aussi des prisonniers politiques, dont plusieurs ne lui étaient pas étrangers. Le docteur Édouard Rousseau, Augustin-Norbert Morin, Adolphe Jacquies, Étienne Parent, Jean-Baptiste Fréchette, Barthélémi Lachance, Louis-Pierre Chasseur et John Teed se retrouvèrent tous emprisonnés à Québec durant l'incarcération de l'ex-shérif. On ne saurait oublier ici Napoléon Aubin, détenu durant cinquante-trois jours, au début de 1839, pour avoir publié dans *Le Fantasque* un poème de Guillaume Barthe dédié aux prisonniers politiques déportés aux Bermudes. On se souviendra ici que l'auteur des *Anciens Canadiens* l'avait accueilli à Saint-Jean-Port-Joli, en compagnie de son fils Philippe, au mois de février 1836[2].

* * *

Philippe Aubert de Gaspé ne se plaignit guère de sa détention du point de vue physique[3]. Ce qui ne signifie pas qu'elle fut facile. Il est vrai que la prison de Québec où il fut détenu avait de la classe. Construite entre 1810 et 1814, d'après un plan de l'architecte François Baillairgé, sur le site d'un ancien fort érigé par Frontenac au XVIIe siècle, elle figurait parmi les édifices les plus intéressants de Québec.

---

2.   Napoléon Aubin fut aussi incarcéré brièvement en compagnie de Philippe Aubert de Gaspé fils les 23 et 25 février 1838.
3.   Il en est question dans une requête adressée au gouvernement en 1841.

Ancienne prison de Québec, située sur la rue Saint-Stanislas, où fut incarcéré Philippe Aubert de Gaspé. (ANQ-Québec, coll. initiale.)

Ayant servi de collège après l'ouverture de la prison des plaines d'Abraham en 1867, cet immeuble est aujourd'hui connu sous le nom de Morrin College et abrite depuis de nombreuses années la bibliothèque de la Literary and Historical Society of Quebec. Situé sur la rue Saint-Stanislas, entre les rues Sainte-Anne, Sainte-Angèle et Dauphine, il est fait de maçonnerie de pierre et ressemble aux gros édifices administratifs britanniques construits à l'époque en Amérique du Nord. Flanqué de deux ailes, le corps principal du bâtiment est orné de pilastres surmontés d'un imposant fronton et d'une entrée de style classique au-dessus de laquelle se trouvait au siècle dernier un balcon où l'on pendait les condamnés à mort.

L'intérieur était naturellement plus sévère. Trois de ses quatre étages comptaient des cellules regroupées symé-

Cellules de l'ancienne prison de Québec. État actuel. (Coll. de l'auteur.)

triquement en plusieurs endroits autour d'une petite salle commune, question de favoriser la réhabilitation. On a raconté qu'à l'exception des prisonniers politiques qui disposaient de cellules généralement bien éclairées les détenus vivaient pour la plupart dans des cellules obscures, entassés les uns contre les autres, couchaient plus souvent sur le plancher que sur la paille et se partageaient des latrines qui n'étaient rien de plus que des trous creusés dans la terre à l'extrémité d'un étroit passage. On a aussi parlé de prisonniers bien portants à leur arrivée rue Saint-Stanislas et qui, après y avoir vécu dans des conditions malsaines, en ressortirent d'une maigreur squelettique. Deux lettres de Thomas Ainslie Young, l'une du 11 juin 1839, l'autre du 18 juin suivant, font d'ailleurs état d'une congestion à la prison de Québec qui, à ses yeux, justifiait, du moins temporairement, l'ouverture d'un deuxième établissement. Enfin, l'inscription macabre qui se trouvait à cette époque à l'entrée de l'édifice rappelait à ceux qui connaissaient le latin que la prison de Québec au XIXᵉ siècle n'était pas, malgré son apparence, un hôtel de luxe. On l'a traduite de la façon suivante: L'an du seigneur 1810, dans la cinquantième année du règne de George III, le puissant seigneur James Henry Craig, chevalier du Bain, étant gouverneur de la Province. Puisse cette prison venger les bons de la perversité des méchants[4].

* * *

Par la voix d'un personnage de son roman, M. d'Egmont, Philippe Aubert de Gaspé a raconté dans les *Anciens Canadiens* les tortures psychologiques qu'il a endurées pendant son emprisonnement. Sa famille nombreuse ne pouvant demeurer seule à Saint-Jean-Port-Joli, il fallut fermer le manoir seigneurial et trouver un logement à Québec. À compter de 1838, la mère de Philippe, son épouse, sa belle-mère, une de ses tantes et au moins neuf de ses

---

4.   Pierre-Georges Roy, *À travers les Anciens Canadiens de Philippe Aubert de Gaspé*, Montréal, G. Ducharme, 1943, p. 80.

La rue Sainte-Angèle où vécut la famille de Philippe Aubert
de Gaspé durant son emprisonnement. (Coll. de l'auteur.)

enfants demeurèrent à proximité de la prison sur la rue
Sainte-Angèle[5]. Le fait de se savoir séparé de sa famille par
la largeur d'une rue aurait pu être avantageux, mais ce ne fut
pas le cas, comme le raconte l'auteur des *Anciens Canadiens*:

> Le prisonnier éprouve un singulier besoin pendant le premier
> mois de sa captivité: c'est une inquiétude fébrile, c'est un
> besoin de locomotion continue! Il se lève souvent pendant ses
> repas, pendant la nuit même pour y satisfaire: c'est le lion

5.   C'est ce qu'atteste le testament de madame Allison, née Thérèse Baby,
signé le 24 mars 1839 en présence du notaire L. Panet. George Gale, dans
Historic Tales of Old Quebec, publié en 1923, p. 25, affirme pour sa part que
l'auteur des *Anciens Canadiens* vécut un certain temps au numéro 1813 de la
rue Sainte-Angèle, au coin de la rue Dauphine. Quant à Luc Lacourcière, à
partir d'une lettre datée du 6 avril 1842 annonçant le décès de Marie-Louise
Tarieu de Lanaudière, il affirme que la famille de Gaspé vécut au numéro 20
de la rue Sainte-Anne, durant l'emprisonnement de l'ex-shérif. Il est vrai que
sa famille vécut à cette adresse, comme l'affirme Lacourcière, mais vraisemblablement uniquement après sa libération en 1841.

Élizabeth-Zélie Aubert de Gaspé (1818-1893). (Coll. privée.)

Philippe-Ignace-François Aubert de Gaspé (1814-1841).
(F. Daniel, *Histoire des grandes familles françaises du Canada.*)

dans sa cage. [...] Je comptais sans la main de Dieu appesantie sur l'insensé, architecte de son propre malheur! Deux de mes enfants tombèrent si dangereusement malades, à deux époques différentes, que les médecins désespérant de leur vie, m'annonçaient chaque jour leur fin prochaine. C'est alors, ô mon fils! que je ressentis toute la douleur de mes chaînes. C'est alors que je pus m'écrier comme la mère du Christ: «approchez et voyez s'il est douleur comparable à la mienne!» Je savais mes enfants moribonds, et je n'en étais séparé que par la largeur d'une rue. Je voyais, pendant de longues nuits sans sommeil, le mouvement qui se faisait auprès de leur couche, les lumières errer d'une chambre à l'autre; je tremblais à chaque instant de voir disparaître ces signes de vitalité, qui m'annonçaient que mes enfants requéraient encore les soins de l'amour maternel. J'ai honte de l'avouer, mon fils, mais j'étais souvent en proie à un tel désespoir que je fus cent fois tenté de me briser la tête contre les barreaux de ma chambre[6].

Deux événements, l'un normalement joyeux, l'autre toujours triste, eurent lieu durant l'emprisonnement de Philippe Aubert de Gaspé. Sa fille Zélie, née en 1818, épousa à Québec, le 28 octobre 1840, Louis-Eusèbe Borne, résidant aux Îles-de-la-Madeleine. M. Borne mourut cependant peu après, laissant une fille qui devint en 1864 l'épouse de l'honorable T.-J.-J. Loranger, juge de la Cour supérieure. L'événement triste, l'ex-shérif l'apprit en ouvrant dans sa cellule une lettre datée du 9 mars 1841 et signée par un de ses anciens camarades de classe demeurant à Halifax, Thomas Pyke. Après avoir écrit qu'il avait rencontré son fils Philippe, sans le sou, et qu'il lui avait trouvé de l'emploi comme professeur, Pyke ajoutait que ce dernier avait par la suite obtenu du travail dans un des journaux de la ville et que tout laissait croire qu'il deviendrait un motif de consolation pour ses parents lorsque la Providence en décida autrement: «après une

---

6. *Les Anciens Canadiens*, p. 178. De l'arrière de la prison, où se trouvaient plusieurs cellules, on pouvait voir très bien à l'époque les maisons de la rue Sainte-Angèle.

courte maladie de vingt-quatre heures, il fut délivré des peines de ce monde dimanche soir, le 7 mars[7].»

Cette lettre de sympathie fut bientôt suivie par une autre qui rappela à Philippe Aubert de Gaspé la cruauté de ses créanciers. Le propriétaire de la maison où avait habité son fils, à Halifax, lui demandait de lui faire parvenir quatre louis pour acquitter une dette que le jeune journaliste avait contractée à son endroit, sans quoi il lui faudrait conserver ses effets personnels et les vendre éventuellement à l'encan[8].

* * *

Comment Philippe occupa-t-il son temps en prison? Il n'a pas répondu à cette question. On peut imaginer cependant qu'il passa beaucoup de temps à réfléchir, à lire, à écrire et peut-être à élaborer des plans pour le jour où il recouvrerait la liberté. Un document inachevé qu'a pu consulter l'auteur du présent ouvrage indique qu'il songea sans doute plus d'une fois à demander aux autorités sa libération. Susanne Allison, son épouse, le fit pour lui dès le 24 juin 1838, adressant une lettre pleine d'émotion à lord Durham qui venait d'arriver à Québec. L'année suivante, le gouvernement se montra favorable à sa libération s'il pouvait «donner caution qu'il paierait la somme de 1170 livres, sans intérêt[9]». Ce qu'il ne put faire. Deux ans s'écoulèrent avant que d'autres démarches soient faites. Le 16 juillet 1841, une requête en bonne et due forme préparée par lui était déposée devant le Parlement[10]. L'Assemblée en ayant confié l'étude à un comité présidé par le procureur général Ogden, un rapport très favorable à l'ex-shérif émana de ce

---

7.   Lettre rédigée en anglais citée par Luc Lacourcière, «Aubert de Gaspé, fils (1814-1841)», *Cahier des Dix*, vol. 40, 1975, pp. 301 et 302.
8.   Archives privées.
9.   *Journaux de l'Assemblée législative de la Province du Canada du 14ᵉ Juin au 18ᵉ Septembre*, 1841, p. 310. Pour la lettre de S. Allison voir ANC, RG4 b20, vol. 25, pp. 9215-9224.
10.   *Journaux de l'Assemblée législative de la Province du Canada*, 1841, vol. 1, p. 214. La pétition a aussi été déposée au Conseil législatif.

Chambre du Comité, Assemblée }
Législative, 3e Aout, 1841. }

M. *Christie*, du Comité Spécial auquel a été référée la Pétition de *Philippe Aubert De Gaspé*, ci-devant Shérif du District de *Québec*, avec pouvoir de faire rapport par Bill ou autrement, a présenté à la Chambre le Rapport du dit Comité, lequel a été lu de nouveau à la table du Greffier, comme suit :

Il appert, d'après les papiers qui ont été soumis de la part du Pétitionnaire, qu'il est incarcéré depuis le mois de Mai 1838, conformément à un jugement rendu contre lui le 20 Juin, en faveur de la Couronne, pour la somme de £1169 14 courant.

Il paraît à votre Comité que M. *De Gaspé* a donné à la Cour du Banc du Roi à *Québec*, en Mai 1836, un État de toutes les propriétés mobilières et immobilières qu'il possédait alors, ou qu'il s'attendait devoir posséder par la suite, afin de se prévaloir des limites accordées aux autres Débiteurs insolvables, d'après les dispositions de l'Acte Provincial du *Bas-Canada*, de la 6e *Guill*.4, chap. 4, et dont un jugement de la Cour du Banc du Roi de *Québec* avait déclaré qu'il avait droit de se prévaloir.

Ce jugement a néanmoins été renversé par la Cour d'Appel, dans le mois de Novembre 1836, la Cour ayant décidé que ce Statut ne devait pas s'étendre aux Débiteurs de la Couronne.

Sans vouloir mettre en question la justesse de cette décision de la Cour d'Appel, votre Comité regarde la position de M. *De Gaspé* comme très cruelle. L'abandon de tous ses biens, présens et à venir, l'aurait soustrait à l'emprisonnement, s'il eut dû à tout autre qu'à la Couronne. La prérogative de la Couronne, dans le cas actuel, ne peut être révoquée en doute,—néanmoins, il paraît à votre Comité, que l'exécution rigide de la Loi, qui retient M. *De Gaspé* emprisonné depuis plus de trois ans, sans avantage pour la créance publique, et sans même aucune perspective d'avantage, devrait avoir un terme, surtout, puisqu'il paraît que la santé de M. *De Gaspé* souffre matériellement de son long emprisonnement. Votre Comité a devant lui la preuve, par une Lettre de M. le Secrétaire Civil *Goldie*, datée à *Montréal*, le 15 Août 1839, de la position favorable ou est le Gouvernement de décharger M. *De Gaspé*, en donnant caution qu'il paierait £1170, sans intérêt ; ce que M. *De Gaspé* n'a pu faire ; et votre Comité ose exprimer l'espoir que le Gouvernement est encore dans les mêmes dispositions. Il est persuadé qu'il n'entre pas dans les vues de l'Exécutif de donner à la Loi un effet cruel et oppressif, ou même la semblance de l'oppression ; et que le Gouvernement voudra bien concourir dans toute mesure que les deux autres branches pourront passer pour terminer l'emprisonnement de ce Monsieur.

;;Dans cette persuasion, et considérant le long emprisonnement de M. *De Gaspé*, son âge avancé, et le mauvais état de sa santé par suite de son long emprisonnement ; et considérant aussi, qu'il a donné en Cour, et sous serment, un État fidèle par écrit de tous les Biens et Propriétés qu'il possédait au monde, dans la vue de se libérer de ses Dettes, votre Comité recommande qu'il soit passé un Acte pour le soulagement de ce Monsieur, et il présente en conséquence un Bill à cet effet.

M. *Christie* a alors présenté à la Chambre un Bill pour le soulagement de *Philippe Aubert De Gaspé*, lequel a été reçu, et lu pour la première fois.

Ordonné, Que le dit Bill soit lu une seconde fois Jeudi prochain.

groupe restreint. Lu à l'Assemblée par le député Robert Christie, qui connaissait ses finances pour lui avoir vendu la Maison des Bains et l'avoir rachetée pour un de ses clients, ce rapport prenait soin de ne pas condamner explicitement ceux qui s'étaient déjà penchés sur ce dossier, mais il n'hésitait pas pour autant à rappeler que la Cour du banc du roi avait déclaré en 1836 que le signataire avait le droit de se prévaloir des limites accordées aux débiteurs insolvables et que «la position de M. de Gaspé leur paraissait très cruelle». Ajoutant «qu'il n'était pas dans les vues de l'Exécutif de donner à la loi un effet cruel et oppressif, ou même une semblance de l'oppression», il terminait ainsi:

> Considérant le long emprisonnement de M. De Gaspé, son âge avancé et le mauvais état de sa santé par suite de son long emprisonnement; et considérant aussi qu'il a donné en Cour, et sous serment, un État fidèle par écrit de tous les Biens et Propriétés qu'il possédait au monde, dans la vue de se libérer de ses Dettes, votre Comité recommande qu'il soit passé un Acte pour le soulagement de ce Monsieur et il présente en conséquence un Bill à cet effet.

Approuvé en première lecture le jour de sa présentation, le projet de loi en question fut lu une deuxième fois trois jours plus tard et adopté sans amendement le 10 août 1841. Enfin, le Conseil législatif ayant donné son accord, il reçut la sanction royale le 18 de ce mois[11].

Philippe Aubert de Gaspé ne fut pas libéré pour autant à cette date. Il lui fallut patienter encore quarante-cinq jours. La Cour du banc du roi, qui s'était pourtant montrée libérale à son endroit en 1836, exigea non seulement qu'il demeure à l'intérieur des limites du district de Québec, ce qui était conforme à la loi autorisant son élargissement, mais aussi qu'il verse un cautionnement de 7000 livres ou de 28 000

---

11. *Statuts du Canada*, 1841-42,-43; pp. 383-385; *Journaux de l'Assemblée législative de la Province du Canada du 14ᵉ Juin au 18ᵉ Septembre 1841*: première lecture (3 août), p. 310; deuxième lecture (6 août), p. 344; adoption (9 août), pp. 352 et 353; Conseil législatif (18 août), p. 416; sanction royale (18 août), p. 724.

dollars. Pour l'ex-shérif, qui avait été incapable de rembourser un peu moins de 2000 livres à la Couronne avant son emprisonnement et qui n'avait plus d'amis, il s'agissait là d'une somme considérable. Elle fut quand même réunie et déposée le 2 octobre par un marchand de Québec, Julien Chouinard, et par William Power qui, depuis 1829, n'avait rien épargné pour aider son beau-père[12]. Le registre de la prison de Québec indique qu'il fut finalement libéré le même jour, sur un ordre du shérif, c'est-à-dire trois ans, quatre mois et quatre jours après le début de son emprisonnement. Âgé de trente-six ans lorsqu'il fut écarté de l'administration, il en avait cinquante-cinq le jour où il put de nouveau circuler librement dans la ville qui avait fait la joie de son adolescence.

---

12. Tel que convenu avant le dépôt de ce cautionnement, Catherine Tarieu de Lanaudière et sa sœur Marie-Louise se portèrent par la suite caution «pour Philippe Aubert de Gaspé pour la somme de sept mille livres envers Julien Chouinard» et hypothéquèrent à cette fin tous leurs biens meubles et immeubles (document signé en présence du notaire R. Lelièvre, le 5 octobre 1841). Ce Julien Chouinard était vraisemblablement originaire de Saint-Jean-Port-Joli.

Seigneur de Saint-Jean-Port-Joli
et autres lieux

(1842-1854)

Traité de façon oppressive par les tribunaux mais avec compréhension par le Parlement du Bas-Canada, Philippe Aubert de Gaspé retrouva les siens au début du mois d'octobre 1841. Le temps n'ayant pas arrêté sa marche, sa famille n'était plus tout à fait celle dont il avait été séparé au mois de mai 1838. Son fils aîné était décédé dans les circonstances pénibles évoquées précédemment. Thomas, qui se destinait à la prêtrise, poursuivait ses études à l'extérieur. Zélie, mariée depuis peu, avait trouvé refuge aux Îles de la Madeleine. Adélaïde, qui dès 1832 avait uni sa destinée à celle du comte de Beaujeu, ne vivait plus que pour Montréal et Côteau-du-Lac. Thérèse Baby, sa belle-mère, avait rejoint son mari dans la mort. Suzanne, devenue madame Power, n'avait guère changé il est vrai. En compagnie de son mari toujours prévenant, elle continuait à s'intéresser à son père, ainsi qu'à ses huit frères et sœurs encore au foyer.

L'abbé Thomas Aubert de Gaspé. (Coll. privée.)

Deux événements rapprochés dans le temps vinrent modifier rapidement l'existence incertaine à laquelle semblait devoir faire face le père de cette famille nombreuse. Au mois d'avril 1842, la mort frappa à deux reprises au numéro 20 de la rue Sainte-Anne où les de Gaspé demeuraient depuis leur départ de la rue Sainte-Angèle. Marie-Louise de Lanaudière, qui ne s'était jamais séparée de sa sœur Catherine, mourut le 4 avril. Neuf jours plus tard, madame de Gaspé, âgée de soixante-quinze ans, s'éteignait à son tour. Philippe ne pleura pas ces jours-là que la mort d'une tante et d'une mère, mais aussi des deux personnes qui en dernier ressort avaient rendu possible sa récente mise en liberté. Par un curieux concours de circonstances, ces décès successifs allaient contribuer toutefois à lui redonner un statut respectable au sein de la société québécoise. On se souviendra que son père lui avait légué à sa mort, en 1823, l'usufruit des deux tiers de tous ses biens meubles et immeubles, ainsi que la jouissance du manoir seigneurial, du domaine et des moulins à eau, le tout à commencer seulement après le décès de sa mère. C'est ainsi que le 14 avril 1842, Philippe Aubert de Gaspé devint seigneur usufruitier de Saint-Jean-Port-Joli et de La Pocatière (Demi-lieue).

Par testament, Marie-Louise de Lanaudière avantagea aussi son neveu, et Susanne Allison, en leur léguant l'usufruit de tous ses biens, à commencer, dans ce cas aussi, après le décès de sa sœur Catherine[1]. Par ce legs, Philippe Aubert de Gaspé devint également coseigneur des fiefs de Saint-Vallier et de Saint-Pierre-les-Becquets[2], et obtint une part des revenus de la baronnie de Longueuil dont sa tante avait hérité d'une fraction[3]. Prévoyante, mademoiselle de Lanaudière, qui avait été témoin des déboires financiers de son neveu, avait pris soin d'ajouter une clause à son testament stipulant que son legs serait annulé si les créanciers de l'ex-shérif s'avisaient de tenter de saisir cet usufruit. Ce qui n'arriva pas.

Catherine de Lanaudière pensa également à son fils au moment de rédiger son testament: tout comme sa sœur Marie-Louise, elle lui légua, ainsi qu'à son épouse, l'usufruit de tous ses biens, la propriété de ceux-ci allant à leurs enfants[4]. Outre ses effets personnels, plusieurs meubles, une

---

1. ANQ-Q, greffe du notaire Simon Fraser, 17 juin 1841.
2. En vertu de ce testament Philippe Aubert de Gaspé reçut l'usufruit d'un huitième de la seigneurie de Saint-Pierre-les-Becquets et de quatorze quatre-vingt-seizièmes de la seigneurie de Saint-Vallier. Quant à la propriété de ces biens, elle échut à ses enfants.
3. Marie-Louise Tarieu de Lanaudière et ses sœurs Agathe et Marguerite héritèrent de leur mère Catherine Le Moyne de Longueuil en vertu d'un testament olographe déposé chez le notaire Antoine A. Parent le 23 octobre 1843.
4. ANQ-Q, greffe du notaire Simon Fraser, 17 juin 1841.

Charlotte-Elmire Aubert de Gaspé,
épouse du juge Stuart (1817-1899).
(Coll. privée.)

Andrew Stuart.
(Coll. privée.)

cinquantaine de pièces d'argenterie, une quinzaine de bêtes
à cornes et vingt et une brebis, madame de Gaspé laissa à ses
héritiers la moitié des seigneuries de Saint-Jean-Port-Joli et
de la Pocatière dont elle était propriétaire, une somme de
quelque soixante livres qui lui était due par ses censitaires et
la petite part de la baronnie de Longueuil dont elle avait
aussi hérité[5].

 Éprouvé en 1842 par la perte de deux êtres chers,
Philippe Aubert de Gaspé eut par ailleurs la satisfaction de
voir une autre de ses filles s'unir à une des grandes familles
du pays. En effet, le 18 juin 1842, un peu moins de deux mois
après le décès de sa mère, Charlotte-Elmire, la troisième de
ses filles, épousa à Québec Andrew Stuart dont le père avait
été solliciteur général du Bas-Canada de 1838 à 1840, et le

5. Philippe Aubert de Gaspé devint ainsi seigneur usufruitier des cinq
sixièmes des seigneuries de Saint-Jean-Port-Joli et de La Pocatière, l'autre
sixième allant aux héritiers de son frère Thomas décédé le 27 mai 1824.

grand-père fondateur de l'Église épiscopale du Haut-Canada. On a écrit qu'il était possible que leur ancêtre lointain descende des Stuart qui donnèrent des souverains à l'Angleterre et à l'Écosse[6]. Reçu au barreau en 1834, Andrew Stuart se fit rapidement une clientèle nombreuse parmi les hommes d'affaires et plaida la plupart des causes importantes dont les tribunaux québécois furent saisis à l'époque. Nommé juge de la Cour supérieure en 1859, il devint, onze ans plus tard, juge en chef de ce haut tribunal[7]. Ce mariage, qui contribua à sa façon à redorer le blason des Aubert de Gaspé, s'avérera également précieux à l'auteur des *Anciens Canadiens* lorsqu'à la fin de sa vie il lui sera difficile de subvenir seul à tous ses besoins.

* * *

Les habitants de Saint-Jean-Port-Joli se sentirent un peu délaissés durant le séjour de Philippe Aubert de Gaspé sur la rue Saint-Stanislas, leur seigneuresse, Catherine de Lanaudière, qui n'était plus jeune, ayant décidé de demeurer durant ce temps à Québec en compagnie de Susanne Allison et de ses petits-enfants. Aussi, c'est avec une satisfaction non dissimulée qu'ils accueillirent leur nouveau seigneur en 1842. Sans habiter le manoir seigneurial à longueur d'année, ce dernier y séjourna avec sa famille du printemps à l'automne de chaque année. Ses randonnées en voiture au village, sa présence assidue à l'église où il prenait place dans le banc seigneurial[8], ses excursions de chasse et de pêche avec ses amis d'antan et sa disponibilité au manoir de Trois-

---

6.   A.H. Young, *The Revd. John Stuart, D.D., U.E.L., of Kingston, U.C. and his Family*, Kingston, Whig Press (sans date), p. 7.
7.   J. Castonguay, *Au temps de Philippe Aubert de Gaspé: Lady Stuart*, Montréal, Éditions du Méridien, 1986, pp. 37 et 73.
8.   Ignace-Philippe Aubert de Gaspé céda à la paroisse de Saint-Jean-Port-Joli, le 14 novembre 1756, un terrain pour bâtir une église et un presbytère et aussi aménager un cimetière, recevant en retour l'usage gratuit d'un banc honorifique, le droit au pain bénit et le droit d'être inhumé dans l'église paroissiale.

Saumons étaient autant de choses qui ne laissaient personne indifférent. Les anciens se remémoraient avec plaisir le temps où les relations entre le seigneur et les censitaires étaient non seulement courtoises mais aussi faciles.

Philippe Aubert de Gaspé, qui s'était révélé un mauvais administrateur lorsqu'il était shérif, s'inspira de la façon dont sa mère géra ses biens lorsque le temps vint de lui succéder. Catherine de Lanaudière, qui avait préféré se faire représenter par William Power lorsqu'il lui fallut faire acte de foi et hommage au gouverneur en 1832, fit fréquemment appel aux services du notaire Simon Fraser dans l'exécution de ses fonctions de seigneuresse. Elle lui confia, par exemple, le 3 mars 1823, l'importante tâche de percevoir tous les arrérages de cens et rentes et de lods et ventes, présents et à venir, et l'autorisa à prendre les mesures pour forcer les débiteurs à s'acquitter de leurs obligations, sans exclure, si nécessaire, la saisie et la vente de leurs biens[9]. Cette procuration, en apparence contraignante, n'eut pas de conséquences fâcheuses. Le notaire Fraser, qui exerçait sa profession à Saint-Jean-Port-Joli depuis 1804, étant un homme pondéré et estimé, les censitaires peu fortunés, et ils étaient nombreux semble-t-il, continuèrent sans être incommodés à remettre au lendemain le paiement de leur dû. Un document préparé vraisemblablement pour le seigneur énumère quatre-vingt-seize transferts de propriétés pour lesquels les lods et ventes, une taxe que devait payer au seigneur l'acquéreur d'une propriété appartenant à un censitaire, n'avaient pas été payés. On y lit cependant que les débiteurs concernés étaient soit pauvres, soit très pauvres ou tout simplement déménagés[10].

Pour administrer ses seigneuries, Philippe Aubert de Gaspé recourut donc lui aussi aux services du notaire Fraser

---

9.   ANQ-Q, greffe du notaire Amable Morin, 3 mars 1823: procuration par Dame Catherine Tarieu de Lanaudière à Simon Fraser.

10.   «Les personnes arriérées qui doivent encore des lods et ventes dans les seigneuries de Port Joli et de La Pocatière», archives de l'auteur.

Le notaire Louis-Zéphirin Duval qui, à Saint-Jean-Port-Joli, géra les affaires des Aubert de Gaspé durant plus de cinquante ans. (Coll. privée.)

et, après lui, à ceux du notaire Louis-Zéphirin Duval. Les greffes de ces deux notaires contiennent plusieurs actes et contrats signés par les Aubert de Gaspé. À elle seule, la signature du père de Philippe apparaît plus de cinquante fois au bas de documents préparés par le notaire Fraser. L'auteur des *Mémoires* dira de ce dernier qu'il «géra les seigneuries de sa famille pendant plus de quarante ans avec autant de probité que d'intelligence[11]».

Louis-Zéphirin Duval, qui exerça lui aussi la profession de notaire à Saint-Jean-Port-Joli, reçut le mandat d'administrer les seigneuries de Saint-Jean-Port-Joli et de La Pocatière le 12 juillet 1852. Philippe Aubert de Gaspé le constitua son

---

11. *Mémoires*, p. 381, note 1.

procureur général et spécial pour «régir, gérer et administrer tant activement que passivement tous les biens et affaires du dit constituant en ce qu'il peut être concerné dans les cinq sixièmes indivis des dits fiefs et seigneuries». Tout comme l'avait fait sa mère, il donna à son mandataire toute l'autorité nécessaire pour sévir contre les censitaires qui négligeaient de payer leur dû, «en un mot faire tout ce qui lui semblera bon pour le profit et avantage du dit constituant[12]».

Après avoir assumé ces responsabilités durant dix-neuf ans, le notaire Duval s'occupa aussi des affaires des enfants du seigneur durant près de quarante ans. Ce vieil original — on raconte qu'il transportait sa valise dans une brouette lorsqu'il devait se rendre à la station pour y prendre le train — descendait de François Duval-dit-Dupontlaut, premier colon à s'établir à l'est de la seigneurie de Port-Joly, là où s'élève aujourd'hui l'église paroissiale[13]. Capitaine de milice, greffier de la Cour des commissaires et membre fondateur de la Chambre des notaires de Montmagny, il appartenait à la poignée d'intellectuels qui fondèrent l'Institut littéraire de Saint-Jean-Port-Joli en 1856, organisme voué à la promotion des arts et des lettres. Par son mariage à Éléonore Verreau, sœur d'Hospice Anthelme Verreau, éducateur, historien et fondateur des Archives nationales du Canada, le notaire Duval s'assura les services d'une collaboratrice qui ne se faisait pas prier pour faire office de clerc et distribuer de bons conseils! Au dire de madame David-Octave Castonguay, la plus jeune de leurs filles[14], il n'était pas rare de voir

---

12. ANQ-Q, greffe du notaire Simon Fraser, 12 juillet 1852.
13. François Duval-dit-Dupontlaut, fils de Guillaume Duval, seigneur du Ponthaut, en Bretagne, prit possession, probablement en 1691, d'une terre de sept arpents de front en bordure du fleuve au centre de ce qui est aujourd'hui le village de Saint-Jean-Port-Joli. Ignace-Philippe Aubert de Gaspé, qui céda en 1756 un terrain à la fabrique pour construire une église et un presbytère et aménager un cimetière, acheta vraisemblablement ce terrain de François Duval père ou de François Duval fils le 1er juillet 1743 (ANQ-Q, greffe du notaire Jacques Pinguet, 1er juillet 1743).
14. Alice Duval épousa à Saint-Jean-Port-Joli, le 23 janvier 1883, le notaire David-Octave Castonguay, un résidant de Saint-Roch-des-Aulnaies qui avait fait sa cléricature chez le notaire L.-Z. Duval.

De gauche à droite, Atala, Philomène, Azéline
et Anaïs Aubert de Gaspé. (Coll. privée.)

les clients trouver des réponses à leurs questions avant
même de pénétrer dans l'étude du notaire. Témoin des
fréquentes visites que faisait le seigneur de Gaspé à son père,
ou son père au seigneur de Gaspé, madame Castonguay
conservait d'agréables souvenirs de cette époque déjà éloignée. «Mon père, le notaire Louis-Zéphirin Duval», confiait-
elle un jour au notaire Jean-Marie Turgeon, «était très lié
avec le seigneur dont il administrait les biens. Presque tous
les jours, durant la belle saison, nous voyions donc arriver M.
de Gaspé ou nous allions lui rendre visite. Je n'étais qu'une
fillette, vous comprenez, et il me taquinait à propos de mes
toilettes et de mes poupées. Il me semble entendre encore
son rire malicieux. En même temps, sa distinction comman-
dait le respect. Je n'ai pas oublié sa coqueluche de septuagénaire[15]».

---

15. Jean-Marie Turgeon, *Les Vendredis de l'Oncle Gaspard*, Québec, 1944, p. 184.

* * *

À compter de 1842, année où il devint seigneur de Saint-Jean-Port-Joli et de La Pocatière, jusqu'au début des années 1850, Philippe Aubert de Gaspé vécut des années relativement paisibles. Il eut bien encore quelques problèmes financiers, mais ils n'étaient pas insolubles cette fois, les rentes qu'il retirait de ses seigneuries lui permettant de satisfaire petit à petit ses créanciers. Il put ainsi acquitter des dettes remontant à l'époque où il était shérif de Québec[16]. Habitué aux réclamations des étrangers, il lui fallut en tant que seigneur apprendre aussi à répondre, et ce durant tout le reste de sa vie, aux demandes des héritiers de son frère Thomas qui n'oubliaient pas qu'en vertu du testament de Pierre-Ignace Aubert de Gaspé ils possédaient une partie, soit un sixième, des fiefs de Saint-Jean-Port-Joli et de La Pocatière. Les notaires Simon Fraser et Louis-Zéphirin Duval aidant, les choses finirent toujours par s'arranger[17].

Si la gestion des cens et rentes ne posait guère de problèmes, celle des moulins à eau parut plus difficile. Un inventaire de quelques greffes de notaire indique que le moulin à eau de la rivière Trois-Saumons, par exemple, changea plusieurs fois de mains. Le capitaine de Gaspé le loua à Louis Barde en 1781[18]; l'honorable Pierre-Ignace Aubert de Gaspé le loua à son tour par bail emphytéotique à Robert Harrower en 1801[19]; Catherine de Lanaudière continua la tradition en

16. Le 5 mai 1846, Lawrence et James Cannon signaient une quittance en faveur de Philippe Aubert de Gaspé pour le paiement d'une somme due à leur père (John Cannon) en vertu d'un acte passé à Québec en 1816. John Cannon était un des signataires de la pétition déposée à l'Assemblée législative le 28 février 1823 par des créanciers du shérif de Québec.
17. Pierre-Ignace Aubert de Gaspé avait légué par testament aux enfants de son fils Thomas le tiers de la moitié de la propriété des seigneuries de Saint-Jean-Port-Joli et de La Pocatière (ANQ-Q, greffe du notaire S. Fraser, 1er décembre 1820).
18. ANQ-Q, greffe du notaire L.-C. Conscient de Saint-Aubin, 1er septembre 1781.
19. ANQ-Q, greffe du notaire F. Têtu, 20 juillet 1801.

1840 en consentant un bail emphytéotique à Charles Harrower[20]; ce dernier le céda ensuite à son neveu, David Harrower, en 1848[21]; enfin, Philippe Aubert de Gaspé, à la suite de difficultés financières éprouvées par David Harrower, reprit le moulin le 20 mai 1854 pour le louer à Jean Thibault le 4 septembre suivant[22]. L'intérêt des Harrower pour ce moulin s'explique, on le sait, par le fait que ces derniers possédaient une distillerie tout près, sur la rive est de la rivière, et que l'exploitation du moulin était normalement rentable[23].

Le moulin du fief de La Pocatière ou Demi-Lieue construit en 1819 par Pierre-Ignace Aubert de Gaspé, à l'intersection du troisième rang et de la route Elgin, changea lui aussi souvent de mains. Philippe Aubert de Gaspé le loua à François Bélanger[24] le 1er mars 1849 et, après le décès du seigneur, il changea de propriétaire au moins huit fois[25].

* * *

Les années qui suivirent le retour au manoir seigneurial furent également marquées par les événements inévitables de l'existence, particulièrement fréquents dans les familles nombreuses, tels que les naissances, les mariages et les deuils. Philippe Aubert de Gaspé et Susanne Allison n'eurent plus d'enfant après 1837. Ils eurent cependant de nombreux petits-enfants. Avant même la naissance de Philomène, la cadette de la famille, ils avaient déjà six petits-enfants et, au cours des années qui suivirent, ils en eurent cinquante-cinq autres. Si on pense que la plupart d'entre eux se marièrent et

---

20. ANQ-Q, greffe du notaire R. Lelièvre, 13 mai 1840.
21. ANQ-Q, greffe du notaire L.-Z. Duval, 8 août 1848.
22. ANQ-Q, greffe du notaire J. Petitclerc, 20 mai 1854.
23. Après le décès de Philippe Aubert de Gaspé, ce moulin passa à Léandre Méthot, puis à Alexandre Bourgault, à Edmond Hudon et à Dolorès Hudon.
24. ANQ-Q, greffe du notaire L.-Z. Duval, 1er mars 1849.
25. Après le décès de Philippe Aubert de Gaspé, ce moulin fut successivement la propriété de Thadée Francœur, père et fils, François Bélanger, Calixte et Auguste Saint-Pierre, Prudent d'Amours, Emile et Dominique Bernier.

Anaïs Aubert de Gaspé (1834-1923),   William Fraser.
épouse de William Fraser.   (Coll. privée.)
(Coll. privée.)

furent aussi prolifiques, on imagine aisément l'importance de la postérité du seigneur de Gaspé. Cependant, comme il eut plusieurs filles, et seulement deux garçons qui se marièrent, son nom ne semble pas s'être perpétué au Canada, comme nom de famille, mais importante est encore aujourd'hui sa descendance[26].

Les noces vinrent aussi, à cette époque, agrémenter la vie des Aubert de Gaspé. À la suite de Suzanne, Adélaïde, Elmire et Zélie, ce fut au tour de Pierre-Édouard, Zoé, Anaïs, Alfred et Atala de contracter mariage. Suivant en cela l'exemple de leurs sœurs Suzanne et Elmire, et aussi de leur père, Zoé, Anaïs et Alfred s'unirent tous les trois à des anglophones, la première à un anglophone de descendance irlandaise, les deux autres à des anglophones de descen-

---

26. On rencontre de nos jours des descendants de Philippe Aubert de Gaspé qui ont pour nom Beaubien, Perrault, Audette, Stuart, Loranger, Power, Chassé, DesRosiers, Taché, Fraser, Lizotte, Alleyn, Taschereau, Vallée, de Salins, de Kersabiec, etc. On rencontre également des descendants de Thomas Aubert de Gaspé, le frère de Philippe, qui portent le nom de Gaudreau, Primeau, Desparois, etc.

Zoé Aubert de Gaspé, épouse
de C.-J. Alleyn (1825-1888).
(Coll. privée.)

Charles-Joseph Alleyn.
(Coll. privée.)

dance écossaise.[27] C'est aussi à cette époque, plus précisément le 10 octobre 1847, que Thomas, le sixième des enfants
du seigneur, fut ordonné prêtre à Québec. Après avoir été
vicaire dans quelques paroisses, il fut successivement curé de
Saint-Éloi (Témiscouata), de Saint-Apollinaire et de Thurso.

L'événement le plus important des années 1840 fut
toutefois malheureux. Après avoir partagé durant trente-six
ans les joies, les peines et les douleurs de Philippe Aubert de
Gaspé et avoir contribué à accroître de façon sensible sa
grande famille, Susanne Allison mourut à Québec le 3 août
1847, atteinte, croit-on, d'hypertrophie du cœur. Elle n'avait
que 53 ans. Des esprits étriqués établirent des liens entre la
maladie qui l'emporta et la conduite de son fils mort à

_____

27. Pierre-Édouard épousa Marie Adélaïde Caron le 21 juillet 1846; Zoé
épousa Charles Alleyn le 15 mai 1849; Anaïs épousa William Fraser le 23 juin
1857; Alfred épousa Madeleine Fraser le 17 mai 1859 et Atala épousa Joseph
Eusèbe Hudon le 10 mai 1869.

Halifax six ans plus tôt...[28] Pour les paroissiens de Saint-Jean-Port-Joli qui assistèrent nombreux à son inhumation dans l'église où elle avait occupé si souvent le banc seigneurial avec sa famille, Susanne Allison avait été toute sa vie une femme dévote et généreuse ayant fait honneur à sa race[29].

* * *

Un événement d'importance nationale, échappant à la volonté de Philippe Aubert de Gaspé, mais qui le toucha profondément, marqua les années 1850. Le régime seigneurial qui, sans être parfait, avait rendu de grands services à la Nouvelle-France fut l'objet d'ardentes critiques au siècle dernier. On lui reprochait surtout de retarder la colonisation, de mettre des entraves à l'industrialisation du Bas-Canada et de perpétuer une forme de servitude inacceptable. On s'en prenait, entre autres, aux lods et ventes qui ne favorisaient pas la mutation des propriétés et à l'obligation qu'avaient les censitaires de faire moudre leur grain au moulin du seigneur. L'Assemblée législative mit finalement un terme à ce long et pénible débat en adoptant, le 18 décembre 1854, une loi abolissant ce système de distribution du sol et de peuplement.

À l'instar des autres seigneurs, Philippe Aubert de Gaspé accueillit cette mesure avec beaucoup de réticence. Conscient que le régime seigneurial avait atteint ses objectifs, non seulement à Saint-Jean-Port-Joli, mais un peu partout le long des deux rives du Saint-Laurent, l'à-propos de cette loi ne lui parut pas évident. Le souvenir de son grand-père et de son père renforçant sa conviction que nombre de seigneurs avaient été non seulement très bons à l'égard de leurs censitaires, mais avaient joué auprès d'eux un rôle de chef, en temps de paix comme en temps de guerre, il se résigna à ce

---

28. L. Lacourcière, «Aubert de Gaspé, fils (1814-1841)», dans les *Cahiers des Dix*, n° 40, 1975, pp. 299 et 300.
29. Susanne Allison fut inhumée dans l'église de Saint-Jean-Port-Joli le 5 août 1847.

changement avec peine et amertume. Sa correspondance avec le notaire Duval, responsable de la préparation du «papier terrier», et un long document à l'intention du commissaire Siméon Lelièvre,[30] chargé de dresser le cadastre de ses seigneuries, laissent transparaître son insatisfaction. Lorsqu'il prendra la plume pour écrire les *Anciens Canadiens*, il le fera aussi avec l'idée de défendre le régime seigneurial. Il brossera un tableau refutant les principales critiques formulées à son endroit et illustrera les avantages qu'il comportait[31]. Il reviendra sur ce sujet dans ses *Mémoires*, insistant sur la nature des liens qui existaient entre les seigneurs et les colons: «Des gens envieux, jaloux, ont soufflé la zizanie, afin de rompre les liens d'affection, fondés le plus souvent sur la gratitude, qui attachaient les censitaires à leurs seigneurs. La nature de l'homme, le taux peu élevé des cens et rentes, les secondaient puissamment pour accomplir cette œuvre malveillante[32].»

La loi qui faisait des censitaires les propriétaires de leur terre et abolissait les droits honorifiques et onéreux autorisait cependant les seigneurs à conserver leur manoir, leur moulin, leur domaine et les terres non encore concédées. Elle prévoyait aussi le versement d'une indemnité financière et la possibilité d'exiger une redevance annuelle (rentes constituées) de la part des censitaires qui ne voulaient pas ou ne pouvaient pas se prévaloir du privilège de se porter acquéreur de leurs terres moyennant le paiement d'un certain prix d'achat[33]. La valeur totale de la seigneurie de Saint-Jean-Port-Joli, selon le rapport du commissaire Lelièvre, s'élevait alors à 30 145,15 $ et celle du fief de La Pocatière à 9 600,32 $[34].

---

30. ANC, MG 18 H 44.
31. Voir sur ce sujet l'intéressante introduction de Maurice Lemire à l'édition des *Anciens Canadiens* publiée par la Bibliothèque québécoise inc., en 1988, pp. 11-21.
32. *Mémoires*, p. 530.
33. M. Trudel, *Le Régime seigneurial*, Ottawa, Les Brochures de la Société historique du Canada, n° 6, 1971, pp. 21 et 22.
34. *Cadastres abrégés des seigneuries du district de Québec*, Québec, George Desbarats, 1863, vol. II, n° 76, p. 24 et n° 77, p. 7.

Banc seigneurial des Aubert de Gaspé à l'avant de l'église
de Saint-Jean-Port-Joli. (Photo Conrad Toussaint.)

Même si la loi privait les seigneurs de leurs droits honorifiques, les marguilliers de Saint-Jean-Port-Joli exprimèrent
leur gratitude aux Aubert de Gaspé en autorisant leur seigneur à conserver sa vie durant le banc spécial qu'avaient
occupé ses ancêtres durant soixante-quinze ans. Geste
louable mais bien inutile, rappelle, le 5 février 1906, le notaire
Duval à Alfred Aubert de Gaspé, puisque ce banc appartenait à sa famille à perpétuité:

> J'ai une nouvelle à vous apprendre un peu difficile à croire,
> mais bien que trop vraie, la Fabrique de St Jean Port Joli qui
> doit donner l'exemple d'honnêteté à sa paroisse s'est permise
> de vendre votre banc dans l'Eglise à la criée hier au sortir de
> la grande messe, qui a été adjugé à un nommé Ernest Fortin
> pour le prix minime de $15.

> Feu Mr votre grand père en faisant par devant le Notaire
> Noël Dupont le 14 novembre 1756 une donation à la fabrique
> de l'emplacement pour la bâtisse de l'Église, sacristie et

presbytère [...] a fait en la dite donation la réserve suivante
que je copie mot à mot sur la donation elle-même: Cette
donation faite par le dit donateur aux charges et conditions
suivantes, que le dit donateur s'est réservé et se réserve,
savoir, un Banc Seigneurial contre les balustres dans la dite
eglise du coté de l'Epître lorsqu'elle sera bâtie sur le dit
terrain mentionné, et que *le dit Banc sera à perpétuité annexé à
l'ainé de la famille* du dit donateur[35].

Le banc seigneurial des Aubert de Gaspé fit couler beaucoup d'encre avant et après cette lettre du notaire Duval. Son
histoire aux épisodes multiples pourrait sans doute trouver
place dans une monographie paroissiale.

---

35. Lettre de L.-Z. Duval à Alfred Aubert de Gaspé, 5 février 1906. Archives
de l'auteur.

CHAPITRE 11

Gestation et naissance
des *Anciens Canadiens*

(1856-1863)

La famille de Gaspé séjourna régulièrement à Saint-Jean-
Port-Joli après la mort de Catherine Tarieu de Lanaudière,
mais l'automne venu, une fois les récoltes rentrées, elle
retournait ordinairement à Québec et y demeurait jusqu'au
printemps. Les plus jeunes des filles du seigneur pouvaient
ainsi fréquenter le célèbre couvent des Ursulines comme
l'avaient fait leurs aînées, Suzanne et Adélaïde, à l'époque où
leur père était shérif. Zoé, Azéline et Atala y furent inscrites
comme demi-pensionnaires à compter de 1838, et Anaïs et
Philomène à partir de 1846 et 1847 respectivement[1]. Saint-
Jean-Port-Joli n'avait que des écoles de rang ou l'équivalent
au XIXᵉ siècle. Le couvent des sœurs de Saint-Joseph de
Saint-Vallier n'ouvrit ses portes qu'en 1903.

---

1. Seuls les noms d'Elmire et de Zélie n'apparaissent pas au fichier des
étudiantes des Ursulines. Cette absence s'explique par le fait que les de Gaspé
vivaient à Saint-Jean-Port-Joli lorsqu'elles furent d'âge scolaire.

Après sa libération, Philippe Aubert de Gaspé demeura quelque temps sur la rue Sainte-Anne, tout près de l'établissement de la rue Saint-Stanislas où il avait été détenu trop longtemps. Cherchant à oublier cet environnement où il avait beaucoup souffert moralement, il alla s'établir au nord de la ville, sur la rue des Remparts. C'est ce que rappelle une lettre qu'il adressait à sa fille Adelaïde le 17 mai 1844: «Viens passer un mois, deux mois, avec nous, nous avons une maison très spacieuse, No 16, rue des Remparts, où nous tâcherons de te mettre à ton aise: c'est l'endroit le plus retiré de Québec[2].» Il demeura également par la suite sur les rues Sainte-Famille et Saint-François[3], autant de rues situées à peu de distance du séminaire, de la cathédrale, de la rue du Parloir et de l'ancienne école de James Tanswell. Ce retour dans un quartier où il avait été heureux ne fut pas qu'un simple changement de lieu. Il fut un véritable retour aux sources marqué par un renouveau sur le plan social. Reprenant contact avec les Québécois de langue française qu'il avait forcément négligés depuis nombre d'années, il s'éloignait du même coup de la communauté anglophone avec laquelle il avait beaucoup frayé et travaillé du vivant de son père. Bien qu'il conservait quelques bons souvenirs de cette époque mouvementée, qu'il prendra soin d'ailleurs de consigner dans ses *Mémoires,* il se tiendra dès lors à distance de l'administration et des fonctionnaires qui l'avaient traité sans ménagement; il ne fréquentera plus les mess des régiments britanniques en garnison à Québec; il ignorera la milice qui l'avait rayé de ses rangs lorsque ses difficultés financières furent connues et s'abstiendra en général de prendre part aux activités sociales auxquelles, plus jeune, il prêtait volontiers son concours.

Le seigneur de Gaspé ne passa pas pour autant les mois d'hiver entre les quatre murs de sa résidence du Vieux-

---

2. Citée par P.-G. Roy, *À travers les Anciens Canadiens...,* p. 82.
3. Selon *The Quebec Directory,* il habita plusieurs années sur la rue des Remparts, puis au numéro 20 de la rue Sainte-Famille de 1861 à 1864 et au numéro 1 de la rue Saint-François à compter de 1866.

La rue Sainte-Famille. Philippe Aubert de Gaspé habitait au numéro 20
de cette rue au moment de la publication des *Anciens Canadiens*.
(ANQ-Québec, coll. initiale.)

Québec. S'adonnant à la lecture, il y demeura sans doute de
longues heures, mais en sortait quotidiennement pour faire
des promenades, bouquiner et rencontrer des amis partageant les mêmes intérêts que lui. Ses marches sur les remparts le ramenaient plusieurs années en arrière. Il lui semblait revoir le *Lauzon*, le premier traversier à vapeur à faire le
service entre Québec et la Pointe-Lévis. Sorti des chantiers en
1818, il avait fait «une vraie révolution dans les habitudes
des citoyens de la bonne ville de Québec, dont plus des trois
quarts n'avaient jamais mis pied sur la rive sud du fleuve
Saint-Laurent. Chacun voulait visiter cette plage inconnue»,
note l'auteur des *Mémoires*[4]. Sur la rue des Glacis, il lui

4. *Mémoires*, p. 540.

arrivait de chercher à revoir le célèbre théâtre des marion-
nettes qui, malgré ses indiscutables succès, avait disparu
pendant son incarcération[5]. À la Canardière, il se retrouvait
par la pensée en l'heureuse compagnie de ses confrères du
séminaire les jours de congé hebdomadaire[6]. Sans doute lui
arrivait-il aussi de penser à Coq Bezeau, à son ami Lafleur,
à Ives Chôlette et à beaucoup d'autres amis d'enfance.

* * *

Philippe Aubert de Gaspé n'attendit pas d'être sexagé-
naire, ni même d'avoir atteint la maturité, pour s'intéresser
aux arts et aux lettres. Durant son séjour au séminaire, il
s'initia à l'histoire et à la littérature latine et française. À
l'école de John Jackson, il découvrit les auteurs de langue
anglaise et traduisit des passages de Sterne, Walter Scott,
Pope et Shakespeare. Chez Jonathan Sewell, son professeur
de droit, dont il eut le loisir d'utiliser la riche bibliothèque, il
put lire des auteurs tels que Volney, presque introuvable à
Québec. Avec la Société littéraire de Québec, dont il fut un
des fondateurs et le premier vice-président, il fit sienne la
cause des lettres et écrivit possiblement ses premiers textes.
C'est ainsi que dès l'âge de vingt-six ans, maîtrisant l'anglais
et le français, il fut nommé traducteur et secrétaire du Bas-
Canada. Plus tard, durant sa retraite prolongée à Saint-Jean-
Port-Joli, il fit de la lecture son passe-temps favori et contribua, croit-on, à la préparation du roman de son fils,
L'Influence d'un livre[7].

L'intérêt de Philippe Aubert de Gaspé pour l'histoire et
les lettres en général était partagé par plusieurs de ses concitoyens qui aimaient se réunir pour évoquer des souvenirs,
tirer des leçons, parler littérature et faire des projets. Le
magasin de Charles Hamel, au numéro 84 de la rue Saint-

---

5. *Ibid.*, pp. 454 et ss.
6. *Ibid.*, p. 454.
7. L. Lacourcière, «Aubert de Gaspé, fils (1814-1841)», dans *Cahier des Dix*,
n° 40, 1975, p. 284.

Jean, n'était pas étranger à ce phénomène. Ce vieux célibataire, fin, courtois et un peu efféminé, s'adressait à une clientèle bien particulière. Aux personnes dont la piété invitait à la consommation, il offrait des statuettes, des cierges, des crucifix, des missels et des chapelets. Les pauvres comme les riches pouvaient satisfaire chez lui leurs besoins. À ceux qui appréciaient le raffinement en matière de boire, il proposait dans un coin obscur de robustes bouteilles de liqueur fine dont les noms, «Grande Chartreuse» et «Bénédictine», avaient la vertu de ne pas choquer ses clients dévots. Bien plus, à l'arrière, dans une pièce à part, il mettait à la disposition des intellectuels un ensemble d'ouvrages dont plusieurs n'étaient pas marqués au sceau des autorités ecclésiastiques. Il n'en fallut pas davantage pour que son établissement devienne un lieu de rassemblement pour les historiens, les archéologues et les «vétérans des lettres». Ayant formé une sorte de cénacle baptisé le «Club des anciens», ces férus d'histoire en vinrent à se réunir tous les jours durant les mois d'hiver, entre 1850 et 1860. «On trouvait là causant ensemble», écrit Hubert LaRue, «d'anciens marchands, vétérans des affaires: *long John* Fraser, Henry Forsyth, père, Benj. Lemoine, père; des historiens et archéologues tels que F.X. Garneau, G.B. Faribault, Philippe Aubert de Gaspé, le commissaire général Jas. Thompson, George Alford, le major Lafleur[8]». On ne saurait dire si Philippe Aubert de Gaspé a écrit autre chose que des documents concernant ses affaires personnelles durant son emprisonnement. Il est probable que non. On peut penser cependant qu'il songea à le faire à l'époque du «Club des anciens» et que la plupart des sujets traités dans les *Anciens Canadiens* et dans les *Mémoires* ont fait l'objet de narrations ou de discussions dans le magasin de Charles Hamel[9]. Il en fut question à tout le moins avec

---

8.   Hubert LaRue, *Voyage sentimental sur la rue Saint-Jean*, Québec, C. Darveau, 1879, p. 98. Voir aussi: J.M. LeMoine, *Picturesque Quebec: A sequel to Quebec past and present*, Montreal, Dawson Brothers, 1882, pp. 156-157.
9.   L. Lacourcière, «L'enjeu des Anciens Canadiens», dans *Cahier des Dix*, nº 32, 1967, p. 232.

Barthélemi Faribault dont les connaissances, selon son propre témoignage, lui furent précieuses pour la rédaction de ses chapitres sur la Corriveau et Salaberry[10].

Mais Charles Hamel ne fut pas le seul à contribuer par son commerce à l'essor des lettres à Québec au milieu du XIXe siècle. Après lui, les frères Crémazie firent beaucoup et même davantage. Joseph fut le premier à exercer la profession de libraire. Son établissement demeura cependant modeste jusqu'à ce que son frère Octave, après avoir acquis une bonne culture littéraire au Séminaire de Québec et avoir développé un goût pour les lettres, décida de se joindre à lui. En 1844, la petite librairie de Joseph Crémazie, devenue la librairie «J. et O. Crémazie», prenait son envol. Trois ans plus tard, elle quittait ses locaux de la rue Sainte-Famille pour aller s'établir au numéro 12 de la rue de la Fabrique et devenir au cours des années qui suivirent un des principaux foyers de la culture française à Québec. On passait à la librairie Crémazie pour prendre connaissance des acquisitions récentes et acheter des volumes, mais aussi pour discuter littérature. «Aux abords de 1860, écrit Réjean Robidoux, l'arrière-boutique de la librairie Crémazie était une sorte de cénacle où passaient et parfois se réunissaient ceux qui participèrent au mouvement littéraire, désigné plus tard sous le titre un peu trop catégorique d'école de Québec[11].»

Octave Crémazie comptait plusieurs jeunes parmi ses clients et ses admirateurs. Il avait aussi des amis parmi les «anciens Québécois» qui se réunissaient au magasin de Charles Hamel. François-Xavier Garneau, Barthélemi Faribault et Philippe Aubert de Gaspé, tous les trois du «Club des anciens», étaient du nombre. Garneau et Faribault avaient fait leurs preuves dans le monde des lettres: le premier en tant qu'historien, le second en tant que bibliographe étaient des figures de proue dans leur domaine respectif. Quant au seigneur de Gaspé, malgré son âge respectable, il

---

10. *Ibid.*, p. 229.
11. Réjean Robidoux, «Octave Crémazie», *DBC*, X, p. 221.

s'apparentait aux jeunes dont les projets étaient encore en phase de gestation. Après avoir parlé de son ouvrage à son ami Faribault, il en parla aussi à Crémazie qui voulut y contribuer en composant un poème sur Québec qui apparaît au début du premier chapitre[12]. Il en fut également question avec les responsables des *Soirées canadiennes*, une revue littéraire fondée par quelques habitués de la librairie Crémazie et qui publia dès ses premières livraisons, au mois de mars 1862, des extraits des chapitres 3, 4, et 5 des *Anciens Canadiens*.

Le manuscrit de Philippe Aubert de Gaspé fut également connu à Saint-Jean-Port-Joli avant d'être achevé. On craignait, confiait madame Castonguay au notaire Turgeon[13], qu'en raison de sa «coqueluche de septuagénaire» M. de Gaspé ne puisse terminer son travail. On présume que les membres de l'Institut littéraire, dont le notaire Duval était vice-président et le seigneur de Gaspé vraisemblablement l'inspirateur, ne demeurèrent pas non plus étrangers à ce projet.

* * *

Le manuscrit original des *Anciens Canadiens* et le manuscrit des fragments publiés au début de l'année 1862 dans les *Soirées canadiennes*, dont nous avons fait la découverte dans de vieux papiers de famille en 1980, nous permettent de préciser la date où Philippe Aubert de Gaspé mit en chantier son premier ouvrage. Incertain de la réaction du public face à son travail, il voulut sonder l'opinion de la critique avant de franchir le Rubicon. C'est pourquoi il accepta l'invitation que lui était faite de publier séparément quelques extraits de son ouvrage. Conservant intact le manuscrit des *Anciens Canadiens* qu'il était à rédiger, il fit des copies des fragments qu'il désirait publier[14] et les remit à

---

12. *Ibid.*, p. 224; L. Lacourcière, «L'enjeu des Anciens Canadiens...», p. 230.
13. Témoignage de madame A.-D. Castonguay à Jean-Marie Turgeon, *Les Vendredis de l'Oncle Gaspard...*, p. 184.

Le professeur Luc Lacourcière exhibe des documents sur les Aubert
de Gaspé. La table proviendrait de la cellule de l'auteur des
Anciens Canadiens à la prison de Québec. (Coll. de l'auteur.)

l'éditeur des *Soirées canadiennes* à la fin de l'année 1861 ou au
début de l'année 1862, en prenant soin d'ajouter une note
indiquant qu'il s'agissait là d'extraits d'épisodes des *Anciens
Canadiens* qu'il se proposait de publier prochainement[15]. Ce

---

14. On trouve dans les *Soirées canadiennes* (1862) un fragment important du
chapitre 3 (Une nuit avec les sorciers), un fragment également important du
chapitre 4 (La Corriveau) et la presque totalité du long chapitre 5 (La débâcle).
15. Cet avertissement se trouve au début des fragments des chapitres 3 et 5,
quoique dans ce dernier cas il est raturé.

qui signifie qu'en 1861 Philippe Aubert de Gaspé avait déjà écrit plusieurs chapitres de son volumineux ouvrage. Considérant son âge avancé, le fait qu'il en était à son premier livre et qu'il n'exerçait pas le métier d'écrivain sans quelque peine, comme l'atteste le manuscrit original qui comporte plusieurs ajouts, ratures et corrections[16], on peut conclure qu'il débuta probablement la rédaction de son ouvrage au plus tard en 1860.

La lecture du manuscrit original des *Anciens Canadiens* nous permet aussi de faire une hypothèse quant à la date la plus hâtive du commencement de ses travaux. Philippe Aubert de Gaspé écrit au tout début du premier chapitre du volume publié en 1863 qu'il a commencé «le métier d'auteur à soixante et seize ans». Or, ces mots ne se trouvent pas dans le manuscrit original, ni d'ailleurs l'anecdote où il est question de la rencontre sur la rue Saint-Louis d'un ami lui reconnaissant beaucoup d'esprit qui l'incita à voler chez son libraire pour acheter «une rame de papier foolscap» et à se mettre à l'œuvre[17]. Il semble bien que ce soit là des additions faites peu avant l'impression de l'ouvrage en 1863[18]. Le passage où l'auteur écrit que son travail, «tout canadien par son style», est celui d'un «septuagénaire», se trouve cependant dans le manuscrit original et y est parfaitement intégré[19].

---

16. Le manuscrit original des *Anciens Canadiens* a été remis par l'auteur du présent volume aux Archives du Séminaire de Québec le 30 octobre 1987 et celui des fragments publiés dans les *Soirées canadiennes* aux Archives nationales du Canada le 3 novembre 1988. Quant au manuscrit qui a servi à l'édition de 1863, il a été remis au père Alphonse Gauthier du Collège Bourget de Rigaud, le 29 septembre 1937.
17. *Les Anciens Canadiens*, pp. 5 et 6.
18. L'abbé H.-R. Casgrain a écrit avoir recommandé des modifications aux premières pages et à la conclusion du manuscrit (*Souvenances canadiennes*, chap. XXIV, p. 21). Il est donc possible que ce soit là des additions suggérées par lui en janvier 1863.
19. *Les Anciens Canadiens*, pp. 7 et 8.

On doit donc retenir, à la lumière de ces textes, que Philippe Aubert de Gaspé était septuagénaire lorsqu'il a commencé à écrire les *Anciens Canadiens*. Il n'avait pas pour autant soixante-seize ans. Né en 1786, il a donc vraisemblablement commencé son ouvrage entre 1856 et 1861 et certainement pas après 1861[20].

* * *

Septuagénaire, Philippe Aubert de Gaspé comptait de nombreux enfants et petits-enfants auxquels il écrivait chaque année à l'occasion des fêtes[21]. À la fin de l'année 1862, les nouvelles ne faisant pas défaut, la tâche fut plutôt facile. À Anaïs, qui depuis son mariage à William Fraser demeurait au manoir seigneurial de Rivière-du-Loup, il donne des nouvelles de la «chère Zoé condamnée à garder le sopha peut-être pendant un mois et plus», d'Elmire qui «se cherche une servante pour remplacer Salomé qui se marie», d'un membre de la famille parti pour les «États du Sud au siège de la guerre», de la Cour que les Fraser espèrent avoir à Rivière-du-Loup, et aussi, naturellement, du manuscrit des *Anciens Canadiens* qui est presque terminé. Une rencontre est prévue à ce sujet pour le 3 janvier:

L'abbé Casgrain descend à la R. Ouelle, il sera de retour le 2 de janvier et le lendemain je commencerai à lui faire la lecture

20. L'abbé Casgrain, pour qui l'origine des *Anciens Canadiens* est indissociable de l'épigraphe de Charles Nodier mise en tête des *Soirées canadiennes*, situe le début du travail de composition de Philippe Aubert de Gaspé après le 21 février 1861. Le professeur L. Lacourcière, qui n'a pu consulter les manuscrits découverts en 1980, a montré qu'aussi bien le lien entre les *Anciens Canadiens* et l'épigraphe de Nodier que la date retenue par l'abbé Casgrain sont inadmissibles. La date est trop tardive pour être réaliste et le lien entre l'épigraphe et l'origine des *Anciens Canadiens* présuppose que Philippe Aubert de Gaspé découvrit cet auteur en 1861 alors qu'il le connaissait déjà en 1837. Il en est de même «de la révélation première que Casgrain aurait eue du manuscrit»: il s'agit là d'une de ses vantardises («L'enjeu des Anciens Canadiens...», pp. 223-248).
21. Lettre de Philippe Aubert de Gaspé à Raoul de Beaujeu, le 2 janvier 1864, dans P.-G. Roy, *À travers les Anciens Canadiens...*, p. 234.

de mon ouvrage: c'est convenu. Mon roman est augmenté d'un quart depuis que tu l'as vu; j'achève un long chapitre tout nouveau et supplémentaire, qui sera assez drôle et surtout de la manière que je l'introduis. J'ai beaucoup allongé aussi mon dernier chapitre qui finit d'une manière dont jamais littérateur ne s'est avisé[22].

Pourquoi Philippe Aubert de Gaspé voulut-il faire la lecture de son manuscrit à l'abbé Casgrain? Pour répondre à cette question, il faut retourner quelque peu en arrière. L'entente entre les membres du «Comité de Collaboration» des *Soirées canadiennes* fut plutôt éphémère. Tôt après la fondation de la revue, des problèmes administratifs les avaient divisés et, au cours de l'automne de 1862, l'éclatement de l'équipe s'était produit. Joseph-Charles Taché, qui jouait le rôle de rédacteur en chef, avait démissionné le 10 octobre, suivi bientôt en cela, mais pour des motifs différents, par Antoine Gérin-Lajoie, Hubert LaRue et l'abbé Casgrain. Bien plus, ces derniers, avec l'abbé Jean-Baptiste-Antoine Ferland et Octave Crémazie, avaient décidé de mettre sur pied une seconde revue: *Le Foyer canadien*. Poursuivant plus ou moins le même but que celui des *Soirées canadiennes*, les fondateurs de la nouvelle publication s'étaient assurés la collaboration du seigneur, dont les textes publiés le printemps précédent avaient suscité beaucoup d'intérêt. Ce n'est donc pas à un ami seulement que M. de Gaspé commença à faire la lecture de son ouvrage à compter du 3 janvier 1863, mais avant tout à un représentant du *Foyer canadien* intéressé à en patronner la publication.

Le manuscrit étant volumineux, il y eut plusieurs séances de lecture au presbytère de Notre-Dame où demeurait l'abbé Casgrain depuis deux ans. Le seigneur de Gaspé, qui avait élu domicile depuis quelques années au 20 rue Sainte-Famille, s'accommoda aisément de la situation. L'abbé recommanda quelques changements au premier chapitre et à

---

22. Lettre de Philippe Aubert de Gaspé à Mme Fraser, R. du Loup, le 28 décembre 1862, dans *BRH*, 58, 3 (juillet-août-septembre 1952), pp. 115 et 116.

La débâcle. (*Les Anciens Canadiens*, éditions Beauchemin.)

la conclusion, Philippe les fit volontiers, semble-t-il, et ajouta quelques notes explicatives ici et là.

Les choses allèrent par la suite à une rapidité étonnante. *Le Foyer canadien* étant non seulement très favorable à la publication de l'ouvrage, mais aussi impatient de le voir paraître, la signature du contrat entre l'éditeur, Desbarats et Desbishire, et l'auteur se fit sans délai, le seigneur de Gaspé recevant sur le champ «quatre cents piastres», ce qui était une somme non négligeable à l'époque. La composition du texte se fit en peu de temps, l'abbé Casgrain acceptant d'en corriger les épreuves[23]. Enfin, le mois d'avril commençait à peine que les quelque mille exemplaires qui constituaient la première édition sortaient des presses et disparaissaient en quelques mois des étagères des libraires. À Québec, comme à Saint-Jean-Port-Joli[24], l'ouvrage de Philippe Aubert de Gaspé fut l'événement littéraire de la décennie, laissant déjà présager l'intérêt soutenu qui allait en faire le premier classique de la littérature québécoise, «le seul livre de la période pré-romanesque auquel nous sommes encore attachés», écrira Gilles Marcotte[25].

Le récit qui a pour cadre la ville de Québec et le manoir seigneurial de Saint-Jean-Port-Joli se situe à l'époque de la Conquête. Les deux personnages principaux, Jules d'Haberville, d'origine française, et Archibald Cameron de Locheill, un orphelin écossais, étudient au même collège à Québec. Devenus amis, ils passent chaque année leurs vacances au manoir seigneurial d'Haberville. Se destinant à la carrière militaire, le premier dans l'armée française, le second dans l'armée anglaise, ils quittent le Canada pour l'Europe en 1857. Deux ans plus tard, contre toute attente, ils se retrouvent en Nouvelle-France sur les champs de bataille et naturellement sous des drapeaux différents. De Locheill, qui fait partie d'un détachement de l'armée anglaise descendu à la Rivière-Ouelle, remonte la côte en direction de la Pointe-Lévis. En raison de l'opposition rencontrée au moment du

---

23. L'abbé Casgrain s'est attribué un rôle d'intermédiaire important dans ce dossier (*Souvenances canadiennes*, chap. XXIV, p. 16).

24. L'Institut littéraire de Saint-Jean-Port-Joli, qui figurait au nombre des clients des librairies Crémazie, Hardy et Brousseau et du magasin de Charles Hamel, se porta acquéreur dès leur parution de plusieurs copies des ouvrages du seigneur de Gaspé. Disposant d'une bibliothèque et d'une salle de lecture, ses membres pouvaient y lire, outre de nombreux volumes, *Le Courrier du Canada*, *Le Canadien*, *La Minerve*, *Le Pays*, *Le Journal d'agriculture*, le *Courrier des États* et le *Morning Chronicle*, rappelle le livre de comptes de cette société en milieu rural (Archives de Gilles Saindon, Saint-Roch-des-Aulnaies).

25. Gilles Marcotte, *Une littérature qui se fait*, Montréal, Éditions HMH, 1962, p. 14.

débarquement, il a reçu l'ordre «de mettre le feu à toutes les habitations de ces chiens de Français» que lui et sa compagnie rencontreront sur leur passage. Parvenu à Saint-Jean-Port-Joli, il se retrouve bientôt à proximité de la «demeure où pendant dix ans il avait été accueilli comme l'enfant de la maison: où, pauvre orphelin proscrit et exilé, il avait trouvé une autre famille». Il hésite, un atroce combat intérieur s'engage, mais l'honneur militaire a finalement raison de lui: la nuit venue, le manoir seigneurial et ses dépendances sont la proie des flammes. La guerre terminée, Jules se reconcilie avec Arché. Avec les années, les autres membres de la famille font de même. Alors que Jules épouse une jeune Anglaise rencontrée sur un navire le ramenant au pays, sa sœur Blanche d'Haberville refuse sa main à Arché. Bien qu'elle l'aime aussi profondément qu'elle est aimée, l'honneur lui rend insupportable l'idée d'une telle alliance: «capitaine Archibald Cameron de Locheill, il y a maintenant un gouffre entre nous, que je ne franchirai jamais.»

Ce récit, paradoxal pour un écrivain qui a épousé la fille d'un officier britannique et dont trois enfants ont uni leur destinée à des anglophones d'origine écossaise et deux autres à des familles irlandaises, laisse parfois songeur. Doit-on y voir un signe de la difficile cohabitation des anglophones et des francophones au pays? Si on considère les difficultés éprouvées par Philippe Aubert de Gaspé qui, sous l'influence de son père, a voulu se frotter à l'administration anglaise, on éprouve de la difficulté à rejeter cette hypothèse du revers de la main. Si, d'autre part, on s'arrête à considérer ce que l'on sait des relations entre lui et son épouse, et entre ses enfants et leurs conjoints anglophones, on est peu enclin à penser que des facteurs personnels auraient pu influencer de la sorte le déroulement de son récit, tout particulièrement son dénouement. D'ailleurs, l'auteur des *Anciens Canadiens* ne fait-il pas dire à Blanche d'Haberville qu'il est naturel et souhaitable «que les races française et anglo-saxone, ayant maintenant une même patrie, vivant sous les mêmes lois, après des haines, après des luttes séculaires, se rapprochent

Dîner au manoir seigneurial. (*Les Anciens Canadiens*, éditions Beauchemin.)

par des alliances intimes[26]?» Doit-on voir par ailleurs, dans cette intrigue, un simple prétexte pour peindre la vie rurale des anciens avec leurs légendes, leurs mœurs, leur langue, leur histoire et leurs traditions? Aux yeux de l'abbé Casgrain, on l'a dit, c'était la réponse de Philippe Aubert de Gaspé à l'invitation des *Soirées canadiennes* et de Charles Nodier «de raconter les délicieuses histoires du peuple avant qu'il ne les ait oubliées». Ne pourrait-on pas croire également qu'il s'agissait là d'un prétexte pour plaider la cause du régime seigneurial[27] et de l'ancienne aristocratie, et pourquoi pas aussi la cause de l'auteur lui-même, surtout si l'on songe au chapitre dix où le bon gentilhomme explique à Jules d'Haberville les circonstances qui ont entraîné sa ruine financière et son incarcération?

---

26. *Les Anciens Canadiens*, p. 337.
27. Voir sur ce sujet l'introduction du professeur Maurice Lemire à l'édition des *Anciens Canadiens* publiée aux éditions Fides en 1988, pp. 7-21.

Il ne semble pas invraisemblable que, subjectivement, tous ces facteurs aient été présents à la rédaction de cette œuvre, les mobiles incitant à l'action étant souvent complexes, parfois inconscients et généralement indissociables. Quoi qu'il en soit, objectivement, on trouve dans les *Anciens Canadiens* un vivant tableau de la vie des seigneurs et des censitaires au cours du siècle qui suivit la Conquête. Sur un fond historique, les mœurs de l'ancienne aristocratie et les traditions populaires y sont peintes avec une simplicité qui en facilite l'intelligence et un charme qui sollicite discrètement l'assentiment. Dans cette perspective, cet ouvrage n'est pas qu'un trésor de connaissances sur la vie des anciens Canadiens, mais aussi un instrument de réhabilitation pour l'ex-shérif et de réconciliation pour le régime seigneurial[28].

---

28. Pour le professeur Paul Wyczynski, *Les Anciens Canadiens* touchent à la fois au roman historique, au roman de la terre, au roman d'aventures et constituent «un témoignage direct sur une époque, une précieuse relation de la vie canadienne dans la seconde moitié du XVIIIᵉ siècle et la première du siècle suivant» («Évolution du roman canadien-français», dans *Le Roman canadien français*, collection «Archives des lettres canadiennes», Montréal, Fides, 1971, p. 14).

Les *Mémoires* du parfait gentilhomme

(1863-1866)

Durant la deuxième décennie du XIXe siècle, tous les Québécois ou presque entendirent parler de Philippe Aubert de Gaspé. Avocat, shérif, officier de milice, fils de conseiller législatif et descendant d'une famille illustre, il était de toutes les activités importantes de la ville et son nom apparaissait régulièrement dans les pages de la *Gazette de Québec*. Il y signait en particulier des avis d'exécution de jugements. À la suite de sa destitution comme shérif, en 1822, il leur devint cependant beaucoup moins familier et finalement à peu près étranger. Son nom cessa de paraître dans l'*Almanach de Québec* et dans les répertoires d'adresses de la ville. Ce n'est que vers 1850 qu'on s'habitua de nouveau à sa silhouette sur les remparts, à proximité du monastère des Ursulines et aux abords de la cathédrale Notre-Dame et qu'on remarqua sa présence assidue chez les libraires et à la bibliothèque provinciale. S'étant signalé en 1862 par sa contribution aux *Soirées canadiennes*, il souleva l'année suivante l'enthousiasme de ses concitoyens par la publication de son roman, *Les Anciens Canadiens*. La parution de cet ouvrage, qui le réhabilita complètement aux yeux de ses compatriotes, lui valut une première place, et pour plusieurs années à venir, parmi les auteurs québécois.

L'accueil que la critique réserva aux *Anciens Canadiens* n'avait rien d'équivoque. Pour Hector Fabre, nommé à la rédaction du *Canadien* en 1863, «ce fut un jour unique et qui restera une date dans notre histoire littéraire que celle où l'on vit apparaître au seuil des lettres canadiennes cet auteur qui débutait à 70 ans par un roman. Il n'y eut qu'un cri d'admiration lorsqu'on sentit cette fraîcheur d'imagination, quel charme de style régnait dans ce livre qui devint tout de suite le plus populaire de nos ouvrages[1]». Dans *La Minerve* du 21 août 1863, l'abbé Casgrain parla pour sa part «d'épopée nationale» et d'un ouvrage «qui immortalisera avec toutes ses traditions et souvenances, ses gloires et ses larmes, la plus glorieuse page de notre histoire». L'enthousiasme de Nazaire Petit ne fut pas moindre. S'il dévora «ventre à terre» les chapitres des *Anciens Canadiens*, «c'est que M. de Gaspé a un talent de narrateur inimitable. Souvent, en quelques lignes, il vous présente un tableau où rien ne manque, où tout est parfait, description, narration, dialogue[2]». Plus tard, on dira même de cet ouvrage qu'il est la Chanson de Roland de la littérature québécoise.

Disparue rapidement des rayons des libraires, la première édition fut suivie d'une deuxième dès 1864[3]. Bien plus, la même année, Georgiana M. Pennée, répondant en cela au désir des anglophones de Québec alors plus nombreux que les francophones, publia une première traduction anglaise de cet ouvrage. Intitulée *The Canadians of Old* et éditée elle aussi

---

1. Cité dans *Biographies et portraits d'écrivains canadiens*, Montréal, Librairie Beauchemin, 1913, p. 93.
2. Cité par H.-R. Casgrain, dans *Philippe Aubert de Gaspé*, Québec, 1871, pp. 75 et 76.
3. Revue et corrigée par l'auteur, cette deuxième édition fut publiée à Québec, chez G. et G.-É. Desbarats (1864).

Philippe Aubert de Gaspé).

chez Desbarats[4], elle donna lieu à l'extérieur du pays à une critique des plus favorables. On a écrit que les éloges qu'en firent, par exemple, *The London Review* et *The Dublin Review* surpassèrent ceux pourtant enthousiastes de la critique québécoise[5]. On compte de nos jours plus de vingt-cinq éditions anglaises et françaises des *Anciens Canadiens* et une édition espagnole[6]. Les dernières éditions françaises sont récentes. Les Éditions internationales Alain Stanké en publièrent une en 1987 et les Éditions Fides en 1988.

Le roman de Philippe Aubert de Gaspé remporta également un succès immédiat auprès des étudiants. Tandis que les bibliothécaires des collèges se faisaient un devoir d'acquérir une ou plusieurs copies, les professeurs de lettres

---

4.   On doit aussi à Charles G. D. Roberts une traduction anglaise de cet ouvrage. Elle fut publiée à New York par D. Appleton and Company en 1890. Cette traduction, comme celle de madame Pennée, servit à quelques autres réimpressions. *Seigneur d'Haberville (The Canadians of Old), A Romance of the Fall of New France*, publié à Toronto en 1929 par The Mission Book Company, est une édition revue et corrigée du texte de madame Pennée par M.T.-G. Marquis.

5.   *A Man of Sentiment, The Memoirs of Philippe-Joseph Aubert de Gaspé 1786-1871*, translated and annotated by Jane Brierly, Montréal, Véhicule Press, 1988, p. 31, et *Biographies et portraits d'écrivains canadiens...*, p. 98.

6.   L'abbé Casgrain qui avait apporté des modifications au texte de *L'Influence d'un livre* d'Aubert de Gaspé, fils, imprimé chez G. et G.-É. Desbarats en 1864, publia la troisième édition des *Anciens Canadiens* en 1877. Les initiatives de ce dernier dans le monde de l'édition donnèrent lieu à un procès canonique inusité à Québec (Réjean Robidoux, «Fortunes et Infortunes de l'abbé Casgrain», dans «Archives des Lettres canadiennes», Éditions de l'université d'Ottawa, 1961, pp. 220 et ss.). Faute de documents, on a cru également que la quatrième édition fut publiée par l'abbé Casgrain sans les autorisations requises. Ce qui ne fut pas le cas. Le 19 août 1885, Georges E. Desbarats céda ses droits de publication des *Anciens Canadiens* à Alfred Aubert de Gaspé, le fils de l'auteur (greffe du notaire E.G. Simard, n° 1787, 19 août 1885). Ce dernier, après avoir enregistré (4 septembre 1885) ses droits au bureau de l'Agriculture à Ottawa, les céda à son tour, d'abord par convention sous seing privé signée le 12 septembre 1885, puis par acte notarié, à MM. Cadieux & Dérome pour une période de dix ans commençant le 12 décembre 1885 (greffe du notaire Charles Alphonse Léveillé, 9 juin 1886). Or, on sait que la quatrième édition fut publiée par la maison Cadieux et Dérome en 1886. Alfred Aubert de Gaspé céda également ses droits pour une période de dix ans à MM. C.O. Beauchemin & fils le 12 mai 1896.

s'empressaient de le commenter en classe. Le Collège de l'Assomption voulut faire davantage. Deux professeurs ayant conçu un drame dont les principaux épisodes provenaient des *Anciens Canadiens*, il le présenta au public à sa distribution des prix du 12 juillet 1865. M. de Gaspé, invité à cette cérémonie, reçut alors un accueil triomphal: «Le bateau à vapeur qui le transporta de Montréal à l'Assomption, écrit l'abbé Casgrain, était pavoisé, et de chaque côté de la rivière, l'auteur fut accueilli à son passage par des salves de mousqueterie. À son arrivée au collège, les élèves, rangés sur deux haies, le reçurent par des hourras frénétiques[7].»

Philippe Aubert de Gaspé n'eut jamais la parole facile. C'est lui qui l'affirme[8]. Aussi, appelé à dire quelques mots à la fin de la représentation, il choisit de lire un court texte dans lequel il dit son regret de ne pouvoir exprimer toute la gratitude qu'il éprouvait pour la faveur inattendue qu'on lui avait faite et combien les interprètes l'avaient transporté aux beaux jours de sa jeunesse et fait vivre durant trois heures avec les amis que son imagination avait créés[9].

* * *

La réaction des intellectuels et du public en général à la parution des *Anciens Canadiens* modifia l'existence de Philippe Aubert de Gaspé. Non seulement retrouva-t-il une part de la vivacité qui avait caractérisé ses jeunes années, mais aussi l'énergie nécessaire à la poursuite de ses travaux. Son manque d'aptitude et de goût pour l'administration l'avait amené très tôt à confier la gestion des fiefs et seigneuries dont il avait la jouissance à ses notaires successifs, Simon Fraser et Louis-Z. Duval, et à louer les moulins à eau de Trois-Saumons et du troisième rang. Peu après la parution de

---

7.   H.-.R. Casgrain, *Philippe Aubert de Gaspé...*, p. 86.
8.   *Biographie et oraison funèbre du Revd. M. F. Labelle et autres documents relatifs à sa mémoire, ainsi qu'à la visite de Philippe Aubert de Gaspé, Ecr., au Collège l'Assomption*, Montréal, Imprimerie de la Minerve, 1865, p. 67.
9.   *Ibid.*, p. 68.

son premier ouvrage, il fit de même avec la ferme seigneu-
riale. L'ayant d'abord louée à Charles Harrower[10], puis à son
fils Édouard[11] qui mourut en 1862, il signa un bail avec
Alexandre Vallée, un agriculteur de Saint-Jean-Port-Joli. Le
17 juillet 1863, il loua tout ce qui se trouvait sur ce qu'avait
été le domaine seigneurial, en se réservant une partie du
manoir, le jardin potager se trouvant au sud-ouest de ce
dernier, la production des arbres fruitiers, un cheval et une
place dans les dépendances. Quant à Alexandre Vallée, il
s'obligea en retour «à établer, nourrir et soigner convena-
blement» le cheval de M. de Gaspé, à transporter ce dernier
en temps convenable chez sa belle-fille demeurant dans la
paroisse voisine[12] et à livrer à cette dernière des produits de
la ferme[13].

Libéré ainsi d'à peu près tous ses soucis d'ordre matériel
et stimulé par les remarques de ses amis qui lui reprochaient
de n'avoir pas commencé à écrire quarante ans plus tôt,
l'auteur des *Anciens Canadiens* entreprit la rédaction d'un
second ouvrage:

> Comme, malgré mon expérience, je n'ai jamais pu me persua-
> der qu'on voulût mortifier quelqu'un de cœur joie, et encore
> moins un vieillard, j'ai pris la remarque en bonne part, et je
> me suis mis à écrire[14].

Penché durant de longues heures sur la petite table
d'acajou que lady Dorchester avait donnée à sa mère en souvenir des rapports d'amitié qui unissaient les deux familles,
Philippe Aubert de Gaspé entreprit d'écrire cette fois «l'histoire de ses contemporains» en se servant comme cadre de
l'histoire de sa propre vie:

---

10. Bail à ferme consenti par Mr de Gaspé à Charles Harrower (ANQ-Q,
greffe du notaire Simon Fraser).
11. Édouard Aubert de Gaspé cultiva la terre familiale du 1er mai 1854 au
22 novembre 1862, date de sa mort.
12. Il s'agit là de l'épouse de son fils Édouard.
13. Bail à ferme consenti par Mr de Gaspé au sieur Alexandre Vallée, 17
juillet 1863 (Archives de Gilles Saindon, Saint-Roch-des-Aulnaies).
14. *Mémoires*, p. 6.

Je ne puis écrire l'histoire de mes contemporains sans écrire ma propre vie liée à celle de ceux que j'ai connu depuis mon enfance. Ma propre histoire sera donc le cadre dans lequel j'entasserai mes souvenirs[15].

Après avoir fait œuvre de romancier, à la façon de Walter Scott, il se fait donc mémorialiste, un peu à la manière de Jean-Jacques Rousseau dans les *Confessions* et les *Rêveries du promeneur solitaire*. Il fait son autobiographie; mieux, il se raconte mais en émaillant son récit de souvenirs, de scènes et d'anecdotes de la société qu'il a connue et fréquentée. Ce faisant, il ne fait pas que peindre cette société à une période déterminée de son histoire, mais, implicitement, invite le lecteur à une réflexion sur les questions fondamentales de l'existence[16]. Loin des essais contemporains souvent perçus comme des tentatives de règlement de compte ou d'expression de traumatismes refoulés, le texte qu'il rédige n'est pas une *catharsis*, mais un ouvrage serein et bienveillant, un effet de la mémoire sélective du parfait gentilhomme. Il n'est pas aveugle pour autant, ni moins véridique. Il ignore ou feint d'ignorer ceux qui ont contribué à sa descente aux enfers ou rien fait pour l'en sortir, mais n'hésite pas à écrire de Jonathan Sewell qu'il était «un des hommes les plus estimables qu'il eut connus». Tout en se trouvant incompétent pour commenter les déchirements vécus par ses compatriotes à l'époque de son incarcération, il écrit plusieurs paragraphes élogieux sur Louis-Joseph Papineau qu'il avait côtoyé au Séminaire de Québec. Il parle des «grands» de son époque, mais aussi, et longuement, de ses humbles compagnons et amis de Saint-Jean-Port-Joli. Laurent Caron et Romain Chouinard font à eux seuls l'objet de trois chapitres[17].

---

15. *Ibid.*, p. 6.
16. Jane Brierly a remarqué de nombreuses affinités entre de Gaspé et Rousseau, tant du point de vue des sujets traités que de la manière de le faire (*A Man of Sentiment...*, pp. 31 et 32).
17. Les chapitres sept, treize et quatorze.

Généralement fidèle à son plan de travail, il parle beaucoup de son époque, mais tout en se racontant. Son enfance au manoir seigneurial, sa jeunesse turbulente à Québec, les années passées à l'étude et à la pratique du droit et sa vie d'adulte à Saint-Jean-Port-Joli, après son départ de Québec en 1824, occupent plusieurs chapitres. Le souvenir des événements récents ou pénibles s'estompant et s'effaçant rapidement de la mémoire du septuagénaire, il est par ailleurs plutôt discret sur la période qui suivit sa libération et la mort de sa mère. Il emplit néanmoins plusieurs centaines de pages de papier *foolscap* identique à celui de son premier manuscrit[18].

* * *

Au début de l'année 1865, malgré plusieurs crises de découragement qui auraient pu mettre un terme à ses travaux[19], il est assez avancé pour assumer qu'il pourra compléter son ouvrage. Le 17 février, il rencontre Georges-Édouard Desbarats, celui-là même qui, deux ans plus tôt, avec son père, avait publié ses *Anciens Canadiens* et signe un contrat qui ne manque pas d'intérêt. L'auteur vend à l'éditeur la propriété et la jouissance d'un ouvrage intitulé *Mémoires des Contemporains* pour une période de dix ans à compter du premier jour de mai 1865, moyennant la somme de cinquante louis payable à la livraison du manuscrit et une autre somme de cinquante louis payable lors de la mise en vente de l'ouvrage. L'éditeur s'engage en outre à remettre à l'auteur vingt-cinq exemplaires de l'ouvrage au moment de sa publication[20]. On aura remarqué que le titre ici mentionné n'est pas celui qu'on lira sur le volume au moment de sa parution:

---

18. On peut consulter aux Archives du Séminaire de Québec les quelques chapitres dont nous avons fait la découverte en 1980.
19. *Mémoires*, p. 558.
20. Philippe Aubert de Gaspé céda par la suite ses droits sur cet ouvrage à son fils Alfred, à compter du 17 mai 1865 (greffe du notaire Alexandre Benjamin Sirois, 10 janvier 1867).

Philippe Aubert de Gaspé. (Coll. privée.)

Mémoires des Contemporains sera alors amputé de deux mots pour devenir simplement *Mémoires*. La lecture de la préface, écrite en fonction du premier titre, suggère un certain embarras de la part de l'auteur: «Si j'osais risquer un *Irish bull* (un calembour irlandais), écrit Aubert de Gaspé, je dirais que mon plus ancien contemporain étant moi-même, je dois d'abord m'occuper de mon mince individu», ajoutant quelques lignes plus loin, «je ne puis écrire l'histoire de mes contemporains sans écrire ma propre vie liée à celle de ceux que j'ai connue depuis mon enfance[21]». Le nouveau titre dissipera

---

21. *Mémoires*, p. 6.

une possible ambiguïté créée par le mot «contemporains», mais la préface demeurera inchangée.

En présence de sa fille Atala, demeurée célibataire, Philippe poursuit sans relâche son travail de rédaction au cours des mois qui suivent la signature de son contrat avec Desbarats. Il se sent bien et l'écrit à son petit-fils Raoul de Beaujeu: «J'ai rarement joui d'une meilleure santé que celle que j'ai maintenant; tous ceux que je rencontre m'en félicitent. Je marche plus lestement que je ne l'ai fait depuis longtemps, [...] je prends beaucoup d'exercices, voilà le principal; j'oubliais l'appétit qui est excellent. Que peut-on désirer de plus[22]?» La santé aidant, il écrit à une cadence impressionnante pour un homme presque octogénaire. Les paragraphes s'ajoutent aux paragraphes, les chapitres aux chapitres, si bien que le 1er septembre 1865, deux ans et quatre mois seulement après la sortie des presses de son premier ouvrage, il peut écrire à l'abbé Casgrain, auquel il fait la lecture de son manuscrit, tout comme il l'avait fait pour les *Anciens Canadiens*: «Je crois vous avoir écrit que j'avais terminé mon dernier chapitre, que je puis même vous envoyer par la prochaine poste si vous le désirez. Puisque les autres chapitres ont trouvé grâce auprès de vous, j'ai toute confiance que vous serez satisfait de lui[23].»

Pendant ce temps, chez Desbarats, on n'avait pas attendu que le texte soit terminé pour en commencer la composition et on expédiait régulièrement des épreuves à l'auteur. Commencée au cours du printemps ou de l'été, la correction des épreuves se poursuivit durant plusieurs mois, au grand déplaisir d'Aubert de Gaspé qui détestait ce genre de travail. Une lettre que ce dernier adressait à Raoul de Beaujeu, le 10 février 1866, nous permet de croire qu'elle s'étendit vraisemblablement jusqu'à la fin de février: «J'ai

---

22. Lettre de Philippe Aubert de Gaspé à Raoul de Beaujeu, 12 janvier 1865, dans P.-G. Roy, *À travers les Anciens Canadiens...*, p. 236.
23. Lettre de Philippe Aubert de Gaspé à l'abbé H.-.R. Casgrain, 1er septembre 1865, ASQ, Fonds Casgrain, 0449, vol. 2, n° 17.

commencé à corriger la semaine dernière le dernier chapitre de mon ouvrage, et j'espère le terminer sous peu de jours et en être débarrassé, car j'en ai pardessus la tête de ces épreuves à n'en plus finir[24].»

La parution des *Mémoires*, un volume de cinq cent soixante-six pages réparties en dix-sept chapitres[25], ne causa pas d'effet de surprise. Les lecteurs savaient à quoi s'attendre de l'auteur des *Anciens Canadiens*. Cet ouvrage ne manqua pas cependant de plaire à la critique. Perçu par son auteur comme un travail dont le seul mérite était d'être un complément à son premier volume, il fut rapidement considéré comme une pièce maîtresse de la littérature québécoise. Réédité lui aussi plusieurs fois et traduit en anglais par madame Jane Brierly en 1988, il figure aujourd'hui parmi les rares volumes publiés au Canada au siècle dernier qui suscite de l'intérêt en dehors du cercle des spécialistes. Il est encore lu au Québec, mais aussi ailleurs au pays et à l'étranger.

Cette publication valut à son auteur, déjà perçu comme le premier romancier québécois, d'être également considéré comme le meilleur et le plus aimable de nos conteurs.

---

24. Lettre de Philippe Aubert de Gaspé à Raoul de Beaujeu, le 18 février 1866, dans J. Castonguay, *La Seigneurie de Philippe Aubert...*, p. 141.
25. Philippe A. de Gaspé, *Mémoires*, Ottawa, G.-É. Desbarats, Imprimeur-Éditeur, 1866. Après la mort de son père en 1865, Georges-Édouard Desbarats alla s'établir à Ottawa où il travailla pour le gouvernement. C'est ce qui explique que les *Mémoires* ne furent pas publiés à Québec en 1866, mais bien à Ottawa.

CHAPITRE 13

La révélation d'un troisième ouvrage
(1866-1869)

Composer un ouvrage de l'importance de *Mémoires* ne fut pas une tâche facile pour un octogénaire venu tardivement à l'écriture. Philippe Aubert de Gaspé n'a pas cherché à le dissimuler. Au moment d'en écrire le dernier paragraphe, il avoue simplement qu'aux prises avec le découragement il a été tenté d'interrompre cent fois son travail. Bien plus, il donne à entendre qu'avec les *Mémoires* il va mettre un terme à son activité littéraire: «Je brise ma plume trop pesante pour ma main débile, écrit-il, et je finis par ce refrain d'une ancienne chanson: «Bonsoir la compagnie[1].» Si l'on en croit la lettre qu'il écrivit à son neveu, Raoul de Beaujeu, le 18 septembre 1866, la publication elle-même de cet ouvrage, avec l'interminable correction d'épreuves qu'elle comporta, ne fut pas non plus de nature à l'encourager à poursuivre son œuvre.

---

1. *Mémoires*, p. 559.

Quoi qu'il en soit, ceux que la lecture des dernières lignes des *Mémoires* avait pu attrister n'eurent pas à attendre bien longtemps pour retrouver le sourire. Reposé et stimulé par l'accueil réservé à son volume, Philippe Aubert de Gaspé ne tarda pas à remplacer la plume qu'il avait brisée. Bien que la critique lui fut favorable, il se trouvera quand même un lecteur pour envoyer deux lettres au *Journal de Québec* qui piquèrent sa curiosité et peut-être son amour propre. Dans sa première missive, publiée le 18 septembre 1866, le lecteur pointilleux faisait remarquer que l'auteur des *Mémoires* avait omis de dire dans son ouvrage que c'est à Ives Cholet que la cité de Québec était redevable de la statue du général Wolfe qui ornait l'encoignure des rues du Palais et Saint-Jean. Dans sa seconde, il revenait à la charge pour affirmer que la statue en question avait été commandée par un aubergiste du nom de Hipps et que des officiers du 15e régiment britannique avait fourni une image au sculpteur Cholet pour l'aider dans son travail[2].

Bien qu'habitué à se fier à son exceptionnelle mémoire, de Gaspé voulut cette fois défendre son point de vue en faisant appel à des autorités et à des documents de première main. Le résultat de son travail fut publié dans le quatrième tome du *Foyer canadien* qui parut à l'automne de cette année-là. Dans un article d'une dizaine de pages, l'auteur des *Mémoires* rétablissait les faits en démontrant que ni Yves Cholet, ni son frère Hyacinthe n'avaient pu, compte tenu de leur âge, sculpter la célèbre statue du général Wolfe[3].

Sa contribution au *Foyer canadien* en 1866 ne se limite pas à ce texte. Aux légendes qu'il s'était plu à raconter dans les *Anciens Canadiens* et les *Mémoires*, il voulut ajouter le récit de la légende du Grand Serpent, une tradition qui demeura longtemps vivace parmi les Hurons de la Jeune-Lorette. Le

---

2.   *Divers par Philippe Aubert de Gaspé, auteur des «Anciens Canadiens» et des «Mémoires»*, Montréal, C.O. Beauchemin et fils, 1893, pp. 89-92.
3.   Philippe Aubert de Gaspé, «La statue du général Wolfe», dans *Le Foyer canadien*, tome IV, 1866, pp. 513-523. Dans ce texte, il écrit «Cholet».

diable, prenant la forme d'un grand serpent, puis d'un petit vieillard, achète l'âme d'Otsitsot, surnommé le Carcajou, en retour de son aide et d'une bouteille d'eau-de-vie qui ne se videra jamais et le rendra riche. Le Carcajou ne doit pas retourner à la foi chrétienne, sinon le petit manitou se vengera sur lui et sur sa race, et son village demeurera stationnaire[4].

* * *

L'activité littéraire du célèbre conteur au cours des années qui suivirent la publication de ces deux articles dans *Le Foyer canadien* nous est connue, quoique de façon imparfaite, grâce à l'intérêt que porta Alfred Aubert de Gaspé à l'œuvre de son père. Incapable de conserver longtemps le même emploi, Alfred éprouva des difficultés financières toute sa vie. Il l'avoue sans détour dans sa correspondance avec l'honorable Georges Baby, un cousin de son père, auquel il fit fréquemment appel pour obtenir un emploi ou de nouvelles responsabilités au ministère des Postes[5]. Ministre du Revenu de l'Intérieur, puis juge, Georges Baby l'aida volontiers.

Philippe Aubert de Gaspé aida lui aussi son fils. Il le fit au moyen de ses œuvres, les seuls biens dont il n'eut pas que l'usufruit. Le 10 janvier 1867, moins d'un an après la parution des *Mémoires*, il lui céda tous ses droits sur cet ouvrage, «pour en jouir comme bon lui semblera[6]». Ce que fit Alfred qui en publia la deuxième édition. Celui-ci bénéficia aussi des *Anciens Canadiens* dont Georges-É. Desbarats lui céda, également gracieusement, les droits le 19 août 1885[7]. On sait qu'Alfred vendit par la suite le droit de publier et de vendre cet ouvrage aux libraires Cadieux et Dérome et, dix ans plus tard, à la maison C.O. Beauchemin et fils. C'est sans doute

---

4. *Ibid.*, pp. 533-551.
5. Archives de l'Université de Montréal, Fonds P 88 (Collection Baby).
6. ANQ-Q, greffe du notaire Alexandre Benjamin Sirois, 10 janvier 1867.
7. ANQ-M, greffe du notaire E. G. Simard, 19 août 1885.

DIVERS

PAR

PHILIPPE AUBERT DE GASPÉ

AUTEUR

DES " ANCIENS CANADIENS " ET DES " MÉMOIRES "

PREMIÈRE ÉDITION

MONTRÉAL
C. O. BEAUCHEMIN & FILS, LIB.-IMPRIMEURS
256 et 258, rue Saint-Paul
—
1893

ainsi que, plusieurs années après la mort de l'auteur des *Anciens Canadiens* et des *Mémoires*, Alfred Aubert de Gaspé se retrouva en possession des manuscrits de son père. On croit qu'il en détruisit plusieurs et que le mérite d'avoir sauvé du naufrage ce qui en restait revint à sa fille Blanche[8]. Ce qui est certain c'est qu'on n'a pas retrouvé le manuscrit des *Mémoires*, si ce n'est quelques chapitres, ni les notes explicatives du manuscrit original des *Anciens Canadiens*, ni les textes publiés par Alfred sous le titre *Divers* en 1893[9].

---

8. J. Castonguay, «Les souvenirs d'un bon gentilhomme», postface de l'édition des *Anciens Canadiens* publiée par les Éditions internationales Alain Stanké ltée, Montréal, 1987, pp. 302 et 303.

9. *Divers par Philippe Aubert de Gaspé, auteur des «Anciens Canadiens» et des «Mémoires»*, Montréal, C.O. Beauchemin et fils, 1893.

Cette dernière publication est cependant instructive quant à l'activité littéraire de Philippe Aubert de Gaspé durant les dernières années de sa vie. *Divers* contient les deux articles qui parurent dans *Le Foyer canadien* en 1866, mais aussi deux textes qu'Alfred Aubert de Gaspé dit avoir découvert dans les papiers de sa famille[10]. Le premier, qui loue l'hospitalité traditionnelle des aborigènes du Canada, raconte l'histoire d'une esclave iroquoise qu'un Abénaquis céda un jour au capitaine Jean-Baptiste Couillard de Lespinay, seigneur de Saint-Thomas (Montmagny) et de Saint-Pierre, en retour d'un fusil de chasse et d'une corne ornée de plaques d'argent. «La jeune indienne, raconte l'auteur, sut bien vite gagner la confiance de ses maîtres, et se prit d'affection tendre et maternelle pour l'enfant doux et aimable qu'on lui donna à amuser et qu'elle appela son fils[11].» Elle vécut cinquante ans au manoir seigneurial des Couillard de Lespinay. «Ressemblant par les qualités précieuses de l'âme et du cœur» à celui dont on lui avait confié la garde durant sa jeunesse, elle s'éteignit trois jours avant la mort de son protégé, dont elle avait pressenti la fin prochaine[12].

Quant au second texte, il a trait à un ancien chef malécite qui avait l'habitude de planter chaque été son *wiggam* le long de la grève, à proximité du manoir des Aubert de Gaspé. Toujours sombre et rêveur, le vieil indien n'échangeait que quelques paroles avec ceux qu'il rencontrait. Néanmoins, l'auteur des *Mémoires* réussit avec le temps à gagner son amitié et à entrer dans son intimité. Encore jeune, le Loup-Jaune, c'était là son nom, avait appris de sa mère la voix des bois, des lacs et des montagnes, et de son père l'art de la chasse et de la guerre. Il devint ainsi un grand chef, un terrible chasseur et un guerrier redoutable. Son cri faisait trembler la forêt, sa flèche allait percer l'aigle dans les nuages

---

10. *Ibid.*, p. 7.
11. *Ibid.*, p. 46.
12. *Ibid.*, pp 9-52.

Le Loup-Jaune sur la grève du manoir de Saint-Jean-Port-Joli.
(*Divers*, éditions Beauchemin.)

et sa hache faisait tomber les ennemis des Malécites comme les feuilles sèches pendant la tempête. Fait prisonnier par les Iroquois, il avait été cependant torturé plus d'une fois mais, pouvant «faire parler l'écho» (il était ventriloque), il avait su échapper chaque fois à la mort[13].

Dans la présentation qu'il fait des quatre textes contenus dans *Divers*, Alfred Aubert de Gaspé avertit le lecteur qu'il s'agit là «des derniers écrits d'un octogénaire qui est décédé avant d'avoir eu l'avantage de pouvoir les repasser[14]». Cette affirmation n'est pas exacte. Les deux textes publiés d'abord dans *Le Foyer canadien* avaient certainement été revisés par l'auteur. Quant aux deux autres, on ne saurait dire qu'ils étaient les derniers écrits de Philippe Aubert de Gaspé. Parmi les documents dont Alfred de Gaspé avait hérité de son père se trouvait un texte qui semble avoir échappé complétement à son attention. Ce texte a pourtant l'avantage d'expliquer l'existence d'au moins trois des quatre récits con-

13. *Ibid.*, pp. 55-88.
14. *Ibid.*, p. 7.

tenus dans *Divers* et de les situer par rapport à la production littéraire du célèbre conteur au cours des dernières années de sa vie. Bien plus, il nous apprend que Philippe Aubert de Gaspé, loin d'avoir brisé sa plume, avait entrepris, à l'âge de quatre-vingt-trois ans, de composer un troisième ouvrage. Le coin de Fanchette n'étant pas encore vide, il avait commencé un second volume de chroniques ou de mémoires.

Ce texte ignoré, volontairement ou non, par Alfred de Gaspé contient un intéressant prologue à ce que devait être ce dernier ouvrage. Dialoguant avec un ami, sous prétexte de demander l'avis d'un expert, l'auteur explique les motifs qui l'ont amené à reprendre la plume. D'abord, l'âge n'a rien à faire avec son projet: Fontenelle ne bouillait-il pas d'esprit quoique centenaire? Puis, le public a bien accueilli ses premiers ouvrages et il n'a pas raison de redouter la critique. Enfin, il a encore bien des anecdotes à raconter.

À la suite du prologue vient un premier chapitre consacré aux aborigènes du Canada qui indique vraisemblablement l'orientation que l'auteur voulait donner à cet ouvrage. On peut aisément assumer ici que les textes publiés dans *Divers*, où il est question en particulier des Malécites, des Hurons, des Abénaquis et des Iroquois, avaient été expressément composés pour figurer à la suite du premier chapitre et former ainsi un ensemble dans lequel l'auteur, après avoir traité des aborigènes en général, abordait des sujets analogues mais de portée plus restreinte[15].

Quoi qu'il en soit, Philippe Aubert de Gaspé n'eut pas la santé, ni le temps nécessaires pour terminer son troisième ouvrage. Il avait quand même réussi à en écrire plusieurs chapitres et ce que l'on en sait aujourd'hui ne saurait qu'aider à évaluer l'ensemble de l'œuvre du bon gentilhomme et en particulier les travaux qui suivirent la publication des *Mémoires*.

---

15. Ce texte est publié *in extenso*, avec quelques autres inédits, en appendice au présent volume.

CHAPITRE 14

Les dernières années du célèbre conteur
(1868-1871)

Le manoir de Saint-Jean-Port-Joli, qui avait connu une grande animation durant la première moitié du XIXᵉ siècle, devint calme et paisible, presque inanimé, à la fin des années 1860. Ainsi en fut-il de la résidence des Aubert de Gaspé à Québec. Les mariages, les départs et les décès avaient réduit le bon gentilhomme à vivre presque seul. Au moment de la publication des *Anciens Canadiens* en 1863, seuls quatre de ses enfants n'étaient pas mariés: Thomas, Azéline, Philomène et Atala. Thomas vivait sur la rive sud, où il desservait la paroisse de Saint-Apollinaire, Azéline demeurait à Montréal, où elle mourut en 1864, et Philomène avait élu domicile à Côteau-du-Lac chez la comtesse de Beaujeu, sa sœur. Seule Atala partageait encore l'existence de son père. À ses côtés durant les beaux jours de la parution de ses ouvrages, Atala était encore là lorsque l'âge commença à modifier sensiblement la perception que le vieux conteur avait de l'existence et à réduire sensiblement ses forces.

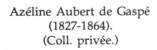

Azéline Aubert de Gaspé
(1827-1864).
(Coll. privée.)

Philomène Aubert de Gaspé
(1837-1872). (ASQ, photo W. B.
Edwards Inc. 0297, p. 35.)

La vie de Philippe Aubert de Gaspé, de l'enfance au seuil de la vieillesse, exception faite pour la période qui suivit sa destitution comme shérif, fut marquée par la confiance et l'enthousiasme, voire l'insouciance. Ne s'occupant, lorsqu'il était jeune, «ni du passé, ni encore moins de l'avenir[1]», il conserva longtemps «une foi robuste en lui-même[2]». Mais, après la publication des *Anciens Canadiens*, l'idée de vieillissement sembla l'envahir progressivement. On commença à rencontrer de plus en plus fréquemment sous sa plume les termes septuagénaire, octogénaire, vieillard, vieillesse, mort et tombe.

Le mot qu'il adressa aux étudiants du Collège de l'Assomption en 1865, lors de la présentation de la pièce de théâtre tirée de son roman, ne laissa guère de doute sur son évolution psychologique. Même s'il avait eu l'occasion au cours de sa vie de prendre la parole en public, il préféra ce

1. *Mémoires*, p. 12.
2. *Les Anciens Canadiens*, p. 176.

jour-là lire un texte écrit pour la circonstance, alléguant que «les infirmités inhérentes au vieil âge, la perte de la mémoire, des mots propres et des expressions précises» ne lui permettaient pas d'improviser. «J'ai peu d'espoir, Messieurs, disait-il, de conserver longtemps le souvenir de votre gracieuseté: le septuagénaire ne vit que pour la tombe la plus prochaine; mais quelque soit la durée de sa vie, elle aura l'effet de dissiper les sombres nuages qui attristent, de temps à autre, l'existence d'un vieillard[3].»

On a vu que le dernier paragraphe des *Mémoires* n'est guère plus optimiste, pas plus d'ailleurs que le prologue qu'il rédigea pour son troisième ouvrage. Bien que non dépourvu d'humour, ce dernier texte est celui d'un homme un peu triste qui ne se fait pas d'illusions sur sa fin prochaine:

> Évohé! esprit somnolent de la vieillesse. Rappelle à ma mémoire les anecdoctes des anciens jours que j'ai omises. Transporte moi de nouveau et pour la dernière fois, hélas! aux jours heureux de mon enfance et à ceux si bruyants de ma jeunesse. Le temps passe. La tombe sourde et silencieuse ne proclame qu'une vérité terrible, l'éternité[4].

Au nombre des papiers conservés par son fils Alfred se trouvait aussi un document de quelques lignes qu'on aimerait citer ici. Nostalgique, Aubert de Gaspé se remémore avec tristesse les jours de sa jeunesse passés sur les rives du Saint-Laurent:

> Oh! beaux jours de ma jeunesse dont il ne me reste que le souvenir, vous êtes évanouis pour toujours. Poésie de l'âme tout est éteint. Je revois chaque année les scènes grandioses qu'offrent les rives de votre majestueux Saint-Laurent. Je me promène encore le long de ses rives par une belle nuit canadienne, mais je suis mort à toutes ses jouissances[5].

---

3. *Biographie et oraison funèbre du Révd. H.F. Labelle...*, pp. 67 et 68.
4. Prologue du troisième ouvrage de Philippe Aubert de Gaspé écrit vraisemblablement en 1869 et reproduit en appendice au présent travail.
5. Archives de l'auteur.

* * *

À compter de 1868, la vie parut encore plus difficile au vieil auteur. À la lassitude inévitable qu'entraîne le grand âge commencèrent à s'ajouter les malaises physiques. La correspondance qu'il entretenait avec ses filles à cette époque en font foi. Avant 1868, il n'était jamais question de santé dans ses écrits mais, à compter de cette année-là, il en fut tout autrement. Quelques mois après le départ de son fils Thomas de la paroisse de Saint-Apollinaire, où il était curé, pour celle de Saint-Joseph de Lévis[6], où il allait assumer de moindres responsabilités, il se plaignit fréquemment de sa santé. Le 27 juillet 1868, par exemple, en repos chez son gendre William Fraser, à Rivière-du-Loup, il écrivait à sa fille Elmire une longue lettre dans laquelle il lui faisait part de la chaleur qui continuait à l'accabler et à lui enlever tout courage, ajoutant que son système nerveux avait été naturellement beaucoup ébranlé par la catastrophe qui venait d'arriver. On ne saurait dire de quel événement il s'agissait, bien que la suite de la lettre laisse entendre qu'il s'agissait d'un problème familial qu'Elmire aida à résoudre[7].

Un grand bouleversement attendait l'auteur des *Anciens Canadiens* en 1869. Atala, déjà âgée de quarante ans, décida de mettre fin à son célibat. Elle épousa, à Rivière-du-Loup, où elle avait pris l'habitude de séjourner avec son père durant l'été, le docteur Joseph-Eusèbe Hudon, veuf de Hermine-Julie Blanchet[8]. Événement heureux en soi, ce mariage eut, il va sans dire, des conséquences fâcheuses pour le vieux conteur. Pendant qu'Atala réunissait ses effets

---

6. L'abbé Thomas Aubert de Gaspé, qui, selon son biographe, semblait avoir un petit quelque chose en commun avec dom Balaguère des *Lettres de mon moulin* d'Alphonse Daudet, quitta la paroisse de Saint-Apollinaire au début du mois de janvier 1868.
7. Philippe Aubert de Gaspé à madame juge Stuart, Gaspé Bassin, 27 juillet 1868 (Archives privées).
8. Leur mariage eut lieu à la paroisse Saint-Patrice de Rivière-du-Loup le 10 mai 1869.

Eugénie Atala Aubert de Gaspé (1829-1887).
(Coll. privée.)

personnels pour aller s'établir au village de Fraserville (Rivière-du-Loup), celui-ci devait dire adieu à sa demeure du Vieux-Québec, à son cabinet de travail et à la plupart des livres qui lui avaient procuré tant de satisfaction durant sa vie.

À partir de ce moment, il dut partager son existence entre les résidences de ses filles Elmire et Anaïs qui lui avaient ouvert grandes leurs portes. Durant l'hiver, il continua ainsi à demeurer à Québec, plus précisément à Edgehill, la villa des Stuart située à Mount Pleasant, à l'ouest de la ville[9], et quand venait le printemps il se retrouvait chez les

---

9.   Edgehill était situé à l'ouest de l'actuelle avenue Salaberry, au nord du chemin Sainte-Foy.

Les enfants de Philippe Aubert de Gaspé

Suzanne (1812-1882) + (1829) William **Power** (1800-1860), avocat (1826), député de Gaspé (1832-1838), juge (1840).

Philippe fils (1814-1841), journaliste et écrivain, décédé célibataire à Halifax.

Adélaïde (1815-1895) + (1832) G. **Saveuse de Beaujeu** (1810-1865), seigneur de Soulanges, conseiller législatif (1848-1865).

Elmire (1817-1899) + (1842) Andrew **Stuart** (1812-1891), avocat (1834), juge à la Cour supérieure (1859), juge en chef (1885).

Zélie (1818-1893) + (1840) Louis-Eusèbe **Borne** (?-1842), marchand aux Îles-de-la-Madeleine.

Thomas (1820-1889), prêtre (1847), curé de Saint-Éloi, Saint-Apollinaire, assistant à Saint-Joseph de Lévis, curé à Thurso, retiré à Lévis.

Pierre-Édouard (1822-1862) + (1846) Marie-Adélaïde Caron, agriculteur à Saint-Jean-Port-Joli.

Zoé (1825-1888) + (1849) Charles **Alleyn** (1817-1890), avocat (1840), maire (1854), député de Québec (1854-1860) et de Québec-Ouest (1860-1867), ministre (1857-1862).

Azéline (1827-1864), célibataire, décédée à Montréal.

Atala (1829-1887) + (1869) Joseph-Eusèbe **Hudon**, médecin à Rivière-du-Loup (sans descendance).

Alfred (1831-1907) + (1859) Madeleine **Fraser**, employé du ministère des Postes (1854-1884).

Anaïs (1834-1923) + (1857) William **Fraser** (1830-1908), seigneur de Rivière-du-Loup.

Philomène (1837-1872), religieuse, décédée à Rochefort (France).

... et quelques-uns de ses descendants

POWER
Suzanne (1830) + (1854) Charles **Sharples**
Maria (1832) + (????) Edward **Murphy**, sénateur
William (1835), décédé à Chicago
Thérèse (1837) + (1856) Paschal-Y. **Taché**, fonctionnaire
Michael (1839), établi au Colorado
Dominick (1842), décédé dans les Rocheuses
Augustus (1847), avocat, fonctionnaire fédéral
Isabella (1850) + (1872) Georges **Duval**

SAVEUSE DE BEAUJEU
Catherine (1836) et **Blanche** (1843), religieuses
Philippe-Arthur (1845)
Georges-Raoul (1847), député fédéral et provincial
Marie-Alice (1851) + (1870) A. **Siochan de Kersabiec**
Yvonne (1853), religieuse

STUART
Henry Macnab (1843), avocat (sans descendance)
Suzanne (1844) + (1864) Louis **Beaubien**, député fédéral et provincial
Andrew Charles (1846), avocat (sans descendance)
Alma (1848) + (1896) Francis **McLennan** (sans descendance)
Maud (1850) + (1879) William G. **Lemesurier**
James de Gaspé (1853), marié en Ontario
Gustave George (1853), marié à Londres
Mary Grace (1862) + (1888) Louis A. **Audette**

BORNE
Zélie (1841) + (1864) T. J. J. **Loranger**, député et juge

AUBERT DE GASPÉ
Adélaïde (1847) + (1878) Cyprien **Moreau**, capitaine
Édouard (1848), établi au Connecticut
Philippe (1850), décédé à Pittsburg
Alfred (1853), célibataire
Thomas (1854), établi aux États-unis
Suzanne (1856) + (1878) Firmin **Bélanger**
Julienne (1857) + (1880) comte **Quiquerand de Beaujeu**
Charles (1858), décédé au Connecticut

ALLEYN
Margaret (1850) + (1871) John **Sharples**, conseiller législatif
Richard (1852), médecin à East Angus, célibataire
Charles (1854), célibataire
Zoé (1855) + (1877) Thomas-L. **Taschereau**, avocat
J.-Edmond (1857), avocat, ass.-greffier du Conseil législatif
Miriam (1865) + (1889) C. A. E. T. **Taillebois de Preston**

AUBERT DE GASPÉ
Philippe-Alfred (1860)
Blanche (1861)
Marie-Adèle (1865)
Marie-Louise (1867)

FRASER
Malcolm Philippe (1859)
Joseph William (1863)
André Archibald (1867)
Alice-Marie (1870) + (1891) Hector **Prévost** (sans descendance)

Manoir seigneurial de Rivière-du-Loup. Vue actuelle. (Coll. de l'auteur.)

Fraser à Rivière-du-Loup, où l'air salin semblait mieux lui convenir.

Les mois qui suivirent le départ d'Atala, on le devine, ne marquèrent pas d'amélioration. Le 3 septembre, alléguant «son grand âge et ses infirmités toujours croissantes», il se vit contraint à regret de décliner l'invitation qui lui était faite d'assister au mariage de son cher neveu, Raoul de Beaujeu[10]. L'été 1870, sur lequel il comptait pour reprendre un peu de forces, fut aussi décevant. «Je suis tantôt bien tantôt mal, tantôt faible tantôt plus fort», confiait-il à sa fille Elmire le 15 août; «en un mot je suis malade de mes 84 ans, et toute la rhubarbe et le céné du monde ne me rendront pas la santé[11]».

10. Philippe Aubert de Gaspé à Raoul de Beaujeu, 3 septembre 1869, dans P.-G. Roy. *À travers les Anciens Canadiens...*, pp. 242-243.
11. Philippe Aubert de Gaspé à Mme A. Stuart, 15 août 1870 (Archives privées).

Edgehill (Mount Pleasant), villa de sir Andrew et lady Stuart.
(Archives des sœurs missionnaires de l'Immaculée-Conception.)

De retour à Edgehill au mois de septembre, le bon vieillard continua à décliner. À la fin du mois de novembre, Atala
et Anaïs, qui s'interrogeaient sur la santé de leur père, reçurent une lettre qui débutait néanmoins de façon encoura-
geante: «J'ai le plaisir de vous annoncer que je suis beaucoup
mieux, y lisait-on, et à peu près libéré de ma dernière
attaque, laquelle sans être aussi cruelle que les précédentes
ne m'en avait pas moins fait beaucoup souffrir». Le dernier
paragraphe ne fut toutefois pas long à tamiser la lueur
d'espoir créée par cette introduction inhabituelle. «Aurais-je
encore le bonheur de vous revoir tous le printemps prochain,
à Rivière-du-Loup? ajoutait le grand malade. Je l'espère
toujours sans trop y croire. J'écris bien mal, je crains bien de
ne pouvoir écrire comme par le passé. Pas de nouvelles de la
chère Philomène[12].»

---

12. Philippe Aubert de Gaspé à mesdames Hudon et Fraser, le 20 novembre
1870 (Archives privées).

Philippe Aubert de Gaspé ne revit pas sa chère Philomène, la plus jeune de ses filles. Elle avait quitté le Canada pour la France et ne revint jamais au pays. Elle mourut sœur de Charité à Rochefort, le 17 mars 1872[13]. Le bon gentilhomme ne revit pas non plus Rivière-du-Loup, ni Saint-Jean-Port-Joli qui avaient tant charmé son enfance et ses vieux jours. Entouré de ses enfants, il s'éteignit à Edgehill le 29 janvier 1871, à l'âge de quatre-vingt-cinq ans.

L'abbé Casgrain, qui avait été témoin de ses succès littéraires, était aussi à son chevet ce jour-là. Il a écrit par la suite une notice nécrologique dans laquelle il raconte les derniers moments de celui qu'il appelait respectueusement son vieil ami.

> «La douceur de M. de Gaspé, sa patience au milieu d'atroces souffrances, écrit-il, furent inaltérables jusqu'à la fin [...]. Ce fut un spectacle navrant et consolant à la fois de voir ses enfants et petits-enfants, venir, l'un après l'autre, baiser une dernière fois le front glacé du vieillard, qui adressait à chacun une parole affectueuse. Enfin, il joignit les mains, leva les yeux, les referma, et, comme son Sauveur, poussa un profond soupir et ce fut tout. La pâleur de la mort s'étendit sur sa figure, qui devint placide et blanche comme un marbre[14].»

> «Comme le manoir de Saint-Jean demeurait fermé durant l'hiver», racontait madame Castonguay au notaire Jean-Marie Turgeon, «et que notre ami avait demandé d'être inhumé auprès de sa femme, Susanne Allison, de son père, de sa mère, de son grand-père et de sa grand-mère, le notaire Duval lui ouvrit son salon et c'est chez nous que le vieux gentilhomme passa sa dernière nuit sur la terre[15]».

Bien que l'inhumation eut lieu en plein cœur de l'hiver, les habitants de Saint-Jean-Port-Joli attelèrent leurs chevaux pour se rendre des quatre coins de la paroisse dire adieu à leur seigneur. C'est ainsi qu'à côté des Aubert de Gaspé, des

---

13. P.-G. Roy, *La famille Aubert de Gaspé*, Lévis, 1907, p. 173.
14. L'abbé H.-R. Casgrain, *Philippe Aubert de Gaspé...*, pp. 105, 106 et 110.
15. «Une contemporaine de P.A. de Gaspé», dans *L'Événement*, 30 juillet 1951.

Dessin de Louis-Georges Gagnon représentant le village
de Saint-Jean-Port-Joli en 1871. À l'extrême-gauche, la maison
du notaire L.-Z. Duval. (Coll. privée.)

Stuart, des Alleyn, des Loranger, des Fraser et des Hudon,
venus de Québec ou de Rivière-du-Loup, se retrouvèrent ce
jour-là les Dubé, les Dumas, les Verrault, les Pelletier, les
Caron, les Fortin, les Castonguay, les Duval, les Chouinard et
beaucoup d'autres. La plupart de ces derniers n'avaient pas
lu *Les Anciens Canadiens*, ni les *Mémoires*, dans lesquels le
célèbre conteur rend hommage à leurs vertus, mais tous
savaient qu'il ne les avait pas traités comme on traite de
simples censitaires. «Monsieur Philippe», comme ils aimaient
l'appeler familièrement, repose au milieu d'eux depuis le 1er
février 1871[16].

16. Les biens dont Philippe Aubert de Gaspé avait la jouissance revinrent à
ses enfants, ou à leurs descendants, le jour de sa mort. Le partage devant se
faire en douze parts égales, ces derniers décidèrent, d'un commun accord, de
s'en départir. C'est ainsi que, le 15 juillet 1872, Narcisse Duval, le frère du
notaire du même nom, acquit pour la somme de 4008 piastres les «cens et

* * *

L'extraordinaire réussite de Philippe Aubert de Gaspé est sans précédent. Après avoir connu la reprobation de ses concitoyens et avoir vécu à l'ombre durant quelques années, pour des motifs discutables il est vrai, il a su attirer sur lui la sympathie, le respect et l'admiration des grands comme des humbles. N'ayant que l'usufruit ou la jouissance de quelques fiefs et seigneuries, dont il avait confié la gestion à son notaire et loué les moulins et les espaces cultivables, il réussit par sa personnalité attachante et ses écrits remarquables à redorer le blason du régime seigneurial et à en devenir le symbole incontesté. Bien plus, devenu auteur à l'âge de soixante-seize ans, il sut, en publiant un ouvrage appelé à devenir le premier classique de la littérature canadienne, s'élever au premier rang des écrivains de son époque. Seigneur et homme de lettres, Philippe Aubert de Gaspé le fut, mais d'une manière hors de l'ordinaire.

---

rentes constitués» qui en faisaient le successeur légitime de Philippe Aubert de Gaspé à Saint-Jean-Port-Joli. Le même jour, l'honorable Thomas J.J. Loranger acheta pour sa part le manoir et ses dépendances pour les revendre immédiatement à Moyse Leclerc, pour la somme de 4001 piastres. Toujours le 15 juillet 1872, Thadé Francœur acquit quant à lui, au coût de 1301 piastres, le moulin à eau situé à l'extrémité est du troisième rang de Saint-Aubert. Quant au moulin se trouvant à l'embouchure de la rivière Trois-Saumons, il fut acheté par Léandre Méthot, pour la somme de 11 970 piastres, le 22 février 1873 (ANQ-Q, greffe du notaire Louis-Zéphirin Duval, 15 juillet 1872 et 22 février 1873).

Aujourd'hui à Saint-Jean-Port-Joli

Philippe Aubert de Gaspé repose sous le banc seigneurial de l'église de Saint-Jean-Port-Joli depuis plus d'un siècle. L'intérêt pour tout ce qui se rattache à ce célèbre écrivain n'est pas près de s'éteindre pour autant. Non seulement continue-t-on à lire ses ouvrages, mais aussi à faire des recherches sur sa vie et les lieux où il vécut.

La Corporation Philippe-Aubert-de-Gaspé constituée en 1987 et dont le premier objectif est de faire connaître l'auteur des *Anciens Canadiens* compte à son actif plusieurs réalisations importantes. Tout en faisant des recherches historiques, elle regroupe, à intervalles réguliers, plusieurs personnes partageant son idéal, dont un certain nombre de descendants du dernier seigneur de Saint-Jean-Port-Joli. Depuis 1988, elle a fait l'achat du domaine où s'élevait son manoir et, grâce à l'aide du ministère des Affaires culturelles et de la M.R.C. de L'Islet, a entrepris des recherches archéologiques et restauré le vieux four à pain qui échappa au triste incendie du 30 avril 1909.

Dirigées par l'archéologue Richard Fiset, les fouilles ont donné jusqu'à maintenant d'intéressants résultats. En plus d'avoir mené à la découverte de quelque quarante mille artefacts, elles ont permis de connaître les dimensions exactes du manoir seigneurial, les diverses étapes de sa construction et

Cellier découvert sur le site du manoir seigneurial au cours des recherches archéologiques de 1990. (Ministère des Affaires culturelles du Québec.)

le mode de vie de ses habitants. Elles ont aussi mis au jour un étonnant cellier de pierre datant vraisemblablement du Régime français. Aux yeux de monsieur Michel Gaumond, de la direction du patrimoine au ministère des Affaires culturelles, il s'agirait là d'une construction inusitée d'un grand intérêt.

La Corporation Philippe-Aubert-de-Gaspé, présidée depuis sa fondation par monsieur André Thibault et dont Me Louis de la Chesnaye Audette, arrière-petit-fils de l'auteur des *Anciens Canadiens*, assume la présidence d'honneur, songe à établir bientôt un centre d'interprétation.

Saint-Jean-Port-Joli se souvient.

Inédits de Philippe Aubert de Gaspé

FRAGMENTS D'UN TROISIÈME OUVRAGE

Prologue

L'auteur. Bonjour, mon cher ami; heureux de vous rencontrer, je cherchais un homme et je l'ai trouvé.

L'ami. Grand merci du compliment; vous êtes plus heureux que Diogène; mais parole d'honneur j'igno-
rais que ce phœnix fut si facile à trouver dans
notre bonne ville de Québec.

L'auteur. Vous êtes trop modeste. J'ai un petit projet en
tête; mais je ne veux rien faire sans consulter un
littérateur éminent; ma bonne étoile m'a fait vous
rencontrer et je n'agirai que d'après vos conseils.

L'ami. Il est inutile, monsieur, de m'en dire davantage;
je vois à votre air capable que vous vous propo-
sez d'écrire un troisième ouvrage; c'est un sujet
très délicat: et permettez-moi de me recuser.

L'auteur. Vos scrupules vous font honneur, monsieur,
mais il me fallait prendre l'avis d'un littérateur
distingué, *homo litteratus* ou *litteratus homo*, si
vous le préférez, j'ai eu le bonheur de vous rencontrer, vous êtes hypothéqué, comme aimait
dire Molière, à la source par devoir et par état et
je ne lâcherai point que lorsque vous m'aurez
donné votre avis.

L'ami. Il a le diable au corps. Puisque vous êtes (entre le
doute) si tenace, monsieur, permettez-moi de
vous demander, au préalable, quel âge vous avez
maintenant?

L'auteur.	L'âge n'y fait rien, mais puisque vous y tenez, j'ai pris quatre vingt trois ans le 30 octobre dernier.
L'ami.	Bel âge pour se reposer. Vous vous rappelez sans doute un certain archevêque de Grenade et ses homélies dont parle Gil Blas.
L'auteur.	Vous citez, monsieur, une belle autorité que celle de sieur Gil Blas, un niais que chacun mystifie à qui mieux mieux, et auquel on fait manger de la merluche pour de la morue, c.a.d. du poisson salé pour du poisson frais; et un ragout de matou pour un civet de lièvre.
L'ami.	Vous oubliez que ce n'est pas Gil Blas qui a écrit ses propres aventures, mais Lesage, un écrivain célèbre.
L'auteur.	Votre écrivain célèbre n'était pas sage lorsqu'il a écrit l'épisode du respectable archevêque de Grenade qu'il aurait dû respecter.
L'ami. (entre le doute)	Le malheureux fait des calembours.
L'auteur.	N'avez-vous pas l'exemple de Fontenelle qui bouillait encore d'esprit quoique centenaire.
L'ami.	C'est vrai, mais, sans vous offenser vous n'êtes pas Fontenelle.
L'auteur.	C'est fort heureux car je serais âgé de deux cent douze ans bien commis et je ne songerais pas à écrire un autre livre.
L'ami.	Ce serait malheureux!
L'auteur.	J'ai écrit deux ouvrages que le public a très bien accueillis.
L'ami.	Sauf quelques critiques qui ont prétendu peut être à tort que certaines de vos phrases ne trouveraient pas grâce devant l'Académie française.

L'auteur.   Autre belle autorité, monsieur, que votre aca-
            démie. Ignorez-vous, monsieur, que le peuple
            invente et forme les langues et que les académies
            les déforment. Nos académiciens n'ont-ils pas
            fait disparaître en partie cette belle et expressive
            langue des Celtes que nous tenions de nos
            ancêtres, pour y substituer des mots dérivés du
            latin, du grec et de toutes les langues de l'Eu-
            rope! Et ici au Canada, Grand Dieu, à quelques
            rares exceptions, il faut être bien versé dans la
            langue anglaise pour comprendre le français de
            nos littérateurs.

L'ami.   Ma foi vous m'en direz tant que je vous conseille
            d'écrire au plus vite.

L'auteur.   J'étais certain d'avance de votre approbation, et il
            me tarde d'avoir une plume entre les doigts.

Je me suis confessé à lui de ma propre fronde. Je n'étais
pas sérieux lorsque j'ai consulté ce jeune pédant, mais s'il
s'imagine que je n'ai pas senti les coups de griffes qu'il m'a
donnés, il se trompe fort, s'il croit, oh, mon fils, qu'en jouant
le rôle de Géronimo dans la comédie de Molière, il a trouvé
son Sganarelle. Je ne sais maintenant comment sortir de ce
dilemme, si je n'écris pas il va croire que ce sont les petites
flèches qu'il m'a décochées qui m'arrêtent et si j'écris je cours
grand risque de m'exposer à la critique sévère des littéra-
teurs. Il est bien vrai qu'il me restera pour toujours une
consolation dans ma déconvenue. Maints écrivains d'un vrai
mérite ont été de tout temps en butte à la critique des sots,
tandis que des œuvres sans esprit et sans mérite réels ont été
préconisées par eux. D'ailleurs je ne me tiens pas pour battu;
le coin de Fanchette n'est pas encore vide et j'aurai bien du
malheur si je n'y trouve pas matière à écrire un second
volume de chroniques.

Evohé! esprit somnolant de la vieillesse.

Rappelle à ma mémoire les anecdotes des anciens jours que j'ai omises! Transporte moi de nouveau et pour la dernière fois, hélas! aux jours heureux de mon enfance et à ceux si bruyants de ma jeunesse. Hâte-toi! Le temps presse. La tombe sourde et silencieuse ne proclame qu'une vérité terrible, l'éternité!

CHAPITRE PREMIER

Les aborigènes

Plus tard, les traditions seront effacées; un peuple récent foulera, sans les connaître, les tombes des vieux Français; les témoins des anciennes mœurs auront disparu.

CHATEAUBRIAND

Ceux qui écrivent maintenant l'histoire des anciens aborigènes du Canada ne peuvent le faire qu'en compulsant les anciennes chroniques de l'Amérique du Nord, mais moi, octogénaire, je vais les peindre tels qu'ils étaient il y a cent cinquante ans. J'ai connu, en effet, un grand nombre des mêmes hommes de cette race maintenant éteinte qui a joué un si grand rôle dans les guerres de cette colonie quarante ans avant la cession du Canada à l'Angleterre. Peuple nomade c'était encore la même vie errante dans nos vastes forêts, sur les bords de nos lacs et sur les rives de notre majestueux Saint-Laurent. Des chefs, des guerriers, au regard sombre, à la démarche fière, portaient encore le riche et élégant costume qu'ils revêtaient dans leurs visites au grand Ononthio de la Nouvelle-France. Et si d'honorables cicatrices témoignaient de leur valeur dans les fréquents combats qu'ils avaient livrés aux ennemis de leurs alliés français, les membres mutilés d'un certain nombre de guerriers attestaient, aussi, les supplices atroces qu'ils avaient soufferts de leurs barbares ennemis.

J'ai beaucoup pratiqué les sauvages pendant mon enfance et même pendant ma jeunesse; ces aborigènes étaient encore des alliés puissants que le gouvernement avait intérêt à ménager en cas de guerre avec nos voisins. D'amis qu'ils étaient ils pouvaient devenir des ennemis redoutables s'ils tournaient leurs armes contre nous. Aussi le gouvernement avait-il soin de leur faire chaque année des présents considérables pour réchauffer leur loyauté envers la couronne d'Angleterre. Il me serait difficile de fixer l'époque à laquelle notre souverain mit un terme à cette espèce de tribut qu'il payait à la loyauté des Peaux-Rouges, car ce ne fut que par degré et au fur et mesure que la civilisation décimait la race indienne que les cadeaux diminuèrent graduellement de valeur pour cesser dès que leur bon père George III pût se passer de leurs services.

J'ai dit plus haut que j'ai beaucoup pratiqué les sauvages pendant mon enfance et pendant ma jeunesse. Les rives du fleuve Saint-Laurent étaient couvertes pendant l'été des pirogues d'écorce de bouleau de ces arborigènes qui se rendaient à Québec pour y recevoir leurs présents, ou qui retournaient ensuite dans leurs villages, ou dans leurs forêts pour y passer l'hiver. Mais comme le temps n'a aucune valeur pour ces philosophes sans-souci; ils mettaient souvent quinze jours à faire une route qu'ils auraient pu terminer dans une seule journée. Il est bien vrai dire que vivant au jour le jour, il leur fallait camper souvent pour se procuer des vivres chez les visages pâles.

Ils choisissaient de préférence pour camper les grèves sablonneuses, celles du domaine seigneurial et de nos deux voisins du sud-est, courant une dizaine d'arpents jusqu'à la rivière Port-Joli, leur offraient, en tout temps, trois anses de refuge d'un accès facile. Aussi puis-je affirmer qu'il s'écoulait à peine une journée pendant la belle saison de l'été sans que nous eussions la visite de nos amis sauvages. Il est même probable que mon grand-père ayant guerroyé pendant trente ans contre les Anglais avec nos alliés sauvages, ceux qui lui avaient survécu se considéraient encore chez leurs amis lorsqu'ils plantaient leurs *wiggams* sur le domaine de son fils. Mais s'ils usaient sans gêne de l'hospitalité que le seigneur du lieu leur accordait, ils le faisaient avec beaucoup de discrétion. Exemple.

Deux ou trois sauvagesses entrent dans la cuisine du manoir avec chacune un bidon d'écorce de bouleau à la main, et le dialogue suivant s'engage avec ma mère. «Voulez-vous manger?» — «Non, venir chercher du rette (lait) et faline (farine) pour *sagamité* (bouillie) pour *baboujine* (petit enfant).» — «Avez-vous faim?» — Oh! oui. — «Alors commencez par manger et vous aurez ensuite du lait et de la farine.» Elles auraient cru manquer de discrétion à manger et en même temps demander des vivres pour leurs enfants.

Mon père aimait les sauvages pour leur honnêteté. Je suis certain, disait-il, qu'ils ne m'ont dérobé ni fruits, ni légumes quoiqu'ils passent et repassent de jour et de nuit au milieu de mes champs à patates, blé-d'Inde, citrouilles et fèves de mes vergers. Il entre pourtant un matin d'une humeur détestable et dit, ces chiens de *Canaouas* que je croyais si honnêtes m'ont volé des patates cette nuit et je vais de ce pas leur laver la tête d'importance. — Voilà bien du bruit dit ma mère pour une chétive terrine de patates! Viens déjeuner et pardonne leur ce grand crime. — Tu comprends que ce n'est pas la perte de quelques misérables légumes qui me mit en colère, mais je suis peiné de perdre la confiance que j'avais dans une race d'hommes dont mon père m'a tant vanté la probité et dont j'ai moi même fait l'épreuve.

Comme mon père se préparait à sortir, je crus prudent de leur avouer que j'avais donné les malencontreuses pommes de terre au vieux Loup-Jaune. Évidemment soulagé, il me reprocha de ne pas l'avoir averti plus tôt, et partant exposés les honnêtes sauvages à des soupçons injurieux pour un larcin dont ils étaient innocents.

Ma tante Charles de Lanaudière me contait que son père Le Chevalier de Saint-Luc étant surintendant des sauvages à

Montréal, non seulement leurs écuries, étables, hangars et cours étaient encombrés d'Indiens pendant l'été, mais aussi la cuisine, le vestibule et autres chambres du premier étage de leur maison. Les portes des maisons, ajoutait-elle, restaient toujours ouvertes à cette époque même pendant la nuit, je rentrais souvent très tard avec ma sœur en sortant d'un bal, ou d'autres parties de plaisir, et il nous fallait passer sur le corps des sauvages endormis pour monter dans nos chambres. Et chose extraordinaire quoiqu'ils rôdassent souvent, avec le sans façon des Peaux-Rouges, dans les chambres où étaient nos bijoux, nos argenteries, nous ne nous sommes jamais aperçus du plus petit larcin. Mon père disait souvent «ma maison est sous la garde de mes amis».

Ma mère élevée dans la ville de Québec et transportée après son mariage, à l'âge de dix-huit (ans), à la campagne dans un lieu aussi isolé que l'est le manoir de Saint-Jean-Port-Joli, fut d'abord saisi d'effroi, le matin, à la vue d'une demi-douzaine de sauvages, à la mine farouche, dont elle ne soupçonnait même pas la présence sur son domaine, et qui entrant dans le salon lui présentèrent la main en criant qui! qui! ma sœur. Elle poussa un cri; et elle allait fuir, pensant sa longue chevelure blonde en danger, quand son beau-père et son mari acourant à sa voix, et après l'avoir raillé de sa frayeur, accueillirent leurs amis les Peaux-Rouges avec la plus grande cordialité.

Ma mère, qui connaissait toutes les horreurs commises par ces barbares, fut longtemps avant de surmonter la frayeur que lui causaient les vieux Indiens, qu'elle appelait les vieux *croquignoles*; c'est ainsi qu'elle appelait ceux auxquels il ne restait que quelques lambeaux d'oreilles taillées en branches comme nos beignets canadiens.

Quant à moi et mon frère nous passions une partie de la journée étant enfants à jouer avec les jeunes sauvages, les provoquant à la course, à tirer l'arc et à d'autres exercices; et aussi à faire endiabler les jeunes sauvagesses.*

---

*   ANC, Fonds Aubert de Gaspé, Famille, MG 18 H 44.

LÉGENDE DU PÈRE GODRAULT

Je vais la donner au lecteur, s'il est possible, dans le langage naïf du père Godrault, qui travaillait souvent chez mon père, surtout pendant la fenaison, car tout vieux qu'il fut, il avait été soldat dans la compagnie même de mon grand-père, il n'en était pas moins un rude faucheur. C'était un répertoire vivant de toutes les légendes du pays, en sorte qu'il ne manquait pas d'auditoire sa journée achevée.

Il est bon de vous dire que les habitants de la paroisse de St Pierre de l'Isle étaient bien pauvres dans le commencement; ils n'avaient guère les moyens de bâtir une église. Le curé qui les desservait dans une toute petite chapelle en bois ouverte à tous les vents, avait beau leur dire: c'est honteux pour vous autres d'être logés à votre aise, tandis que votre Dieu ne l'est pas; ils répondaient toujours: c'est bien vrai monsieur le curé, mais comment faire? Ce n'est pas la volonté qui nous manque, mais ce sont les moyens. Vous savez qu'il y a eu mortalité depuis deux ans sur nos chevaux, et que le peu qui nous reste n'ont plus que les accoutrements qu'on pourrait voir le soleil se lever à travers de leurs chétifs corps, les pauvres bêtes. Comment voulez-vous, monsieur le curé, charrier la pierre qui est si éloignée. Essayez donc à plumer un crapaud pour voir si vous lui arracherez des plumes? Le curé disait toujours commencez mes enfants, ne vous méfiez pas de la divine providence et vous verrez que Dieu vous viendra en aide. Les habitants se mettent donc à l'ouvrage, mais ça n'avançait guère; les hommes ne manquaient pas de courage, mais les bêtes étaient sur les dents. Si donc qu'un matin le curé se rend sur le terrain où l'église devait se bâtir et trouve les habitants qui fumaient leur pipe d'un air découragé. Allons donc, les enfants qu'il leur dit, l'ouvrage n'avance guère à ce qu'il parait! Que voulez-vous; qu'ils répondirent, nous n'avons plus de pierre; les chevaux n'en peuvent plus et il leur faut du repos. Ils ont été mal hivernés vu la disète de foin, il a fallu faire les semences et c'est tirer du sang des pierres que de les faire travailler. Eh! bien, dit le curé, revenez demain de bonne heure et je vous fournirai un cheval, lui qui ne se fatiguera jamais. Le monde s'en retourna un peu consolé; car ils avaient grande confiance dans leur vieux pasteur. Quelques uns disaient pourtant: où prendra-t-il un cheval: il n'a qu'une vieille rosse et ce n'est pas elle qui sera infatigable et les jeunes gens se mirent à rire: la jeunesse est toujours folâtre.

Le lendemain après le soleil levé tout le monde était au rendez-vous quand le curé parut tenant par la bride un grand cheval noir qui jetait les flammes par les yeux et les narines tant il paraissait ardent; d'ailleurs le curé le menait aussi tranquillement que c'eut été un agneau. Tenez, dit le curé, servez-vous de ce cheval, chargez le tant que vous voudrez; il n'y a pas de charge qu'il ne mène aisément; mais prenez bien garde de ne pas le débrider; me le promettez-vous? Tout le monde le promit. On se mit donc à charrier la pierre avec le cheval; il semblait se rire des charges qu'on lui mettait; si les charettes ou traînes eussent été assez fortes, il aurait mené la charge de dix chevaux; aussi l'ouvrage avançait que c'était une bénédiction. Ce pauvre cheval leur fesait pourtant de la peine; quand il voyait de l'eau, il hennissait, s'en approchait, secouait la tête, regardait le monde d'un air piteux, mais on se ressouvenait de la défense du curé et on lui disait: bois avec ta bride, mon compère, si tu as tant de soif, mais il nous est défendu de te débrider; nous en sommes, vois-tu, bien fachés, mais il faut obéir à notre pasteur. Plus l'ouvrage avançait, plus l'animal faisait entendre à sa façon qu'il avait soif. Il se précipitait dans toutes les petites mares d'eau, se frottait le nez dans l'eau, tirait la langue, geignait que ça en fesait compassion, si bien qu'un bon jour que presque toute la maçonne de l'église était finie, un habitant par compassion lui ôta sa bride. L'animal se mit aussitôt à hennir d'une manière terrible, c'était comme le rugissement d'une bête féroce, il brisa son harnais en morceaux, se monta tout de bout sur ses pattes de derrière, se changea en un tourbillon de flammes et disparut dans les airs en emportant un pan de la muraille de l'église que l'on eut bien de la peine à rebâtir après.

Voilà ce que c'est, dit Godrault, que de ne pas avoir écouté son curé, car ce cheval, comme vous voyez était le diable en personne que les curés font venir quand ils en ont besoin en lisant dans le petit Albert[1]. Une fois le mors de bride dans la gueule, il était comme enchaîné, car le mors est joint en croix, ce qui l'empêchait de s'échapper.

Le père Godrault qui a encore beaucoup de descendants dans la paroisse de St-Jean-Port-Joli me racontait quelque chose de réel et bien plus triste que la légende de l'église de St-Pierre. — Il avait vu un parti de sauvages avec lesquels il fesait la guerre, brûler une femme anglaise, mais laissons le parler lui-même: Nous étions une dizaine de Canadiens allant à la découverte avec une centaine de sauvages, lorsque nous surprîmes un détachement d'Anglais près de leurs établissements, les hommes se défendirent vaillamment et furent tous massacrés; une femme seule eut le malheur de tomber entre nos mains. C'était une belle, belle créature comme j'en ai rarement vue: ces misérables *Canaouas* (nom de mépris pour les sauvages) la dépouillèrent et la firent brûler le lendemain pour se divertir. Nous autres Canadiens fîmes tout notre possible pour la sauver, mais tout fut inutile, nous n'avions pas d'officiers avec nous et étions trop pauvres pour la racheter. On leur fit bien des promesses de leur payer la prisonnière quand nous serions aux habitations, mais tout fut inutile. Car nous n'étions pas les plus forts. Notre caporal Ducros dit Laterreur pleurait de rage. Benoni Francœur lui dit: c'est toi qui commande Laterreur, donne le signal et nous allons la délivrer. Ducros était brave, mais c'était aussi un homme prudent et digne de commander. Je donnerais, dit-il à Francœur, vingt ans de ma vie pour suivre

---

1. Cette croyance que tous les prêtres ont en leur possession l'œuvre d'Albert le petit pour évoquer le diable quand ils en ont besoin était particulièrement répandue autrefois dans les campagnes, mais l'est encore de nos jours.

ton conseil et j'en aurais bien vite échiné une douzaine pour
ma part, mais un soldat qui désobéit à un ordre est désho-
noré et mes ordres sont de ne point me brouiller avec nos
alliés sauvages; nous ne sommes pas déjà trop forts; ayant à
combattre les Anglais presque toujours un contre dix et
quelquefois contre vingt. Tenez Mr Philippe, c'était un spec-
tacle à arracher le cœur de voir cette belle femme attachée
nue à un poteau, avec sa longue chevelure blonde qui la
couvrait presque en entier, entre les mains de ces barbares.
— Six mois encore après je me réveillais la nuit en sursaut
tout baigné de sueurs croyant la voir devant moi et entan-
dant ses cris de *main Got, my God.* Tenez, Mr Philippe, il y a
près de quarante ans de cela, eh bien, il m'arrive encore de
la voir en songe et d'entendre son *main Got.* J'ai vu faire bien
des cruautés à ces *Canaouas,* mais c'était tous des hommes, ça
ne fait pas de la peine comme quand c'est une pauvre
femme. Je ne suis pourtant pas méchant, mais je les aurais vu
griller tous les chiens de *Canaouas* que j'en aurais ri[*].

---

[*]   ANC, Fonds Aubert de Gaspé, Famille, MG 18 H 44. La dernière partie
de ce récit se trouve dans les *Anciens Canadiens* à la fin du chapitre treizième,
mais modifiée.

LE SORCIER MALOUIN

(Le seigneur de Gaspé tente de découvrir qui a blessé le père Francœur. Pendant ce temps son fils Philippe raconte l'histoire du sorcier Malouin)

(Le seigneur de Gaspé) s'adressant à un des fils de Francœur, donnez-moi un compas et sortez avec moi. Les assistants se regardèrent en hochant la tête, ce qui voulait dire monsieur le curé son ami lui aura prêté le Petit-Albert et il va bien vite découvrir le chien de sorcier qui l'a victimé. Ce n'est pourtant pas Malouin, dit Pierre Jean, il est bien vrai qu'il a le Petit-Albert, qu'il parle latin comme un curé et qu'on l'a vu même sortir de l'église avant l'élévation, et qu'il a conjuré le caplan de la baie de Gaspé, mais il est bon homme, il ne cherche qu'à rire et il ne ferait point de peine à un enfant. C'est vrai, dit la mère Jean-Marie Chouinard qui roulait le chapelet près du lit du malade, mais à force de jouer avec le feu on s'y brûle. Chacun baissa la tête en signe d'assentiment à une sentence si incontestable.

Tandis que mon père est à son œuvre de nécromancie, occupons-nous du sieur Malouin que j'ai connu depuis mon enfance jusqu'à sa mort il y a environ quarante ans. Malouin était ce qu'on appelle dans nos campagnes un volontaire, c'est-à-dire un homme qui n'a ni feu ni lieu; son métier était de construire des fours de glaise généralement alors en usage. Malouin était bien accueilli chez tous les habitants; c'était une bonne fortune qu'un tel hôte malgré sa réputation de sorcier. On accourait le soir d'une demi lieue à la ronde pour l'entendre. Il tenait beaucoup à sa réputation de sorcier, ce qui ne l'empêchait pas de tenir beaucoup aussi à sa réputation de prédicateur. Il y a peu de curés disaient les habitants qui prêchent aussi bien que Malouin. J'ai eu le bonheur d'assister un dimanche à un de ses sermons, j'avais alors quinze à seize ans lorsque passant chez notre cinquième voisin Bélanger dit Lacroix, la mère Bélanger me dit: entrez donc Mr Philippe, Malouin va prêcher. Lorsque j'entrai le prédicateur était monté sur une table entourée d'une douzaine de personnes. Il cita d'abord un texte latin tiré de son livre d'heures que j'ai oublié et dit: Lorsque Jésus Christ arriva à Londres en l'année...(c'est un anachronisme de je ne sais combien de siècles), les trois cent mille cloches de cette grande ville sonnèrent tout-à-coup en branle sans l'aide des bedeaux. Les rues étaient si pleines d'hommes et de femmes, d'enfants, de gens charitables qui portaient sur leurs épaules des paralytiques, des aveugles, des boiteux, des cults-de-patte, des possédés, des moribonds, que les maisons éclataient comme du verre. Le Pape, les cardinaux, les évêques, les prêtres, les moines de tous les pays du monde suivaient le bon Jésus en chantant des cantiques qu'on se serait cru dans le ciel. Comme c'est tout ce que je me rappelle de ce mémorable sermon, le lecteur devra se contenter de cet échantillon de l'éloquence de notre sorcier transformé en prédicateur chrétien. La fin d'un homme qui avait joué un si grand rôle dans nos campagnes fut assez triste. Malouin sans être ivrogne faisait de temps à autres des petites débauches avec ses amis, et un soir qu'il sortait d'une auberge avec un de ses amis, ils tombèrent tous deux dans un fossé et s'y endormirent. C'était par une nuit froide du mois d'octobre et lorsqu'on les trouva le lendemain au matin, Malouin était sans connaissance mais son ami était mort. Et comme les sorciers ont la vie dure, Malouin fut rappelé à la vie et vécut encore un assez grand nombre d'années; mais il avait presque perdu l'usage de la parole et il ne l'a jamais recouvré. Les seuls mots qu'il pouvait dire étaient ceux-ci: «Caronet» (nom de l'aubergiste chez qui il avait bu), «il est mort» (faisant sans doute allusion à son cher compagnon de ribote), «que le diable l'emporte! C'est bien de valeur, je ne puis pas parler.» On ne manqua pas d'attribuer cette infirmité à une punition de Dieu que le sorcier méritait à juste titre.

Mon père rentra le compas à main et dit: j'ai découvert, père Francœur, le sorcier qui vous a frappé la nuit dernière.

— Les assistants ne témoignèrent aucune surprise. «Voici, dit mon père, en montrant le compas qu'il tenait en main, le diamètre des deux formes ou pitons qui ornent l'arrière de votre berline, examinons maintenant la blessure et vous verrez qu'elle offre le même diamètre. Vous êtes très sanguin, vous avez eu une attaque d'apoplexie foudroyante et par un bonheur providentiel vous êtes tombé le front sur le piton de votre voiture et il s'en est suivi une hémorragie qui avec l'aide de Dieu vous a sauvé la vie.» Cette explication si naturelle ne plut qu'à demi et les deux tiers au moins de la paroisse de St Jean Port-Joli, de l'Islet et de St Roch n'en ont pas moins resté convaincus que c'était un sorcier sous la forme d'un feu-follet qui l'avait frappé. Francœur a survécu plusieurs années à cet accident, je l'ai bien connu pendant mon enfance; c'était un beau vieillard au teint rose et il avait une cicatrice circulaire au milieu du front d'environ un pouce de diamètre et d'un quart de pouce de profondeur. Comme tous les yeux se portaient naturellement sur cette difformité, il avait pour habitude quand il venait chez mon père de la cacher avec l'extrémité du fouet ou de la canne qu'il tenait en main*.

---

*   ANC, Fonds Aubert de Gaspé, Famille, MG 18 H 44.

PROJET DE DÉDICACE DES *ANCIENS CANADIENS* À L'ABBÉ H.-R. CASGRAIN

M. l'abbé,

Le sentier que j'avais à parcourir lorsque j'ai commencé à écrire les Anciens Canadiens me paraissait jonché de fleurs, mais je dus m'apercevoir bien vite qu'il était au contraire, couvert de ronces et d'épines. Je continuai néanmoins à travailler espérant franchir tous les obstacles de cette route pénible; le bandeau ne me tomba des yeux qu'à la lecture de l'ouvrage quand il fut achevé. Bah! pensai-je: je n'aurai toujours pas perdu mon temps: je laisserai mon manuscrit comme un souvenir affectueux à ma nombreuse famille; et à cette fois je l'enfermai bien précieusement dans un tiroir d'où vous l'avez retiré pour le livrer à l'impression malgré ma répugnance.

Si j'étais capable d'autres sentiments envers vous, Mr l'abbé, que ceux de l'amitié la plus sincère, je vous conserverais de la rancune pour un acte aussi téméraire! N'importe, je me permettrai toujours de vous faire une petite espièglerie en vous dédiant à vous, littérateur distingué malgré votre jeunesse, à vous, protecteur dévoué de la bonne littérature canadienne cette œuvre éphémère.

Vous avouerez, Mr l'abbé, que c'est assez mal reconnaître les excellents conseils que vous m'avez donnés, les soins que vous donnez à l'impression de mon ouvrage, que de chercher à vous rendre solidaire de ses défauts; mais la vieillesse est rancunière.

Ce qui m'empêche pas Mr l'abbé de me souscrire avec une considération très distinguée

Votre serviteur obligé et ami
L'auteur*

---

* ASQ, Fonds Casgrain.

Sigles

ANC   Archives nationales du Canada
ANQ-Q   Archives nationales du Québec – à Québec
ANQ-M   Archives nationales du Québec – à Montréal
ASQ   Archives du Séminaire de Québec
BRH   Bulletin des recherches historiques
DBC   Dictionnaire biographique du Canada

Bibliographie

SOURCES MANUSCRITES

Archives de l'Université de Montréal
Collection Baby, Fonds P58, U-11684.

Archives des Sœurs missionnaires de l'Immaculée-Conception, Pont-Viau
Collection de photographies anciennes.

Archives des Ursulines de Québec
Fichier des élèves.

Archives du Collège Bourget, Rigaud
Manuscrit des *Anciens Canadiens*; documents familles Aubert de Gaspé et de Beaujeu.

Archives du Séminaire de Québec (ASQ)
Fichier des écoliers; Fonds Casgrain; Fonds de photographies; Fonds Verreau; manuscrit original des *Anciens Canadiens*; correspondance variée.

Archives nationales du Canada (ANC)
Fonds Aubert de Gaspé, Famille, MG 18 H 44; RG 4 b20, vol. 25, pp. 9215-9224.

Archives nationales du Québec à Québec (ANQ-Q)
Fonds Pierre-Georges Roy; T11-301, n° 940; greffes des notaires L.C. Conscient de Saint-Aubin, Louis-Zéphirin Duval, Simon Fraser, Roger Lelièvre, Amable Morin, Antoine Panet, Antoine A. Parent, Joseph Petitclerc, Jacques Pinguet, Joseph Planté, Antoine-J. Saillant, Alexandre-Benjamin Sirois, Félix Têtu; documents judiciaires: Fonds

Cour Supérieure, Cour du banc du Roi (1822-1837), Cour du banc de la Reine (1837-1841); «Register of Prisonners Committed to the Common Goal of the City of Quebec» (1838-1841); iconographie: Collection initiale.

Archives nationales du Québec à Montréal (ANQ-M)
Greffe du notaire E. Gamelin Simard.

Archives paroissiales de L'Islet
Registres de baptêmes, mariages et sépultures.

Archives paroissiales de Notre-Dame de Québec
Registres de baptêmes, mariages et sépultures.

Archives paroissiales de Saint-Apollinaire
Registres de baptêmes, mariages et sépultures.

Archives paroissiales de Saint-Jean-Port-Joli
Registres des baptêmes, mariages et sépultures; Arthur Fournier, *Mémorial de Saint-Jean-Port-Joli*, 1923.

Archives privées
Documents conservés par les descendants de Philippe Aubert de Gaspé, quelques antiquaires, l'auteur du présent ouvrage et la Corporation Philippe-Aubert-de-Gaspé.

McCord Museum (Montréal)
Stuart papers.

SOURCES IMPRIMÉES

Almanach de Québec [...] *The Quebec Almanac* [...], publié de 1780 à 1841, excepté en 1841, 1790 et 1793, par divers éditeurs.

AUBERT DE GASPÉ, Philippe. *Divers.* Montréal, C.O. Beauchemin & fils, 1893.

— «La statue du général Wolfe» et «Le village indien de la Jeune-Lorette», dans *Le Foyer canadien*, 1866, pp. 513-551.

— «Les Anciens Canadiens (fragments): Une nuit avec les sorciers, La débâcle», dans *Les Soirées canadiennes*, 1862, pp. 5-64.

— *Les Anciens Canadiens*, Desbarats et Derbishire, 1863, Traduit en anglais d'abord par Georgiana M. Pennée, sous le titre *The Canadians of Old* (1864), puis par Charles G.D. Roberts (1890).

— *Mémoires*, Ottawa, G.-É. Desbarats, 1866. Traduit en anglais par Jane Brierly, sous le titre *A Man of Sentiment, The Memoirs of Philippe Aubert de Gaspé* (1988).

AUBERT DE GASPÉ, fils, Philippe. *L'influence d'un livre; roman historique*, Québec, 1837.

Biographie et oraison funèbre du Révd. M.P. Labelle et autres documents relatifs à sa mémoire ainsi qu'à la visite de Philippe Aubert de Gaspé, Ecr. [...], Montréal, Imprimerie de la Minerve, 1865.

Cadastres abrégés des seigneuries du district de Québec, Québec, Georges Desbarats, 1863.

CAMERON, C. et Trudel, J. *Québec au temps de James Pattison Cockburn*, Québec, Garneau, 1976.

CASGRAIN, Henri-Raymond. *Philippe Aubert de Gaspé*, Québec, Léger Brousseau, 1871.

CASGRAIN, Philippe-Baby. *La vie de Joseph-François Perrault, surnommé le père de l'éducation du peuple canadien*, Québec, C. Darveau, 1898.

Le Catalogue des officiers et élèves du Séminaire de Québec, 1848-1856.

FABRE, Hector. «M. de Gaspé», dans *L'Événement*, 30 janvier 1871.

Journaux de la Chambre d'Assemblée du Bas-Canada, de 1833 à 1841.

Journaux du Conseil législatif de la Province du Bas-Canada, 1841.

LARUE, Hubert, *Voyage sentimental sur la rue Saint-Jean* [...], Québec, Typographie de C. Darveau, 1879.

Quebec Directory (de 1844 à 1870), Québec.

Journaux consultés

La Gazette de Québec, La Minerve, Le Canadien, Le Courrier du Canada, Le Journal de Québec, Le Petit Journal, L'Événement, Morning Chronicle, Quebec Chronicle Telegraph, Quebec Daily Mercury.

ÉTUDES

BAILLARGEON, Noël. *Le Séminaire de Québec de 1760 à 1800*, Québec, Les Presses de l'Université Laval, 1981.

CASTONGUAY, Jacques. «Antoine-Gaspard Couillard», dans *DBC*, VII, pp. 230-231.

— «Ignace-Philippe Aubert de Gaspé», dans *DBC*, V, pp. 33-34.

— *Lady Stuart*, Montréal, Éditions du Méridien, 1986.

— *La seigneurie de Philippe Aubert de Gaspé*, Saint-Jean-Port-Joli, Montréal, Fides, 1977.

— «Les souvenirs d'un bon gentilhomme» dans postface aux *Anciens Canadiens*, Montréal, Stanké, 1987, pp. 301-304.

— «Pierre-Ignace Aubert de Gaspé», dans *DBC*, VI pp. 17-18.

CHOUINARD, André. *Le manoir Aubert de Gaspé*, La Pocatière, Société historique de la Côte-du-Sud, 1985.

CURRAN, Verna Isabel. *Philippe Aubert de Gaspé: His life and works* (thèse de Ph.D., Toronto, 1957).

(DANIEL, François). *Histoire des grandes familles françaises du Canada [...]*, Montréal, 1867, pp. 347-370.

DESCHÊNES, Gaston. *L'Année des Anglais, la Côte-du-Sud à l'heure de la conquête*, Québec, Septentrion, 1988.

— *Portraits de Saint-Jean-Port-Joli*, Sainte-Foy, Les Éditions des Trois-Saumons, 1984.

EDWARDS, Mary Jane. «James Tanswell», dans *DBC*, V, pp. 868-870.

FAUTEUX, Aegédius. *Les Chevaliers de Saint-Louis en Canada*, Montréal, Éditions des Dix, 1940.

GALARNEAU, Claude. «Joseph-François Perrault», dans *DBC*, VI, pp. 744-747.

GRANDBOIS, Alain. «Un type remarquable: Ph. Aubert de Gaspé», dans *Le Petit Journal*, 9 juin 1963.

GREENWOOD, F.M. et LAMBERT, J.H. «Jonathan Sewell», dans *DBC*, VI, pp. 847-856.

GROULX, Lionel. *Histoire du Canada français*, Montréal, Fides, 1967.

HAYNE, D.M. et TIROL, M. *Bibliographie critique du roman canadien-français, 1837-1900*, Québec et Toronto, 1968, pp. 42-60.

HÉROUX, André, «Sir John Caldwell», dans *DBC*, VII, pp. 145-149.

LACOURCIÈRE, LUC. «Aubert de Gaspé, fils (1814-1841)», dans *Cahier des Dix*, n° 40, 1975, pp. 275-302.

— «L'enjeu des Anciens Canadiens», dans *Cahier des Dix*, n° 32, 1967, pp. 223-254.

— «Philippe Aubert de Gaspé», dans *DBC*, X, pp. 19-24.

— «Philippe Aubert de Gaspé», dans *Cahier des Dix*, n° 41, 1976, pp. 191-204. Voir aussi Rapport de la Semaine d'histoire tenue à Québec du 10 au 16 mai 1976, Québec, 1977, pp. 77-91.

LAROQUE DE ROQUEBRUNE, Robert. «Philippe Aubert de Gaspé», dans *L'Action*, 4 avril 1914.

LEMIRE, Maurice, «Introduction», *Les Anciens Canadiens*, Montréal, Fides, 1988, pp. 7-21.

LEMOINE, James McPherson, *Monographies et esquisses*, Québec, Gingras, 1885.

— *Pitturesque Quebec: a Sequel to «Quebec Past and Present»*, Montréal, Dawson Brothers, 1882.

— *Quebec Past and Present, A History of Quebec, 1608-1876*, Québec, Augustin Coté, 1876.

LESSARD, Rénald. «Les premiers bains publics de Québec, 1817-1823», dans *Cap-aux-Diamants*, vol. 1, n° 2, pp. 43-44.

MARCOTTE, Gilles. *Une littérature qui se fait*, Montréal, HMH, 1962.

OUELLET, Gérard. *Ma Paroisse, Saint-Jean-Port-Joly*, Québec, Éditions des piliers, 1946.

PLOUFFE, Marcel. «Thomas Ainslie Young», dans *DBC*, VIII, pp. 1070-1072.

ROBIDOUX, Réjean. «Fortunes et Infortunes de l'abbé Casgrain», dans *Mouvement littéraire de 1860*, Ottawa, EUO, 1961.

— *Le Roman canadien-français. Évolution, témoignages, bibliographie*, Montréal/Paris, Fides, 1965.

— «Octave Crémazie», dans *DBC*, X, PP. 221-224.

ROY, Camille. *Nouveaux essais sur la littérature canadienne*, Québec, L'Action sociale, 1914.

ROY, Léon. *Les terres de la Grande-Anse, des Aulnaies et du Port-Joly*, Lévis, Fortin & fils, 1951.

ROY, Pierre-Georges. *À travers les Anciens Canadiens de Philippe Aubert de Gaspé*, Montréal, G. Ducharme, 1943.

— *À travers les Mémoires de Philippe Aubert de Gaspé*, Montréal, G. Ducharme, 1943.

— *La famille Aubert de Gaspé*, Lévis, 1907.

— *La famille Tarieu de Lanaudière*, Lévis, 1922.

SAINT-PIERRE, Angéline. *L'église de Saint-Jean-Port-Joli*, Québec, Garneau, 1977.

TÊTU, Henri. *Histoire du palais épiscopal de Québec*, Québec, Pruneau & Kirouac, 1896.

TRUDEL, Marcel. *Le Régime seigneurial*, Ottawa, Les Brochures de la Société historique du Canada, n° 6, 1971.

TURGEON, Jean-Marie. *Les Vendredis de l'Oncle Gaspard*, Québec, 1944.

«Une contemporaine de P.A. de Gaspé», dans *L'Événement*, 30 juillet 1951.

WYCZYNSKI, Paul. *Le roman canadien-français*, Collection «Archives des lettres canadiennes», Montréal, Fides, 1971.

YOUNG, A.-H. *The Revd. John Stuart, D.D., U.E.L., of Kingston, U.C. and his Family*, Whig Press Kingston (sans date).

Table des matières

COMPOSÉ EN PALATINO CORPS 11,5
AUX ATELIERS DE L'ÉDITEUR
SELON UNE MAQUETTE RÉALISÉE PAR JOSÉE LALANCETTE
ET ACHEVÉ D'IMPRIMER
SUR PAPIER OFFSET 120M
EN MARS 1991
AUX ATELIERS GRAPHIQUES MARC VEILLEUX
POUR LE COMPTE DES ÉDITIONS DU SEPTENTRION